Incentive Pay and Career Ladders
for Today's Teachers

SUNY Series in Educational Leadership

Daniel L. Duke, Editor

Incentive Pay and Career Ladders for Today's Teachers

A Study of Current Programs and Practices

Richard M. Brandt

State University of New York Press

Published by
State University of New York Press, Albany

For information, address State University of New York
Press, State University Plaza, Albany, N.Y., 12246

Library of Congress Cataloging-in-Publication Data

Brandt, Richard Martin, 1922–
    Incentive Pay and Career Ladders for Today's Teachers : A Study of
Current Programs and Practices / Richard M. Brandt.
        p.   cm. — (SUNY series in educational leadership)
    Includes bibliographical references (p.   ).
    ISBN 0-7914-0399-8. — ISBN 0-7914-0400-5 (pbk.)
    1. Teachers—Salaries, etc.—United States.   2. Merit pay—United
States.   3. Compensation management—United States.   4. Teachers—
United States—Rating of.   I. Title.   II. Series.
    LB2842.2.B7   1990
    331.2'813711'00973—dc20   89-48220
                                                                  CIP

10   9   8   7   6   5   4   3   2   1

Contents

List of Exhibits

Preface

This book is a case study of a movement while it is still taking place. It consists in great part of a compilation of various case histories of state and local district responses to the incentive pay and career ladder movement. While one local district, whose plan I had a hand in designing, is used more than any other to illustrate issues that arise in the planning process and teacher feelings about them, other plans, including several state programs, are also described in some detail and their evolution tracked over the same period. Together, these various case histories permit an interim assessment of how the movement is proceeding and what difference it has made.

In spring 1990, I am not able to tell how long the movement will last, whether it is nearly over or barely beginning. I only know it is very much alive in various places across the country, and achieving consensus about what is happening is not easy. Individuals involved display varied, often heated, reactions to program developments because their own lives are affected by them. What I try to offer in this volume is more objective perspective from an interested, informed, relatively dispassionate observer.

I would like to be descriptive and let events speak for themselves. But I also want to discern the commonalities of issues and solutions across programs and decipher the reasons behind happenings and sentiments. In so doing, and even in the description, I am at least partially aware of my own biases. If I thought that the clamor for reform should not be taken seriously or that incentive pay for teachers was a fundamentally bad idea, I would not have become so involved with districts and states trying to design these programs. I would not have been interested in writing this book. In brief, I do believe that this particular effort, if it can be instituted properly, will improve American education substantially in the years ahead. I realize also that, today, relatively few educators agree with me.

The programs that I describe in greatest detail and draw on most extensively were chosen for several reasons: First, they were among the earliest to begin in this decade and have been operating several years even though most are still not fully institutionalized.

Reactions change sharply after the first year or two. I wanted to concentrate on those that have had a fair trial. Second, substantial descriptive materials and reports were available for study and analysis. With several state programs, third-party evaluations had been conducted and were available for review as well. Third, I was able to visit programs and talk to participants and administrators in charge of them. In several states and districts, I served as consultant, researcher, or outside evaluator. Finally, all states that were committing ten million dollars or more in 1988–89 were included in my tracking process (Cornett, 1988).

While some use is made of journal and book publications about incentive pay, the primary source materials throughout the volume are the case history documents and ethnographic records of visits, observations, and interviews I compiled during my seven-year involvement. I studied many legislative documents, policy directives, manuals, reports, performance scales, records, and evaluation studies as a basis for writing my own descriptions of programs.

In order to improve the accuracy of the program descriptions that appear in chapter 2 and elsewhere, I sent early drafts to school authorities for corrections and recommended changes. I realized that my capsule descriptions were but brief digests of very complicated programs and that not all details could be included. I tried to describe what I thought were the most important features and to exclude factual errors. Although I have sought and considered reactions from program authorities about my accuracy both in reporting and interpreting the information collected, I must assume responsibility for the final content and wording used in the book.

Acknowledgments

School authorities and others who reacted to early drafts of references to their programs and provided needed information included: Mary Amsler, Stephen M. Baker, Susan Barnes, Nila Beard, John W. Bennion, Louann Bierlein, Dolores Bohen, Sharon Bobbitt, Larry W. Brooks, J. Kent Caruthers, Ray Coleman, Lynn M. Cornett, Cristi Denler, Mary I. Dereshiwsky, Daniel L. Duke, David Harrison, Ann Weaver Hart, Lynda Haynes, David Holdzkom, Barbara Kuligowski, George E. Malo, Renfro C. Manning, Ernest W. Martin, Betty McCowan, Richard D. Packard, Robert W. Paskel, Mark Pope-Rolewski, James Salmon, Joseph A. Spagnolo, Jr., Thomas E. Truitt, Joe Vaughn, and Garfield Wilson. I am most appreciative of their efforts to help me set the record straight and keep factual error to a minimum.

I am especially indebted to Daniel L. Duke who, after reading some of my early papers and reports on incentive pay, encouraged me to write such a book. Lynn Cornett and David Holdzkom, as well as Duke, read the entire manuscript and provided very useful suggestions for its improvement.

Special thanks go to Thomas E. Truitt, when he was Superintendent of Schools in Danville, Virginia, for inviting me to serve as continuing consultant during the three years in which a career ladder program was being designed and installed. (Currently Truitt is Superintendent of Florence Public School District One in South Carolina.)

My appreciation is extended to several departmental colleagues at the University of Virginia. As chairman of Educational Studies, Jerry G. Short recognized the importance of including work with schools that were developing such programs in my assignments, which gave me needed time and clerical assistance. Interactions with Donald Ball, Bruce Gansneder, Brenda Loyd, Robert McNergney, and Donald Medley about one issue or another, while not always in agreement, never failed to provide good counsel and extend my thinking. Rebecca Kennedy deserves special thanks for typing and reworking the manuscript with amazing speed and accuracy.

Much of the Danville case study material included in chapters

2, 3, and 4 came from a report that was prepared with funding from the Office of Educational Research and Improvement, U.S. Department of Education under contract number P86–07138. Points of view or opinions, however, do not necessarily represent the official view or opinions of the Office of Educational Research and Improvement. Appreciation is expressed to MGT of America for granting permission to republish, with minor editing, a discussion of compensation practices in business, industry, and the military which I had written for its review of the Florida master teacher program. Permission from Richard Packard to include a reproduction of his readiness model is also appreciated. I also thank the Southern Regional Education Board for granting permission to use selections prepared for publication by the SREB *Career Ladder Clearinghouse*.

Finally, I want to express my gratitude for the warm welcome and splendid cooperation I have received as consultant and investigator from literally hundreds of unnamed teachers, administrators, legislators, school board members, and others with whom I have talked or worked in various states and school districts. Their willingness to give me materials, express their feelings, and cite their ideas has provided me with a rich data base for reviewing and evaluating the incentive pay and career ladder movement. I have great respect for those who have been involved in it—participants as well as program designers and administrators. They have typically complicated their already busy lives in an effort to improve themselves and their school systems.

Richard M. Brandt
Charlottesville, VA

Response to a Mandate

According to Lynn Cornett, who directs the Southern Regional Education Board's *Career Ladder Clearinghouse*:

> Career ladder and other incentive pay programs are the largest educational experiment in the United States today. Hundreds of millions of dollars are being spent, and hundreds of thousands of teachers and school administrators are part of state and local incentive programs to reward teachers and administrators for doing a better job or for taking on additional responsibilities in schools. (December 1987)

Despite the extensive interest and activity, no more controversial recommendation came out of the recent reports on American education than the installation of performance-based pay or master teacher and career ladder programs. Businessmen and many politicians tend to support the idea; educators are wary. Opinions, overall, are highly diverse. The public's simplistic notion that the best teachers are easily identified and should be rewarded with higher pay than other teachers in these days of limited public revenues runs completely counter to long-standing traditions of equal pay for equal education and time in rank. The many issues surrounding this recommendation are complex and not easily resolved.

States and localities have responded to the mandate in different ways. It is time to take stock of what has happened and project what lies ahead. Having been involved extensively in the design, implementation, and evaluation of career ladder and incentive pay programs, I propose in this book to do just that.

I will provide a comprehensive overview of the programs now underway and a description of their major features. At the same time I will display the planning and design process in some detail, and sort out the important and lasting issues that need to be recognized from the many operational decisions that have to be made. The focus will be as much on the motivations and attitudes of the people involved as on operational criteria and program procedures. The ultimate questions to be addressed have to do with the impact and potential impact on schools—how they are organized, how teaching is conducted, and how much pupils learn. Special attention will be devoted to the likely effect on teacher motivation and career aspirations.

Where this movement is leading and what lasting impact it will have on American education remain open questions. Despite many early merit pay and differentiated staffing attempts that failed, the current career ladder and incentive pay movement is still emerging as the 1980s come to a close; and for various reasons, not the least of which are new career opportunities for college-educated women, it may prove more durable.

First, in this introductory chapter, let me return to the education reform scene at the beginning of the decade and review the conditions that led up to this particular mandate.

CALLS FOR REFORM

During the 1970s, grave doubts were raised about the effectiveness of our system of public education. Declining test scores became front-page news. Teacher strikes increased at alarming rates. The volume of letters to the editor rose, with complaints about everything from crime and lack of discipline in the schools to illiterate high school graduates and even illiterate teachers. The charges were many. The public schools were under attack as never before.[1]

While citizen complaints were rising, and the demands for increased accountability as well, educators themselves seemed preoccupied with collective bargaining and equity issues. Their initial response was to oppose accountability proposals in general and state-level testing of students in particular.

No one was prepared for the deluge of reports and specific proposals that materialized from a decade of rising concerns. *A Nation at Risk* in 1983 was only one of the first of several dozen national reports and almost three hundred state reports on the condition of education during the early eighties with recommendations about how to improve it. Most of these reports were directed not so much at educators as at public constituencies, which might then pressure teachers and school authorities into compliance (Haberman, 1987).

In many places comprehensive state and local reform efforts were already underway. Countless numbers of new bills were passed in 1983 and 1984 to enhance school standards and programs. During the entire decade, more than one thousand pieces of legislation affecting teachers, including their pay, were passed. (Darling-Hammond, 1988).

An unprecedented amount of media attention was focused on the reform debate and legislative initiatives. Educational and political leaders seized on the heightened public awareness of the need for change to move swiftly to bring it about.

The Nation Responds report in May 1984 summarized these early activities as follows (p. 11):

> Americans will remember 1983. During that year, deep public concern about the Nation's future created a tidal wave of school reform which promises to renew American education. Citizens, perplexed about social, civic, and economic difficulties, turned to education as an anchor of hope for the future of their Nation and their children. Schools survived an unprecedented firestorm of critical comment and attention from the press to emerge at the end of the year with greater public support than at any time in the recent past.[2]

The main themes of the suggested changes were more rigorous academic standards for students and higher standards and greater recognition for teachers.

Specific recommendations were made in several reports for not only improving teacher salaries but making them performance-based. *A Nation at Risk* stated (p. 30):

> Salaries for the teaching profession should be increased and should be professionally competitive, market-sensitive, and performance-based. Salary, promotion, tenure, and retention decisions should be tied to an effective evaluation system that includes peer review so that superior teachers can be rewarded, average ones encouraged, and poor ones either improved or terminated.

A prestigious task force of governors, business leaders, and educators chaired by North Carolina Governor James Hunt (Task

Force on Education for Economic Growth, 1983) expressed the idea this way (p. 11):

> Boards of education and higher education should cooperate with teachers and administrators on systems for measuring the effectiveness of teachers and rewarding outstanding performance.

Both reports, along with many others, called for the establishment of career ladders that distinguish between beginning and experienced teachers and experienced and master teachers. Within a year, twenty-four of the states were examining career ladder or master teacher programs and six had begun statewide or pilot programs (U.S. Department of Education, 1984).

PUBLIC CONCERNS AND THE BUSINESS PERSPECTIVE

While the mandates were strongly worded and widely endorsed, what they meant in specific new practices and how well they would work once they were in place were far from clear. Something obviously needed to change, but there certainly was no consensus about how it should be done. While improving teacher salaries was almost universally recommended, for example, research on teacher motivation suggested intrinsic rewards were more important motivators than salary (Lortie, 1975). Incentive pay plans might even have more negative than positive consequences (Hatry and Greiner, 1985). To appreciate the problems that lay ahead in working out the planned changes and putting them into practice, we need to examine more closely, first, the nature of the specific concerns of those making the reports and drafting the reform proposals, and second, the origins of their suggestions.

As indicated earlier, the voices of complaint were heard ever more frequently as the decade of the seventies came to a close. Public opinion polls showed a steady decline from one year to the next in judgments about how well the schools were doing. The Task Force on Education for Economic Growth (1983, p. 4) wrote:

> Our future success as a nation—our national defense, our social stability and well being and our national prosperity—will depend on our ability to improve education and training for millions of individual citizens.

More influential than any other theme was a growing perception that the United States was losing its competitive edge on the world scene partly because of deficiencies in its education system. As *A Nation at Risk* stated (p. 7):

> Knowledge, learning, information, and skilled intelligence are the new raw materials of international commerce and are today spreading throughout the world as vigorously as miracle drugs, synthetic fertilizers, and blue jeans did earlier. If only to keep and improve on the slim competitive edge we will retain in world markets, we must dedicate ourselves to the reform of our educational system—old and young alike, affluent and poor, majority and minority. Learning is the indispensable investment required for success in the "information age" we are entering.

There were two interrelated components of the perception that high-quality education was essential for economic competitiveness: Good education was needed to provide a highly skilled, well-motivated labor force. Good schools were necessary to attract new industries to a community and keep old ones.

Improving schools to attract industry and provide the kind of labor desired was especially popular in the Southeast where public school expenditures were below average, at least on a per pupil basis. Particularly anxious to attract new industry, governors in Florida, North Carolina, Tennessee, and Virginia, among others, put school improvement at the top of their priority lists for action and took personal charge of school reform measures. It was no accident either that many of the leaders and members of the task forces to draft proposals were from business and industry.

Education had become too important to be left to the educators. With educators the biggest spenders of state and local budgets and school productivity mediocre at best, it was time to make them more accountable to the society they were supposed to serve. Competition in particular was missing. Whereas business firms competed to stay in business, and individual employees to hold a job, at least in times of retrenchment, similar incentives were seldom found in schools. A dose of competition might be precisely what was needed to stir up a challenge and remove the complacency. Competition was a prominent theme throughout our culture. Why should schools be exempted from having to contend with it?

Ronald Reagan sounded this theme in his 1984 State of the Union Address:

> Just as more incentives are needed within our schools, greater competition is needed among our schools. Without standards and competition there can be no champions, no records broken, no excellence—in education or any other walk of life.

So the nation was considered at risk, and mediocrity rather than excellence was the norm in American education. A strong sense prevailed that the schools could and should do better. The world of business and private enterprise could provide the model. One necessary school ingredient was merit pay. Single out the best teachers, as business identified its most productive workers, for extra pay and faster promotion.

How indeed was compensation used for incentive purposes in the world outside of education? What form did it take in business, industry, and even the military with its rank system? How relevant were the practices used elsewhere to the business of running schools?[3]

Business and industry had long depended on both incentive pay programs and promotional opportunities to attract, retain, and motivate high-quality management personnel. For production workers, too, pay for increased output had a long history. Although performance pay had been supplanted by hourly wage rates for many workers, especially in strongly unionized industries, individual performance was still assessed and tied to pay in many instances. The fisherman's catch and the apple picker's baskets were but two of many examples. Piecework pay still counted in heavy industry when production could be tied to individual performance. Among white-collar workers, the salesperson's commission and the executive's bonus were obvious examples.

The military offered clear examples of career ladder plans for both enlisted and officer ranks. Smaller numbers of people were needed in the higher ranks so promotion became increasingly competitive as one climbed the ladder. Differences existed in how fast one was promoted and, eventually, in how far one went. One's performance in rank, as evaluated primarily by one's supervisors, that is, senior officers, was the principal basis for promotion. Test results, completion of special training, and time in rank were often considered as well.

In the military, incentive pay was a primary recruiting

mechanism. Potential enlistees were frequently offered cash bonuses to join the all-volunteer U.S. Army, for example, along with similar inducements for reenlisting for additional terms. The size of the bonus, furthermore, had a substantial effect on one's tendency to want to sign up. In one study it was found that a $2,000 bonus in the early 1980s apparently made no difference, but $5,000 and especially $8,000 bonuses had considerable effect (Balkan and Groenemans, 1985). An earlier study, which used data collected in 1973 when military duty was not popular, reported that youths were indifferent to pay incentives of $1,000 and $3,000 for enlisting in the navy (Korman et al., 1981). Two obvious implications of these studies for the design of teacher incentive structure plans are to:

- make the size of the performance pay increment substantial if one expects it to succeed
- expect some variation in its inducement effects because of other factors, i.e., perceived working conditions, alternative career opportunities, and economic circumstances in particular.

Several types of merit payment prevail in business and industry:

- *fixed scale increments* in which individuals are allowed to skip a step for superior service (Some school systems are using this form of reward without having to modify their regular salary schedules)
- *variable cash increments* based on performance
- *career progression scales* for promotion to positions with increasing status, responsibility, and pay
- *bonuses* paid as lump sums and not consolidated into salary.

The latter might take the form of stock options, piecework payments, sales commissions, expense-paid vacations, or other one-time rewards.

Merit pay plans are used to communicate corporate values to employees. Those features of job performance that receive emphasis in job descriptions and employee evaluation forms, thereby becoming the explicit criteria for merit pay decisions, serve as powerful directives from management. Just as merit pay provides management with a tool for effecting change in industry, it could help school leaders stimulate instructional improvement in very precise ways. This management potential may underlie some of the resistance of teachers' unions to merit pay proposals.

Either individual performance or company unit performance may serve as the basis for reward distribution, depending on company philosophy. The size of bonuses for top executives in many major corporations is tied to changes in companywide sales, earnings per share, or other corporate accounting indices. With the increased promotion of quality circles and other team activities today, achievement of group performance standards and contributions of individuals to groups are becoming more relevant factors for bonus assessment for individuals at lower organizational levels.

To the extent that teachers are considered part of a team jointly responsible for student learning, rather than individual instructors teaching their own classes, cooperation and sharing should be included among the criteria for evaluating their teaching and schoolwide achievement goals. The merit schools programs are consistent with this philosophy.

After more than a decade of high inflation, merit pay adjustments in the 1980s were beginning to supplant inflation-based increases. A study by the Bureau of National Affairs found that in the United States three-quarters of the 221 companies surveyed that were then paying cost-of-living adjustments (COLAs) intended to eliminate, suspend, or restrict them in future wage negotiations. They would resist job security clauses, expansion of fringe benefits (health care costs in particular were under attack), and other restrictive work arrangements that might automatically inflate labor costs and constrain management's ability to keep companies competitive in the marketplace (Banks, 1985). General Motors, for example, announced that it would eliminate COLAs for all its North America salaried workers at the end of 1985 and would instead base pay increases completely on merit (*Wall Street Journal*, 6 November 1985). Underlying these trends were reductions in the rate of inflation, declining productivity in many industries, and increased competition from abroad where wage costs were considerably lower.

Variations exist from industry to industry and one company to another not only in the overall rise of pay incentives, but also in their form and the criteria used. In corporate conglomerates where divisional autonomy is generally high, for example, division managers are likely to be rewarded more on the basis of specific profit results than their counterparts in large diversified companies like General Electric, where growth has come through internal expansion and management transfers from one unit to another are relatively common. In the latter instance, subjective measures of managerial performance are more likely to be used.

The design of management incentive programs poses special problems for high technology companies with rapidly changing product lines and market priorities. These firms find that traditional evaluation practices do not work. They provide annual incentive awards that reflect not only the company's financial success but also both qualitative and quantitative assessment of each individual's contributions. Making a significant technical contribution may require more than a year's work, and its worth in financial terms can be recognized only indirectly or after an extended period of time (Schuster, 1984).

In contrast to most elementary or secondary schools, where teachers have similar job responsibilities, commercial institutions and the military have natural career ladders built into the various titles and positions that differentiate the work force, especially among professional and executive personnel. It is not necessary to raise salaries from one year to the next for persons holding the same position in order to have an incentive system, but only to tie promotion to performance. The establishment of career ladders for teachers could accomplish the same function as those in industry and the military if the number of openings truly reflects school system needs for responsibilities to be covered, and advancement is based on merit.

The characteristics of a good merit pay program in industry include the following (Sibson, 1974):

- The program should be structured so as to help attract and retain the numbers and kinds of employees required to operate the business. Both the levels and forms of compensation for each group of employees must be reasonably competitive with pay levels and practices that prevail in the various labor markets in which the enterprise competes.
- The program should help to maintain the company in a reasonably competitive position in its product market.
- The nature of the program and the associated administrative time costs must be reasonable and must be in proportion to the other priorities and time demands on the company's financial resources and available management time.
- The program must gain employee acceptance. This does not

necessarily mean that employees must "approve" pay actions, or that compensation policies and practices are somehow subject to popular referendum. It does mean that employees must understand the policies and practices and accept both their concepts and specific actions as being reasonable and impartially administered.

- The compensation program must play a positive role in motivating employees to perform their duties to the best of their abilities and in a manner which supports the achievement of enterprise goals.
- The program must gain acceptance by the firm's "public," which includes owners and, increasingly, the government and to some extent customers, investors, and the general public.
- The compensation program must provide opportunity for employees at every level to achieve their reasonable aspirations in a framework of equity, impartiality, and reasonableness.

In each instance above, parallel principles can be identified for educational institutions. Part of the problem schools face in connection with the first principle, for example, are vastly expanding career opportunities for college-educated women. Bright, talented women graduating from college today are no longer restricted to teaching careers but have the whole range of professional and managerial career options to consider. School systems are now in direct competition for the best of this talent with institutions in every industry. They must respond with appropriate compensation systems if they are to be even moderately successful in attracting and retaining top talent. Just as industry typically turns to merit pay to motivate workers when productivity declines and resources become limited, performance-based pay for teachers would seem to be one way of enhancing the attractiveness of teaching significantly at a time when education faces increased competition for limited tax dollars. It is unlikely that public sentiment would ever favor increasing *all* teachers' salaries 50 percent or more, that is, a sufficient amount to make them reasonably competitive with the private sector; but a merit pay program could offer such possibilities for a good number of teachers. The increase in private sector merit pay programs during the 1980s undoubtedly enhanced public sentiment for increased teacher pay based on performance assessment. In 1985 six Americans in ten favored merit pay for teachers. Although 33 percent said teachers' salaries were too low, a larger number (43 percent) felt they were about right (Gallup, 1985).

Just as teacher incentive structure plans are highly dependent on the quality of assessment instruments and procedures, considerable effort is devoted in the private sector as well to improving the means of performance assessment. In the banking industry, for example, reported trends include (Cole and Smith, 1979):

- clearer and better standards of performance
- improved methods of performance appraisal
- increased training in performance assessment for supervisors
- greater measurement of group as well as individual performance
- more frequent comparisons of one department against another.

The same problems exist with general rating practices in industry as in education: evaluator bias and halo tendencies, ambiguity of feedback, and inflation of scores, among others. To reduce rating problems, many companies have developed more precisely focused rating systems for targeting judgments to specified performance criteria. Jobs are described clearly and classified precisely; then surveys are made to determine how salaries are distributed throughout the industry for similar positions (rank-to-job evaluation) as a means of deciding on a particular salary. Another common procedure assigns points to various compensable factors such as job scope and span of authority in order to derive an overall performance score (point-factor job evaluation) (Schuster, 1984).

Some organizations use multiple judges to reduce the dependency on a single evaluator. Employees are asked to name several other employees who are in a position to evaluate their work and paired-comparison rating procedures are used to obtain judgment from these peers (Edwards and Sproull, 1985).

In drawing parallels between education and industry, differences as well as similarities need to be recognized. The financial well-being of public schools does not depend as directly on the success of their teaching as corporate earnings depend on how well companies produce and market their products. Nevertheless, the wave of criticism of public education during the past decade and the attention paid to standardized test results indicate that schools do undergo regular scrutiny by the public and teachers cannot be immune to accountability demands. To the extent that other institutions than schools provide incentive pay based on performance assessment, educators will be under pressure to do the same.

One other difference that might be noted between teachers and white-collar business employees in particular has to do with attitudes toward competition and achievement-striving. While stereotyping teachers as noncompetitive and business employees as hard-driving, individualistic competitors vastly oversimplifies the comparison, differential tendencies do exist between these two types of employees that must be recognized. Merit pay is likely to have more extensive support in business circles, both from management and employees, than in education.

Merit pay is less likely to be found where unions are strong. The Bureau of National Affairs reports that only 16 percent of unionized plants have merit pay plans, compared with 60 percent of nonunionized plants (Printz and Waldman, 1985). To the extent that teachers are organized tightly along union lines, they can be expected to be at least somewhat resistant to such programs. In contrast to their industrial counterparts, furthermore, most teachers are not accustomed to being compared in any precise, formal way to other teachers. Therefore, considerable anxiety and teacher resistance can be expected from the installation of merit pay programs and the more explicit, more rigorous evaluation practices which they require.

Even in industry, where people tend to work for recognition and money, incentive pay plans that are poorly designed or badly implemented are reported to have serious negative consequences. They lower morale and self-esteem. They often induce unhealthy, cutthroat competition. A well-conceived merit pay plan, on the other hand, can improve not only quality but productivity and morale as well (Printz and Waldman, 1985). Because of different traditions in education and different attitudes toward competitive assessment practices, the importance of careful, thorough planning in the design and implementation of merit pay programs for teachers cannot be overemphasized. Despite the tendency of teachers, hospital workers, and other government employees in particular to resist merit pay, one personnel authority concluded (Thomsen, 1978): "A conceptually sound system of incentives in any organization increases productivity."

The differences between education and private enterprise notwithstanding, the parallels were many and the need to try great. It was time for the private sector to dominate. Before looking at what happened, let me review briefly the long history of merit pay attempts in education and the reasons behind educators' hesitancy to try it again.

EDUCATOR HESITANCY

> For three-quarters of a century, merit pay for teachers has been vigorously debated in many school systems and in almost every state in the nation. (Robinson, 1983)

Not only had the concept been debated, but merit pay programs had been established in hundreds of school districts at one time or another. Some lasted a year or two; others much longer. Some were quite "successful," at least in the minds of local leaders responsible for their continuation. Many others were clear failures— causing dissension among teachers and extra burdens for administrators (ERS, 1979). A 1983 study of forty-seven districts with merit pay programs indicated that 26 percent of their faculties (range: 0 percent to 100 percent) received awards averaging $1,064 (range: $28 to $6,000) (ERS, 1983).

Throughout most of the century, a vacillating interest in merit pay for teachers has reflected the peaks and valleys of public endorsement and concern over the state of education and its leadership. As many as 40 to 50 percent of America's school districts had plans in effect during the 1920s. A steady barrage of complaints about the arbitrary nature of principal judgments and sharply higher pay for men over women and secondary over elementary teachers gradually led to the replacement of merit pay with uniform salary schedules during the thirties and forties. With the Soviet Union's launching of Sputnik in the late 1950s and a widespread disenchantment with "progressive education" came a renewed clamor for paying teachers on the basis of performance. More than 11 percent of the larger school districts (those with more than six thousand students) were operating merit pay programs in 1968. A decade later, however, the Educational Research Service found only 4 percent of school districts with such plans in effect (ERS, 1979). The decline was blamed on two things: difficulties in measuring teacher performance and teacher union opposition (Robinson, 1983).

By 1985, Murnane and Cohen (1986) were able to locate only seven districts with student enrollments of ten thousand or more with plans that had been in effect for at least five years and paid awards of at least $1,000. These were typically wealthy suburban districts with large teacher applicant pools where salaries and working conditions were more attractive than in neighboring districts. Awards were given inconspicuously to almost all teachers, so as to minimize disappointment and competitiveness. No system exists in which salary differentials are based exclusively on differences in performance (Jacobson, 1989).[4]

The claim of educators, when they review the history, is that we have tried merit pay many times before and it seldom works. The problems of fair, accurate measurement of teacher performance are serious and defy easy resolution.

Other related reform suggestions, such as differentiated staffing, master teacher, and career ladder programs have been pursued before as well, without lasting success (English, 1984; Freiberg, 1984). Similar concerns underlie the resistance to these other efforts as well as to merit pay. They are considered divisive and coercive. Individualism and elitism are fostered to the dismay of average and below average performers.

Teachers are not motivated by money, I am told, but by the love of their work and the knowledge of its effects. They already try to teach well, and extra money will not make them try any harder. In fact, merit pay insults their sense of professionalism and serves as a disincentive. Teamwork and cooperation are destroyed by making teaching competitive. Teachers should be working with, not against, each other. The litany of reasons why differential treatment of teachers will not work is virtually endless.

The deeply entrenched, egalitarian norm of the education community has often been in conflict with community desires on evaluation issues. Time and again educators have tried to replace letter grades with other forms of reporting on their students' performances which presumably would be less comparative or norm-based and more informative and personal. They hoped youngsters would improve their reading because of the love and practice of it, not to receive an A. Educators understood the unfairness of comparing unequals and tried to substitute individual improvement as the basic variable to assess in assigning student grades. They wanted children to feel it was safe to fail. They tried to eliminate unnecessary failure whenever possible. Reducing the use of letter grades as the sole mechanism for evaluating children's work was widely endorsed in the educational community. Replacing grades with something else was just as widely rejected by parents, at least in typical middle- and upper-class America.

Profound differences should be noted on one other evaluation matter between what educators think is appropriate and what the public wants. The public judges how well schools are doing in great part by reports of test scores and other indicators of student performance. Many parents and community leaders also think that teachers should be judged, at least in part, by how much their students learn. The legislation that established recent career ladder programs in at least a half-dozen states included student outcomes among the criteria to be used in appraising teachers. Noting many technical and philosophical problems in trying to isolate the influence teachers have on students in consistent, measurable ways, educators have strongly resisted attempts to do so. Very few educator voices can be heard saying it is even possible, much less desirable.[5]

Given the dismal history of teacher merit pay and its almost unanimous rejection by the educational community as an idea worth trying again, it may be puzzling why it became such an important theme in the reform movement. Did not the very people for whom it was suppose to provide an incentive say it was a bad idea and would not work? Societal sentiment at that time was different, however, overwhelmingly in support of merit pay practices. Even some polls at the time suggested teachers favored the basic idea of basing pay on performance (Rist, 1983).[6] In retrospect, however, the polls were asking a "loaded" question, and a socially acceptable response was to agree: "Yes, pay should be based on performance." Once teachers could see the details on how this was to be accomplished, whatever they were, it was seen as a bad idea. They were just hesitant to say so.

By this time, educators were so much on the defensive that the safest strategy was to retreat from any immediate fight over the issue and hope for better days ahead. The reduced enrollments in teacher education programs were catastrophic (drops in a decade from one in five college students interested in teaching to one in twenty). Shortages in fields like mathematics, science, special education, foreign language, and bilingual education were especially great. Something clearly had to be done to regenerate the interest of high-caliber college students in teaching careers. Perhaps merit pay was worth another try. With public sentiment so strongly in favor of the idea, was there any use opposing it?

Despite their objections to merit pay and other reform notions that had been tried and failed before, educators themselves had few fresh ideas about how to improve the schools and solve the many problems they faced. Their primary interest was in more money and more support but not more direction on how to do it. Public patience for continued "hands-off" support had clearly waned. Conditions were ripe for new approaches with others in charge. But the gap in sentiment favoring teacher incentive pay between teachers and the public remained wide.

A DIVERSE RESPONSE

The groundswell of action for educational reform, and to consider and install teacher incentive programs in particular, was unprecedented at all levels. By spring 1984, master teacher or career ladder programs were under examination in half of the states and six had already begun statewide or had pilot programs underway (U.S. Department of Education, 1984). In fiscal years 1983 and 1984, the U.S. Department of Education spent 2.6 million dollars funding seventy-one teacher incentive planning efforts in thirty-seven states and two territories, many at the local level. One grant was made to the Education Commission of the States, which included the establishment of a clearinghouse to explore legal, evaluation, and cost issues related to teacher incentive plans. The Southern Regional Education Board also established a career ladder clearinghouse to facilitate information and technical assistance exchange among those involved in developing incentive programs. School districts through-out the country began considering the idea and in some cases proceeded to implement plans. By 1984–85, almost two out of five (38 %) of all public schools offered one or more teacher incentive programs, more than double the number in existence the previous year (Bobbitt, 1989).

A study of local school districts in Virginia in 1986–87 found great differences in the eleven programs that were then underway (Brandt and Gansneder, 1987). Except for their newness (seven were less than two years old), no two were alike. As designated by the superintendents or their assistants in charge of the plans, six featured merit pay, four, career ladders, and one, a combination. However, one of the merit pay programs was having a career ladder feature added the next year, and two other places were considering similar moves. So, at least in Virginia, the distinction often drawn between merit pay and career ladders was not sharp.

Merit pay is characterized by some kind of monetary supplement for superior teaching. It is awarded as a bonus to those who have performed particularly well over the past year, with the possibility of other bonuses in subsequent years. With it is no increased responsibility or extra assignment.

In Virginia two of the three programs in which mandatory consideration of all teachers was required, rather than allowing them to participate on a voluntary basis, were of the merit pay type. Career ladder programs were all offered on a voluntary participation basis as were four of the merit pay programs. Career ladders typically, but not always, implied extra status and responsibility along with extra money for good or outstanding teaching. For example, in at least two districts, willingness to accept changes in teaching assignments, including transfer to other schools where one's special expertise might be especially needed, was expected of those promoted.

Of the five Virginia plans with career ladder structure, four had barely started; and extra roles for teachers, and possibly extra hours or days of work as well, were not yet fully described. In only one of the plans were participants required to work longer. In this plan, teachers in one of the career ladder classifications were supposed to average one-half hour per day and five days a year more than others, observing and assisting teachers and conducting staff development and curriculum or research activities; the other classification called for no extra duties. Extended hours or days under contract were optional in two plans, not expected at all in one plan, and not yet specified in another.[7]

One's promotion to the next rung on a ladder was usually designated for a longer period than one year—three, four, or five years, perhaps indefinitely. One other feature of all the career ladder plans and at least two merit pay plans was a requirement that teachers have a certain amount of teaching experience, especially in the district itself, before being eligible to participate. In one district ten years were required. In two others, six and seven years respectively were required for the first promotion and three more for the final steps on the ladder.

Teacher incentive pay in Virginia, therefore, is a young and diversified movement. The diversity reflects the full range of settings to be found in the state from Orange County to Fairfax, Danville to Northampton, and Virginia Beach to Bath County. Plans differ greatly with respect to percentages of teachers receiving incentive pay, criteria and data sources used to judge outstanding teaching, the amounts and types of awards, their voluntary versus nonvoluntary nature, and who conducts evaluation.

Teacher evaluation procedures have been improved substantially, especially for the seven plans in which limited numbers of teachers are selected for promotion and/or extra pay. Better evaluation takes more effort and resources. Student performance is at least one criterion and data source in approximately half the plans, the sole criterion in two. In five districts teachers, as well as administrators, serve either as recorders of classroom observation data or as full-fledged evaluators.

The great variation among these eleven plans undoubtedly reflects differences in purpose and intention of those who proposed and endorsed them, but also in political struggles and trade-offs during the planning process. Career ladders on which almost everybody is promoted require a much less rigorous (and less threatening) evaluation system than those in which only a few are selected. When pay is given primarily for extra duties, longer hours, and extended contracts, rather than for teaching extra well, traditional worker pay patterns still prevail; and teacher association leadership is likely to be more supportive.

In this study all 140 districts in the state were surveyed to find out what consideration had been given to teacher incentives and the status of final decisions on whether or not to launch a program. The data clearly indicate that pressure to install incentive pay programs came from the community or its representative body, the school board, not from professional educators. In all eleven districts that had programs underway, the majority of school board members and the community at large was considered in favor of the idea, as was true of at least half of those districts in which planning was still going on but in which a final decision had not been made. Except in the eleven districts, a relatively low degree of interest in having such plans was expressed for all educators, including central administrators. Even in the eleven districts, moreover, the majority of teachers was thought not to favor the idea.

Throughout Virginia, many planning activities in the mid-1980s were focused on teacher incentive plans, even in school districts that did not seriously consider developing programs. Four of every five school boards discussed the topic. Three of five conducted literature reviews, examined plans in operation elsewhere, and received staff recommendations; and half the districts established special task forces to consider possibilities. More than two dozen districts which had studied the idea for at least a year had not yet made a final decision on whether or not to develop a plan. As will be made clear, the diversity of reaction to teacher incentive pay in Virginia is but a small reflection of what happened nationwide.

IMPORTANCE OF THIS STUDY

Incentive pay was one of the major school reform efforts of the 1980s. This book examines how that movement was playing out across the country seven years after the primary call was made in 1983—what form it took, what issues arose as it was put into place, what political struggles ensued, how teachers and others felt about it, what impact it has had, and what its future might be.

By the end of the decade, many recently designed plans were still not fully implemented. More than a few others were in a developmental, pilot-testing and revision stage. Some were encountering substantial budget obligations for the first time as a result of phasing in advanced steps of a career ladder or expanding coverage to new schools or school districts beyond those involved in initial pilot projects. In a number of states, decisions had not yet been made to extend state support for pilot districts beyond the designated experimental period, expand programs to other districts or state-wide, or to shut the whole effort down. Some programs were being reassessed and modified by new leadership resulting from personnel changes in the superintendent's office, on the school board, or in the legislature where other priorities might then seem more exciting. Almost none had stood the real test of time.

What has been learned about planning and implementing such programs? Who should be involved? What needs to be considered? What are the critical issues to be resolved? What variations exist from one plan to another? What continuities prevail in those that succeed and those that fail? How accurately have costs been projected? What impact have these plans had on teacher morale, teacher motivation, principal acceptance, student outcomes, teacher recruitment and retention, community support? What, in general, can be learned by studying what has happened? This book is being written to address such questions.

My primary thesis is that the career ladder and incentive pay movement is an important one that deserves study and analysis. It is in an early stage of evolution; its final form is still uncertain. Close examination of what is happening may improve its chances for ultimate success. To those who argue that incentive pay has been tried before and proved unworkable, there are reasons to think that this time it *may* be different. It has already lasted longer than some people predicted. I am not certain, of course, whether it will be merely one more educational fad of no lasting importance or whether it will result in real structural change in the ways school are organized and teacher responsibilities conducted and rewarded. Its likely future should become more clear, however, after this review and synthesis of what is happening has been completed and at least tentative answers derived to the many questions addressed.

Although hundreds of articles and reports have been written about incentive pay and career ladder programs during the past half-dozen years, only a handful of books have appeared so far (Burden, 1987; Hatry and Greiner, 1985; Johnson, 1985; Klein, 1983–84; ERS, 1979; ERS, 1983). All of these references provide relevant historical background and identify some of the issues involved. None report what actually happened in response to the public outcry for incentive pay that swept the country in the wake of the recent commission reports.

This latter mandate was louder, more forceful, and more universal than ever before, and for that reason, among others, already has been heeded to a much greater extent. It is not just the strength of the mandate, but first, the changing nature of the work force and career opportunities for women, second, the emergence of a research base for identifying effective teaching practices, and third, employment cutbacks of white-collar workers and decreases in the competitive standing of American business and industry in world markets that provide a different underlying context. These and other contextual factors will be considered in my analysis of current career ladder trends and events.

One other reason for examining this movement closely while it is still unfolding is to enhance understanding of the organizational change process itself. Of all our institutions, schools are certainly among those most resistant to change.

Commercial and industrial concerns are expected to change as products and services become outdated and lose their competitive edge. Change, in fact, has been a major feature of twentieth-century living—in family organization and life-style, in community patterns and services, in modes of transportation, means of communication, types of entertainment, and patterns of work. Almost all our institutions have had to change and adapt. More than a few have even disappeared because change and adaptation were insufficient.

Schools too have changed, at least in some ways. They have become bigger, much bigger; they have become more departmentalized, more bureaucratic. The curriculum has expanded tremendously as schools have assumed more of the total teaching responsibility for what children are supposed to learn in the process of growing up. To the basic skills and traditional academic fare have been added driver education, drug abuse, multicultural education, and dozens of other specific subjects that communities expect today's schools to teach (Brandt, 1981).

In other ways, however, they have changed little. Most schools are still organized so that one person teaches a class of twenty or more students one subject at a time. All teachers, whether they have had twenty years of experience or almost no experience, teach approximately the same numbers of classes and students. Under the general direction of school district curriculum guides and textbook materials, teachers plan and conduct lessons, make assignments, and evaluate students as they see fit. Comparing groups of experienced with groups of inexperienced teachers, however, few systematic differences are detectable—in what is being taught, how it is presented, and what is learned. Presumably, classes taught by experienced rather than beginning teachers run more smoothly and children learn more. But such differences are not guaranteed. Consistent differences between two sets of experienced teachers, furthermore, one having taught an average of five years and the other fifteen years, cannot be discerned.

Individual teachers do vary a great deal, of course, in what they teach, how they conduct classes and in how much their children learn; that is, some teachers perform consistently better than others. It is just that these differences are not related to the amount of teaching experience they have had or even to the level of their own education. After the initial two or three years of teaching, the correlation of years of teaching with measures of teaching effectiveness is relatively low. In fact, studies by Schlecty and Vance (1981), among others, indicate that those with the strongest academic backgrounds leave teaching for other pursuits in greater numbers than those with weaker backgrounds.

Despite performance differences that are relatively unrelated to how long one has taught, differences in teachers' salaries have traditionally been based primarily on the years of teaching experience and the amount of college graduate credits earned.

Teacher incentive pay and career ladders, therefore, represent major change in school personnel practices. They have the potential to induce major structural change in organizational patterns that have been in place for a long time. One of the principal questions to be addressed in this volume is determining how much real change is actually taking place in those school systems that have adopted incentive programs. To what extent are teachers who are promoted on career ladders, for example, assuming greater responsibility and status than other teachers? How significant are the pay raises that are based on performance? What effects do the promotions and raises have on teacher morale, professionalism, and career aspirations? What percentages of teachers earn incentive pay or advance to the various levels of the ladder?

In summary then, I will review incentive pay and career ladder developments during the period of the eighties to take stock of what has happened and to derive answers to a number of important questions about their design and impact on the basis of what the evidence seems to indicate at this time. Such a synthesis of recent history ought to provide guidance for those still engaged in developing such programs. It ought also to serve as a benchmark against which later assessments might be made.

OVERVIEW

In this first chapter I reviewed the calls for school reform in the 1980s behind the push for teacher incentive pay. The business theme of rewarding those who work hardest and perform best seemed relevant. The competitive nature of most nongovernment American institutions was manifested both externally in profit and loss reports and internally in differential pay and promotion systems. A second underlying theme was a need to make schools more accountable for what they do. The national reform reports all sprang from a loss of confidence in teachers and school administrators.

I also reviewed briefly the history of teacher merit pay throughout most of this century and the reasons for current rejection of the idea by most educators. Thus, the career ladder and incentive pay movement should be recognized as a community-imposed reform. In those places where plans have been started, educational administrators, recognizing how unpopular the concept is, have to devote considerable time and attention to how planning might best take place and how initial resistance might be overcome. The result is a highly diverse set of programs.

In chapter 2 the full diversity will be made more explicit by the introduction of a program taxonomy featuring six incentive pay models. Sample programs will be used to illustrate each model. Capsule descriptions will be presented of state programs in Tennessee, South Carolina, and Utah, and also local programs in two small, semirural Virginia districts. Key structural dimensions will be described for comparing and contrasting them and other incentive programs.

Chapter 3 will focus on the planning process and approximately thirty issues which are likely to be confronted in the designing of incentive programs. An in-depth study will be presented of how planning was conducted and these issues resolved in one Virginia school system during the initial design stage.

In chapter 4 what happened with respect to these same issues will be traced as the Danville, Virginia, program was implemented during the next two years and all teachers and administrators became involved. Changing sentiments will be highlighted from measures taken at different time periods during early and later implementation. The design and implementation of career ladder programs in another state (Arizona) and one district in particular (Amphitheater) will be described and further information provided from third-party studies of the implementation of Utah programs to permit comparisons to be made of sentiments and procedures.

Chapter 5 will provide a close look at teacher motivation and organizational change processes in order to understand the forces shaping incentive plans in one direction or another and the diversity of responses found in Danville, South Carolina, Utah, and elsewhere. Ethnographic data will be used to cite and discuss likely reasons for teachers' hesitancy to accept such plans. A final section will highlight the power struggles over these programs that I found going on between various constituent groups. Teacher association leadership, for example, not only opposed the original enactment of performance-based pay, with some success, but reduced its influence as the dominant theme in most programs during district and school implementation.

The sixth chapter will provide an interim assessment of the movement and tentative answers to the various questions raised both in this initial chapter and later on. The scope and nature of the response will be summarized. Primary attention will be given to judging how much and what kinds of impact programs have had during the six to seven year period. A brief summary of current incentive pay activity and sentiment will be attempted by citing procedural changes in the early programs and primary features of later ones, and also by reviewing later expressions of educator sentiments.

In chapter 7 I will reassess the public mood to see how strong and enduring the sentiment might still be for this particular reform. I cautiously speak of the future, although I hedge my bets on how long programs will last or how profound their effects will ultimately be on school organization and practice. A final section will spell out a series of policy and procedural recommendations, based on what we have learned, for those who want to start or continue such programs.

The terms "incentive pay," "incentive movement," "incentive programs," and the letters "TIP" will be used as brief umbrella terms to refer to what others might call teacher incentive pay, incentive pay and career ladders, merit pay, pay for performance, teacher incentive pay movement, and so on. All of these terms carry different meanings for different people. When I use any of these umbrella terms, I shall be referring to pay practices (programs or movement) where either the quality of teaching performance provides at least one basis for extra pay, or extra pay is provided for doing something special (working longer hours or additional days, assuming extra responsibilities, teaching in areas where a teacher shortage exists). When "merit pay," "pay-for-performance," or "performance component" is used alone, I shall be referring specifically to extra pay being related to the quality of performance, however it is judged. "Career ladders" typically, but not always, feature performance to some extent in the qualifications required for promotion to steps on the ladder. As will be explained in chapter 2, some career ladders are much more performance-based than others. "Bonuses" are usually supposed to reflect high-quality performance or productivity.

To protect anonymity and enhance readability, I shall adopt the convention of using feminine pronouns when referring to unidentified individual teachers and masculine pronouns for everyone else. It should be understood that I am not attempting to reinforce sex-stereotypes of teachers, administrators, or others.

A Program Taxonomy

The current movement is a diverse one. Incentive pay programs differ in a number of ways, such as: *the type of award* (Whether it is a bonus to be earned annually or a promotion with higher status and salary?); *the size of the award* (Whether it amounts to hundreds or thousands of dollars?); *criteria, measures, and standards* (What teachers have to do? How and by whom they are judged?); and *primary purposes* (Whether to reward only superior teachers, to encourage all teachers to improve, to increase student achievement, etc.?).

Programs cannot always be distinguished by their labels. Some career ladders are highly competitive and designed to reward a select few; others provide opportunities for almost all teachers to be advanced. With some, the basis for promotion is the quality of one's teaching; for others, it is the assumption of extra duties and longer working hours. Bonus and master teacher plans vary in the same ways.

In this chapter, the kinds of programs now in operation will be described along with case histories of representative examples. These case histories are based on data obtained in answers to a series of questions asked of program administrators and used in reviewing program reports and other descriptive documents. Each illustrative program will be described briefly and summary information provided about teacher participation rates, eligibility requirements, assessment methods, costs, and other distinguishing features.

KIND OF PROGRAMS

Superior Teacher Programs

A number of programs are designed to recognize and reward individuals who consistently perform in an outstanding manner with promotion to a higher rank on a career ladder and a substantial salary supplement. Such persons are often but not always expected to take on extra responsibility, such as supervising novice teachers or providing staff development leadership for colleagues. One's potential for such roles may even be included in the selection criteria. However, the primary reason for one's selection is outstanding teaching on a regular basis.

The primary assumption underlying these programs is that some persons are exceptionally good teachers who can be distinguished from other teachers by the quality of their teaching. It is also assumed that identifying and rewarding such individuals should attract and retain the very best teachers for a school district. In addition to teaching well themselves, they should also serve as appropriate models for others to emulate.

The upper two levels of the Tennessee career ladder program exemplify the Superior Teacher Model and will be described below.

Case History: Tennessee Career Ladder Program

Under Governor Lamar Alexander's widely acclaimed leadership, a statewide career ladder program was initiated in 1983 as one component of a comprehensive reform effort. A one-billion-dollar tax package accompanied the legislation and permitted the program to be designed and implemented quickly. The first candidates were promoted to the ladder during 1984–85. Four years later, more than 39,000 people, 84 percent of the state's educators, had received a career ladder certificate, 6,200 at one of the top two levels.

The program was originally designed primarily as a merit pay program[1] to identify and reward superior teachers; and by so doing, to attract and keep the best teachers as one way of improving the quality of education. Governor Alexander's reminder that the best teachers received not one cent more than the poorest teachers was the underlying theme that gave shape to the career ladder.

While the vast majority of Tennessee's tenured teachers, administrators, and other professional specialists (those successfully completing the initial probationary and apprentice years) are now participating in the program at the CL I level and thousands have received training in the evaluation system to improve their teaching, promotion to the upper two levels of the career ladder (II and III) is still done sparingly and only after rigorous scrutiny by an outside peer evaluation team. Only one out of five eligible teachers and administrators holds level II or III certificates. Salary supplements range from $1,000 at CL I to $7,000 for CL III teachers on twelve-month contracts. Along with extra supplements for each level, CL II and III teachers can volunteer and have priority for extended contracts and extra responsibilities during the summer months. The state provides all the funding for teachers' salaries and career ladder supplements.

Although a number of changes have been made in program procedures and the performance assessment system, one is particularly noteworthy. In 1987, the legislature made the career ladder program optional for all tenured teachers (It had been required for those who were certified and first employed in Tennessee after 1 July, 1984), and a licensing system was created to permit those not on the ladder to teach. The career ladder remains an option for those who meet the experience requirements and seek performance-based salary supplements and status.

The performance evaluation system to identify CL II and CL III teachers is the product of extensive research and development on ways to measure what teachers do. It is a highly sophisticated and somewhat costly system, which is intended to recognize and include in the assessment processes the many components of good teaching. The several data sources and instruments used are shown in Exhibit 2.1. Data for each teacher are converted into separate scores for each of five performance domains and various performance indicators.

Exhibit 2.1

Data Sources and Instruments Used in the Tennessee Career Ladder
Evaluation System (from French et al., 1988)

Sources	Instruments
1. Teacher candidate	1. Professional development and leadership summary
	2. Observations (6)
	3. Dialogues (3)
	4. Tests:
	Written test of professional knowledge
	Written tests of reading and writing skills
2. Students	5. Student questionnaires
	(elementary and secondary forms)
3. Principal	6. Principal questionnaire
4. Peer evaluator team (three people)	7. Consensus rating (based on patterns developed over day-long visits by each evaluator)

Note: Peer evaluators administer observations, dialogues, and student questionnaires listed above.

They are then combined to yield one total performance score on a 200 to 800 scale. Passing scores were set at 700 for CLIII and 600 for CLII candidates. To qualify as a candidate for these levels and become a recipient of the outside review, one has to attain 450 or more in each domain and have a history of successful locally conducted evaluations.

Most important, considering the difficulty in distinguishing superior from acceptable teaching, this system apparently works. Fifty (71 percent) of the seventy scores generated by these data sources separated levels I and II teachers in 1985–86 by half a standard deviation or more, and forty-two scores (60 percent) separated levels II and III by the same amount (McLarty, 1987).

Special features of the Tennessee career ladder program include:

- a highly objective, comprehensive summative evaluation system based on multiple instruments and data sources, highly trained peer evaluators from outside the district, an integrated scoring system that combines data from several sources on weighted indicators and distinguishes fairly and consistently between levels I, II, and III
- a high degree of selectivity for superior teachers
- a state designed and operated system at the upper career levels with increased local management at the beginning and lower levels
- state certificates for each step on the ladder that are renewable every ten years
- separate but related criteria and performance indicators for several types of educators in addition to regular classroom teachers, including special population teachers, librarians, psychologists, attendance workers, school social workers, counselors, principals, assistant principals, and supervisors
- a computer printout summary for diagnostic feedback purposes for each level II and III candidate of his/her scores by domain, or indicator, and instrument
- a related career development program for all teachers for mentor, evaluator, and other service roles

Other superior teacher programs can be found in Danville and Lynchburg, Virginia, and at the highest career ladder levels of North Carolina, Texas, and Arizona programs once they become fully operational.

Student Learning Models

In two kinds of programs, student learning is the primary criterion for incentive pay. Measures for assessing student gain are selected, learning objectives specified, and, if they are reached, the teachers involved receive a bonus.

In one model, teachers establish student performance goals, class by class, and subject by subject, or someone else determines their goals and measures for them. They work toward the accomplishment of their goals on an individual basis and receive a bonus if they succeed.

In the other model, schoolwide goals are set and teachers presumably work together to reach them. All teachers in the school, assuming any additional individual requirements are met, receive similar bonuses if student learning targets are reached. The assumption underlying student learning models is that teachers will teach most effectively if they have specific student performance goals to reach and an extra incentive to do so.

Student achievement is specifically mentioned in the legislation establishing career ladder plans in several states, including Arizona, Texas, Utah, and South Carolina. The latter provides clear examples of how student learning models operate.

Case History: South Carolina Teacher Incentive Pay Programs

The number of South Carolina districts operating TIP pilot programs increased from nine in 1985–86 to seventeen in 1986–87, and forty-four in 1987–88, serving approximately 60 percent of the state's students. State funding of this program went from $2.2 million to $12 million in the same period. The program was implemented in all school districts in 1988–89 with funding at $21.5 million.

Originally, three models were piloted, with school districts selecting their preferred option. One model, a career ladder plan, was phased out because extra pay seemed based more on additional work than superior performance or productivity. Of the remaining two models, a *bonus* plan rewards teachers for demonstrating superior performance on each of four criteria (student achievement, performance evaluation, self-improvement, and attendance); and a *campus/individual* plan allows teachers to participate on three levels: collectively in a schoolwide effort to increase student achievement gains above state projected expectations for their particular schools, as individuals in a manner identical to those in the bonus plans, or in both ways.

Under the bonus plan and the individual component of the C/I model, teachers can be awarded between $2,000 and $3,000 annually. Each district decides what the exact amount should be, based on the funding available to the district and the number of teachers who qualify. The maximum amount of an award under the campus component is also $3,000, and "the minimum amount is determined by the total number of eligible teachers in the schools that meet student achievement goals and the available funds which are shared equally among those teachers in the district."[2]

The stated purpose of the plan is to reward teachers "who demonstrate superior performance and productivity." All teachers, media specialists, and guidance counselors who hold continuing contracts are eligible to apply. For those individual applicants who either withdraw during the year or otherwise fail to receive an award, insufficient student achievement gain and not meeting the teacher attendance standard have been primary reasons. Low ratings on classroom teaching performance have also kept some teachers whose schools attained campus awards from receiving their share. Most district performance observation instruments, at the initiation of pilot testing of this program, did not permit sufficiently clear, reliable distinctions to be made between satisfactory and superior teaching to base awards on this criterion. The instruments tended to be formative to help target aspects of teaching that needed improvement. Throughout the pilot test years, districts revised them to distinguish superior performance. A state-designed prototype instrument was developed in 1988–89 to assist districts that did not have one that distinguished superior teaching performance.

In 1987–88, 4,632 teachers were award recipients, one-fifth of the 22,686 teachers eligible to participate in the forty-four pilot districts. The percentages of eligible teachers receiving awards averaged 11 percent in the bonus districts, 14 percent in the career ladder districts, and 25 percent in the campus/individual districts. The award amounts varied considerably, however, with individual awards, under both the bonus and individual component of the C/I model, in the $2,000 to $3,000 range and campus awards between $330 and $2,375. In one district, for example, 67 persons received individual awards of $3,000 and 170 received campus awards of $330. Another fifty to sixty teachers were in schools that won campus awards, but were disqualified by not meeting one or more of the other entry or award criteria specified by the model.

Another feature of these plans should be noted, namely their increased competitiveness as the numbers of participating teachers and schools increase. Participation rates were typically higher in 1988–89; and as more individuals or schools participated, the numbers of participants who tried and failed to receive awards increased also. Under the campus component awards are restricted to teachers who are working in schools whose average student gain scores are in the top quartile in comparison with other schools in the state with similar student populations and demographics. Award amounts are limited by the total amount of state funds received for the program, unless the district itself appropriates funds to supplement state funds. To determine recipients under the bonus model and the individual component, when there are more qualified applicants than awards, local teacher-dominated incentive commit-tees assign points to reflect the difficulty of each applicant's target objectives at the beginning of the year. This point system permits teachers to be ranked at the end of the year on the quality of their accomplishments.

The South Carolina teacher incentive pay program is distinctive in several ways:

- Local districts have a choice of two state-supported models, one based on individual teacher performance only and the other featuring schoolwide incentives but still allowing individuals to seek their own awards, which typically will be larger. As the number of recipients under the campus component increases, the amount of the award decreases.
- More than four out of five teachers in the pilot districts have been eligible to participate each year; but the amount of money provided by the state is purposely limited so that, with the size of individual awards fixed, only a fraction of that number can received awards. In one pilot district, for example, 260 teachers qualified for $2,500 awards in 1987–88, but money was available for only 160. The district had the option of increasing the number of recipients to 200 by decreasing the amount of each award to the state-prescribed minimum of $2,000.
- Although the state distributes funds equally among the districts on the basis of student enrollments, districts have a choice between models and a decision about the size of individual awards (between $2,000 and $3,000). For districts choosing the C/I model, decisions must be made also about

which schools will participate. In both plans, each teacher makes a decision whether or not to participate. Thus, the program provides various choices and stimulates considerable decision-making at the local level.

- Teachers are the dominant constituents on district incentive committees that approve applicants' target objectives and monitor their accomplishments. If there are more applicants than can be recipients, these committees' rankings of teachers' performance on target objectives determine who they will be.

- The use of student gain scores as the most important criterion for determining superior teaching and productivity is quite distinctive. Although school incentive programs, similar to the campus component, are found elsewhere, very few school districts have attempted to emphasize student learning as much in the assessment of individual teacher performance. The selection of appropriate tests and concerns about proper administration and scoring practices, test security, and the equating of standards across subjects, grade levels, and differing student populations represent only a few of the measurement problems that need to be addressed if teachers are to be judged fairly on this criterion.

   South Carolina pilot districts have obtained considerable technical assistance on these matters and adopted a number of procedures designed to improve the quality of student outcome data in relation to teacher performance. Typically, relative gain scores are used to determine whether "expected normative growth" has been exceeded. In some cases, districts have drawn on commercially available, computerized test-item banks to construct their own criterion-referenced pre-post measures and to obtain outside scoring assistance. Where tests are not appropriate, teachers submit plans for collecting pre-post samples of student work and other evidence to document productivity. For teachers of the same subjects and grades, similar measures are devised and administered in a given year. Overall, the state has concentrated a great deal of attention on improving student achievement, one of the major themes of its reform legislation, and developing procedures for using it as a criterion measure of successful teaching.

- Also important as a criterion measure is teacher attendance. That incentive pay recipients cannot miss more than 10 days a year, except for district-authorized professional leave or legally required court appearances, apparently deters many teachers from applying for individual award programs and is a major reason why some withdraw after they apply. In schools receiving campus awards, a substantial number of teachers may also be denied an accompanying bonus because they do not meet the attendance standard.

- Not only are media specialists and guidance counselors included in the teacher incentive program, but a separate program exists for school principals as part of the reform legislation as well as a school incentive program. The campus component of the teacher incentive program operates in conjunction with the school incentive program and has similar standards to be met.

- In some districts, peer teachers are trained to conduct unannounced classroom observations of teacher applicants, and their ratings, along with principals' ratings, determine how well the teacher performance criterion has been met.

- Statewide, teacher incentive money is included along with supplements for advanced degrees as part of total teacher pay in determining whether a legislatively established goal has been met, namely, keeping salaries for South Carolina teachers at least as high, on average, as those in the rest of the Southeast. Currently, that standard is being met, however, even without incentive pay included.

Staff Development Models

Many programs are designed primarily to stimulate teacher behavior in a given direction (increase teacher attendance, participate in staff development activities, pursue graduate degrees, and so on). The purpose of such programs is teacher improvement in knowledge, behavior, and teaching ability. No attempt is made, however, to base pay supplements on improvement in the quality of their overall teaching. Teachers are paid extra for taking part in designated activities or in providing evidence of particular accomplishments such as completing a graduate degree, publishing an article in a professional journal, or giving a report at a conference. It is assumed that participation in professional development activities will make them better teachers.

Incentive pay is given for such purposes in almost all school districts, so the number of examples to choose from here is virtually unlimited. I describe an incentive pay program developed in a small rural Virginia school district to illustrate this model because of its direct focus on the improvement of individual teaching skills as the basis for rewards. It has several unique features and has been exported to a number of other school districts.

Case History: Orange County, Virginia, Pay-for-Performance Program

The Orange County public schools are located in a semirural, small town area approximately ninety miles southwest of Washington, D.C. They consist of one high school, one junior high school, and four elementary schools with a teaching staff of approximately 235. Their pay-for-performance program has been operational since 1983. The teacher assessment system on which it is based is updated annually, but its overall structure has remained relatively unchanged.

The program is designed to help teachers acquire and improve effective teaching skills. Its purpose is to promote staff development by recognizing teacher competency, rewarding teachers for demonstrating it, and providing the means and challenges for its enhancement. At $165 annually, the bonus for successful participation is financially inconsequential, but symbolically important. More important, however, are the clearly targeted instructional assistance teachers receive and the nonthreatening, highly reinforcing manner in which it is given.

The program is organized around twelve professional practice areas (classroom routines, essential techniques of instruction, and others) and fifteen procedures for effective teaching (e.g., circulates among students inviting participation). For each area, the assessment manual describes eight to twelve generic performance indicators of effective teaching and provides examples of how they might be manifested. Participating teachers each choose one broad area to concentrate on for a nine-week period, up to three areas a year. During that time trained peer observers make two classroom visits on the days and with the class the teacher selects. Observers record in objective, narrative language teacher behaviors and actions that exemplify the performance indicators in the target area. Pre-conferences precede the observations for discussion of performance indicators, and post-conferences allow teachers a chance to review the observation report for completeness and accuracy before it is sent to the principal for rating. Thus, peer observers provide the documentation, and principals judge what the record indicates in relation to the standards. Reviewing the two or more observation reports, principals rate each teacher's performance with each targeted practice as "insufficient," "competent" (satisfactory), or "proficient" (superior). A rating review by the central office can be requested if a teacher is dissatisfied with a rating.

Consistently over the years, 98 percent of the teachers have chosen to participate and more than 90 percent have received the small bonuses for achieving proficiency with their professional goals.

Special features of this program include:

- Maximizing the positive and, with very few exceptions, ignoring the negative. Teachers can select the areas in which to be observed and judged. Observers only record what is right (examples of a performance indicator being displayed), never what is wrong.
- Selecting, training, and using a cadre of highly respected teachers to serve as peer observers for providing documentation and formative assistance for other teachers. Approximately 15 percent of all the teachers serve this function in any given year on a released time basis while continuing to teach their own classes as well. They receive thirty hours of training and from $500 to $1,600 extra pay.
- Restricting the role of peer evaluators to observer-recorder which provides the evaluator (the principal) with better documentation than he typically has on his own and gives him time to work with teachers who need special assistance.
- Favorable reactions from teachers with 70 to 80 percent indicating the observation reports make them feel "better about the job" they are doing and more than half of them saying they would recommend the pay program to other teachers. Importantly, half of them typically report that they did some different things this year to become proficient in at least one of their targeted practices.

Area Incentives Model

Extra inducements are sometimes offered to find and keep qualified teachers for certain subjects, grade levels, student populations, neighborhoods, and even entire school districts.

In 1984–85, twenty-eight states funded incentive programs to attract science and mathematics teachers. The most common type of incentive was a loan with a forgiveness clause to provide financial help for those preparing to teach in these fields and also for current teachers to upgrade their science or mathematics backgrounds.[3] Over 3,500 teachers received funds during 1983–85 (Beal et al., 1986).

The retention as well as the attraction of high quality teachers is indeed a serious problem. According to a study of white North Carolina teachers who began teaching in 1976–78, half of them left the field for other pursuits within eight years. One in four left after only one or two years. Chemistry and physics teachers typically went first, half of them being gone within six years. Biology and English teachers also tended to leave sooner than others. Proportionately more teachers with high National Teacher Examination (NTE) scores left teaching than their lower scoring colleagues. Although almost one-third of those who left the field reentered it some years later, those with high NTE scores were least likely to do so (Murnane et al., 1989).

States and school districts offering special pay incentives have other targets as well. New Jersey spent $260,000 in 1988–89 to attract promising high school minority students into teaching. New York spent $1.7 million the year before to attract potential teachers to work with "at-risk" students as part of a teacher opportunity corps. It spent another $4 million on scholarships and fellowships for students preparing to teach in shortage areas. Oregon spent more than a half million dollars on a teacher corps program with education loans to academically talented and minority students and to those willing to teach in remote areas (Cornett, 1987). New York City has a recruiting office in Puerto Rico, and Dallas offers a $1,000 bonus for teachers with bilingual ability (*Wall Street Journal*, 26 September, 1989).

The staffing of inner city schools in large urban school districts is particularly troublesome. Faculty are often relatively young, inexperienced teachers with a high absentee rate. Teacher turnover is high. Transfers out of economically depressed areas are up to ten times higher than those out of advantaged areas. Court testimony in a 1980 Los Angeles case indicated that some inner city high school students had as many as twenty-six different teachers in a single year (Bruno, 1986).

To improve the attractiveness of teaching in such schools, various incentives have been offered such as reduced class sizes and pay supplements. The latter have often been referred to as "combat" or "hazard" pay. Typically, such incentives are only modest in amount, however, because of the budget limitations of most urban school districts.

Bruno and Negrete (1983) studied teacher turnover patterns in a large metropolitan district that gave 11 percent supplements to those who taught in racially isolated schools. They deemed the program "only marginally successful." Teacher turnover rates changed little after the supplements were started. Teachers receiving supplements were required to stay at school longer than teachers elsewhere (two to three hours extra per week). Driving to and from home to school in big city traffic also added complexity and time. So the overall incentive value of the supplement was questionable at best. I have not located programs where the magnitude of pay supplements is sufficiently great to judge the potential effectiveness of combat pay.

Recent information indicates that teacher supply problems may actually be getting worse and increased use of special inducements may be needed to solve them. According to a nationwide survey of more than 40,000 public school teachers in 1987–88, very few (2.2%) were actually receiving extra pay for teaching either in a shortage field (e.g. math, science) or in a high-priority location (e.g. an inner-city school). (NCES, 1990). While forgivable loans apparently attract people into shortage fields and assignments for a few years, greater use of direct salary supplements might be needed to keep them there. The North Carolina study cited above (Murnane et al., 1989) provides substantial evidence that teachers do indeed respond to financial incentives. Their length of stay in teaching was highly dependent on salary. Those with higher salaries ($2,000 above average in 1987 dollars) stayed considerably longer than those with average and especially those with below-average salaries. This trend was found among both elementary and secondary teachers. It was more pronounced with the latter and for those in their first few years of teaching. Those few school districts that offer special pay incentives today, often with the approval of union leadership, to attract and keep good teachers, especially in high priority areas, seem to be taking realistic, promising steps toward the solution of some of their major personnel problems.

High Participation Model

Initial steps on many career ladders and some entire plans appear to be designed so all but a few teachers whose performance is below minimum district standards can participate in the program and receive "incentive pay." Typically, all but 2 or 3 percent of the teachers who have continuing contracts are on the ladder. The pay supplement is usually small in comparison to what it is for those on higher rungs of the ladder. In reality, it amounts to an across-the-board raise for almost everyone.

There appear to be at least two reasons why districts adopt such plans. One is to claim participation in the career ladder movement, both for the school district as a whole and for the vast majority of its teachers. With the public demanding a halt to automatic, equal pay raises for teachers regardless of how well they perform, districts can legitimately say they have changed the pay system to a performance-based one. Teachers who do a good job receive more pay than those who do not.

Without such a plan it is very hard to judge someone's teaching as so poor, after sufficient help has been given, that he or she should be denied a raise which everybody else receives. Unsatisfactory teaching is ill-defined. The evaluation system is too imprecise.

The need to improve evaluation systems and make perfor-mance expectations more explicit led to the establishment of such career ladders. Principals would no longer have to act so completely on their own when not rewarding weak teachers. All teachers would be evaluated against a comprehensive set of standards. Those who came up short would be given special assistance to improve their teaching. No one would receive regular pay increases whose performance was judged unsatisfactory. The new evaluation system would indicate the specific areas of deficiency and reasons why performance-based pay raises were denied.

These programs are minimum-competency oriented. Their focus is on poor teachers—helping them improve or weeding them out so children and the reputation of the schools do not suffer.

Although many programs would serve as appropriate illustra-tion for this high participation model, Hanover County near Richmond, Virginia is used here for this purpose.

Case History: Hanover County, Virginia, Pay-For-Performance Plan

Salary increases for all teachers, counselors, librarians, and other instructional personnel are designed to reflect rises in the cost of living and satisfactory or better teaching performance. Increases in regular salary allocations (e.g. 7 percent) are divided into these two components (e.g. 2 percent for cost of living and 5 percent for performance). All individuals receive annual cost-of-living increases. The vast majority of teaching personnel (97 percent in 1985–86) receive the pay-for-performance increases as well. The primary basis for assessing performance is administrators' ratings of more than forty teaching characteristics after making five half-hour observations and determining how well teacher-selected target objectives have been met. Adopting a performance-based plan was accomplished by improving the evaluation system and using it to decide who would receive a full raise.

The primary reason for labeling this a pay-for-performance plan is to dispel a widely held public perception that teachers have automatic pay raises each year regardless of how well they teach. The step-based salary schedules used in Virginia school districts convey an impression that teachers are not evaluated and the quality of their teaching is not considered in salary decisions. The Hanover County superintendent reports a considerable change in the public's attitude as a result of the formal adoption of this plan. In addition, those few whose teaching was rated as below district standards have either worked hard to improve or voluntarily resigned their positions.[4]

In much the same way, the first step on many career ladders is designed for almost all teachers once they achieve tenure. More than 80 percent of the teachers in Tennessee, Utah, and the North Carolina career ladder pilot districts make the first step once they become eligible to apply.

Full Career Model

Many programs feature extended contract opportunities during the summer months, extra duty pay for free-time and after-school responsibilities during the school year, and extra pay for supervisory or administrative assignments during the school day. Examples of the latter two types, in fact, are found in almost all school districts. Department chairpersons, grade-level coordinators, football and drama coaches, and club sponsors are only a few of the many special roles teachers assume in addition to classroom teaching that may provide salary supplements ranging from a few hundred to several thousand dollars. Summer school teaching also adds income for many teachers, although the rate of pay is often established on a lower hourly basis than one's basic contract.

Increasingly in many districts, nonteaching days for planning and staff development activities are being added to teacher work calendars with additional pay commensurate with the extra time. Opportunities are increasing, also, for teachers to conduct instruction-related assignments after school and in the summer: taking part in staff development activities, developing curriculum materials, conducting research, or performing other school district assignments.

Such job enlargement activities can be intellectually and professionally enriching for talented teachers. They should be distinguished, however, from hall duty, club supervision, or other routine or administrative duties that may supplement pay without necessarily enhancing one's sense of being a respected professional (Duke, 1984).

Job enlargement activities extend and expand teachers' role from classroom instructor alone to fully functioning professional educator. Districts vary, of course, in how people are selected for extended contracts or job enlargement activities and what their assignments will be. In some districts with career ladder programs, priority applicant status is reserved for those highest on the ladder. In others, any teachers can apply and be granted extended contract status. The underlying assumption of the full career model is that some teachers desire year-round employment and a more complete professional role than the classroom alone provides.

The Utah career ladder system is used to illustrate the full career model because its extended contract and job enlargement provisions have apparently had major impacts and been very favorably received by principals and teachers (Nelson, 1986; Garbett, 1987; Amsler et al., 1988). It is a comprehensive program, however, that also features career ladder promotion and bonus payments for exceptional teaching and salary supplements for those in teacher shortage areas. The extended contract provision added several days for planning and staff development. A typical total contract now is for 188 to 192 days, 180 of which are for teaching. The employment period in many districts elsewhere in the country is at least two hundred working days. Existence of eleven- and twelve-month contracts, however, is still very limited in most of the forty Utah school districts. Other noteworthy features of the Utah public education system are the largest average class size in the country and the second lowest per-pupil expenditures (*Education Week*, 10 May 1989).

Case History: Utah Career Ladder System

Legislation in 1983 established state guidelines and funding to encourage local districts to design and implement career ladder programs for their teachers. A sizable amount of money was budgeted ($15 million), and all districts responded by designing plans which were ultimately approved for funding. Underlying purposes for the system were attracting and retaining good teachers, enhancing teacher performance, and improving the quality of the schools.

Programs were structured around four components designed to improve the working conditions and career opportunities:[5] an *extended contract* period for teachers to plan, evaluate, participate in professional development activities, or perform clerical tasks related to instruction without children around; *job enlargement* for teachers to be paid supplements for taking on extra short-term tasks during the school year or in the summer, such as mentoring of new teachers or serving on districtwide curriculum committees (extra curricular and administrative activities were specifically excluded for extra pay under this component for not being sufficiently related to instruction); *performance bonus* based on superior evaluations of classroom teaching and, often, supplementary evidence of student learning; and *career ladder levels* with additional performance expectations and compensation attached to each step up the ladder. The extended contract component is referred to as the horizontal dimension of the system, because all teachers receive the benefit equally. The other three components make up the vertical dimension as teachers participate differently depending on their interest and qualifications.

Within state guidelines, districts vary considerably in funding percentages, criteria, and procedures for each component. Statewide, for example, funds budgeted for extra contract days accounted for 40 percent of the total allocations in 1986–87, with job enlargement (27 percent), performance bonus (22 percent), and career ladder levels (11 percent) making up the remainder. The ranges for districts varied greatly, however, as follows: extended contract (15 to 50 percent), job enlargement (0 to 52 percent), performance bonus (10 to 60 percent), and career ladder levels (0 to 71 percent). State guidelines mandated no less than 10 percent being used for performance bonus payments and not more than 50 percent for extended contracts.

An outside evaluation team reported a substantial reallocation of teacher salaries across the state. Exhibit 2.2 shows the average amount of money earned through each of the components. It also reports an average salary supplement for the 1986–87 year of almost $1,700, 7 percent of the average base salary. The range for these supplements was from zero for thirty-six teachers to more than $7,000 for nine. The vast majority (85 percent) received at least $700 because of the program. Two thousand dollars or more separated the fifteenth and eighty-third percentile groups. This is a major change from traditional salary distribution patterns.

Exhibit 2.2

Salary Distribution among Utah Teachers (based on a sample of 12,817 teachers in ten Utah districts)

	Average	*Std. Dev.*
Base salary	*$23,054.00*	*$5,184.71*
Extended Contract Compensation:	771.52	425.41
(percent of base)	3.65%	1.52%
Career Ladder Levels Payments:	362.73	562.63
(percent of base)	1.39	2.44
Performance Bonus Payments:	146.40	295.76
(percent of base)	.77	1.37
Job Enlargement Payments:	402.00	686.42
(percent of base)	1.21	2.67
Average Total Career Ladder Payments	1,688.86	1,125.34
(percent of base)	7.06%	4.18%

15% of all teachers received less than $700.
17% of all teachers received more than $2,700.
 1% of all teachers received more than $5,000.
.07% (nine) teachers received more than $7,000.
Median Supplementary Payment: $1,574.40

Amsler et al., 1988, p. 13.

The actual amounts one received depended not only on the size of the awards established by the district but the number of components in which one participated. Because everyone did not participate in all components, the actual amounts received for one of the vertical components was typically much larger than the averages shown. Performance bonuses, for example, were usually $600 to $700; perhaps even more.

Eligibility and performance requirements for participation on the performance bonus and career ladder components vary from one district to another. Exhibit 2.3 shows a high participation rate for those eligible for performance bonuses and career ladder levels I and II. Even for level III, half of those who were eligible were participating in it.[6] It is also noteworthy that eligibility requirements prevented more than half of all teachers from even being considered for performance bonuses or the career ladder; and the vast majority

Exhibit 2.3

Participation in Career Ladder Performance Bonus and Levels Components

Basis of Participation	Number in Sample	Percentage
All Teachers	12,817	100.00%
Eligible for Performance Bonuses	5,325	41.55% of sample
Awarded Performance Bonuses	3,844	72.19% of eligibles
Eligible for Lowest Career Ladder Level	5,486	42.80% of sample
Awarded Lowest Career Ladder Level	4,504	82.10% of eligibles
Eligible for second Career Ladder Level	3,364	26.25% of sample
Awarded second Career Ladder Level	2,377	70.66% of eligibles
Eligible for third Career Ladder Level	343	2.68% of sample
Awarded third Career Ladder Level	171	49.85% of eligibles

Amsler et al., 1988, p. 17.

of teachers, 74 percent and 97 percent respectfully, not being eligible for the second and third career ladder levels. Thus, those features of the system that are designed to reward superior teaching are barely functional until teachers have taught for quite a few years.

Special features of the Utah career ladder system, including those noted in the Far West Laboratory report, consist of:

- highly favorable support from teachers and principals overall, especially for the extended contract and job enlargement components
- a job enlargement feature which has brought about the accomplishment of many critical tasks and new curriculum developments. Having a few more days without children has encouraged teachers to perform a number of important planning and clerical duties especially that, in the past, they did not have the time or inclination to do. Many districts are increasing the proportion of their funds supporting extended contract days toward the 50 percent caps
- an interesting diversity of plans and procedures induced by state leadership and funding but implemented in highly variable ways according to local needs and directives
- a comprehensive model with several very different but potentially far-reaching components whose interrelation-

ships may produce a greater synergistic response and effect on education in Utah than the sum total of the several components

- evaluation procedures to distinguish superior from satisfactory teaching which are still difficult to implement and incite the greatest controversy among the four components
- modest state funding increases from $34 million in 1984–85 to $41 million in 1986–87 and again in 1987–88 despite fiscal cuts and revenue losses.

VARIATIONS IN PROGRAMS

Most programs are not pure examples of one type or another from the taxonomy above. Rather they contain features from two or more of the six types identified. Even though South Carolina emphasizes student learning, for example, the major feature of staff development models (to stimulate teacher behavior in a given direction) is clearly included also in the requirement that no teacher who is absent more than ten days a year will be awarded a bonus. Utah has components representing all six program types, even though it was used to illustrate the full career model.

I should also point out again that most multilevel career ladders operate high participation models only at the lowest level. At this level they give teachers the status of being on the ladder because their performance has been judged satisfactory, that is, meeting the many explicit standards established for good teachers. At higher levels, these models are no longer deficiency oriented; they provide higher performance standards and status characteristics of superior or exceptional teaching.

While few pure examples of each type can be found, most programs tend to emphasize one, two, or even more of the six basic features. The taxonomy serves primarily to help one recognize what a specific program actually features.

STRUCTURAL DIMENSIONS

Incentive pay plans can be compared and distinguished from each other by focusing on certain key operating variables. Information was obtained and reported in the capsule descriptions above regarding how these plans differ or are similar on these several structural dimensions. They provide a means for analyzing programs and evaluating how well their purposes are being met.

Purpose

The purposes of most plans are usually stated near the beginning of various documents describing program procedures. They also can be found in the original legislation and policy directives. What teachers have to do, however, to obtain a promotion or pay supplement is not always consistent with stated purposes and needs to be reviewed. One might examine eligibility requirements to see which educator groups are allowed to participate and performance criteria on which they will be judged. How performance is measured, which standards are failed often, how many persons participate, and what new things, if any, are they expected to do if they actually receive incentive pay—these are all relevant factors to be considered in determining what the real purpose of a particular plan is and how closely it matches the stated purpose.

Quality of Performance versus Extra Work

One way of distinguishing among plans, or at least their individual components, is to determine whether they feature extra pay for extra duties and work time, or extra pay for better performance with no added hours or days. The former are often identified with career ladders because, with promotion up the ladder, teachers may be expected to take on more responsibilities which require more time after school or more days in the school year. Bonuses for teachers whose students meet specific instructional goals, as in the South Carolina program, exemplify the merit pay notion; but so does the Tennessee career ladder (despite the name) where those judged best are promoted to the highest levels with no extra duties mandated. Tennessee CLII and III teachers originally did have the only opportunity to earn extra money for extended summer duties as well, but a change was made in 1988 to allow other teachers the same opportunity. This change somewhat reduced the special incentive value of advanced status on the ladder.

It is not the names of plans that provide the distinction but whether or not pay supplements are for higher quality performance or for longer hours and extra duties. Career ladders in which teachers are promoted on the basis of their teaching to higher levels with extra status, pay, and even responsibility, but within the same work hours and time frame as other teachers, are primarily merit pay plans. Other plans, such as the horizontal components of the Utah program, provide teachers, regardless of the quality of their teaching, with extra money for taking on additional responsibilities and working more hours or days.

Promotion versus Bonus or Extra Duty Supplement

Another way of distinguishing among plans is whether teachers are promoted to a new rank and status with extra pay, or receive a bonus for the quality of their performance or an extra duty supplement over a particular time period. The former typically requires closer, more comprehensive scrutiny during the selection process, longer term receipt of extra pay, increased performance expectations and overall responsibilities. Performance bonuses and extra duty pay are typically annual supplements which can be earned year after year, with little change in one's basic performance expectations.

Amount of Awards

The actual size of pay supplements is an important variable. It directly affects the external incentive value of a plan and teachers' willingness to participate in it. It obviously affects the budget and indicates the importance the school governing forces attribute to incentive pay in relation to other priorities.

State or Local Control

Nationally, great variations are found from one state to another in who initiates, funds, and operates teacher incentive pay plans. In places where most money for teacher salaries comes from state sources (Tennessee and North Carolina, for example), development and direction of the plan comes primarily from state legislatures and administrative units. In other states, Utah and Arizona, for example, career ladder funds are distributed to local districts under general state guidelines. In some states, Virginia for example, incentive pay plans are primarily the result of local district initiatives—for funding as well as for operation. It is important to discover where the decision-making authority lies in the development and operation of a plan—what individuals and groups are consulted and which policy-making bodies and individuals make final decisions to operate or not operate the plan and make changes in it as it is developed.

Eligibility Requirements and Participation Rates

One of the most frequently asked questions about an incentive pay plan is: "How many teachers are participating? What proportion of the teaching staff is involved?" One answer is derived simply by dividing the number of teachers receiving incentive pay by the total number in the school district. By itself, however, this answer is often misleading. One ought to ask also for whom the plan was intended: all teachers in the district? beginning teachers? tenured teachers? those with more than ten years experience in the district? part-time as well as full-time? Are counselors, librarians, speech therapists, psychologists, and teachers of the homebound included? How about administrators—principals, vice principals, supervisors, and central staff? Who is and who is not eligible to apply or participate?

If the real question being asked is "How much interest is there in this plan or how selective is it?" then the eligibility requirements have to be clear, and the denominator consists not of all teachers in the district but of the number of persons eligible to be considered.

The numerator of the fraction may vary also. If, for a voluntary plan, the emphasis of the question is on how many individuals are sufficiently interested and have enough expectation of success to apply, the number of applicants becomes the numerator. If selectivity is the real concern, two answers are possible: one derived by dividing the number of persons receiving incentive pay by the number of applicants (or those considered); and the other, by dividing the number of recipients by the number of eligible persons. The latter includes those who selected themselves out. They may not be interested because of the extra work or stress involved in the review process or because they object to the merit pay concept. On the other hand, they may be interested but not sure of the likelihood of their success and not wish to risk failure.

In addition to overall participation rates, similar questions can be asked about each step on a career ladder or each component of a comprehensive incentive pay plan. Eligibility requirements need to be considered in choosing the appropriate population numbers for calculating participation, selectivity, and success or failure rates. Careful attention must be paid to these requirements as well as to which calculations are appropriate when comparing one plan with another.

Measures and Data Sources

One other critical set of features to attend to in examining and comparing plans is the type of data obtained and used in judging who the recipients will be. While the measuring instruments and various data sources deserve a good look, many systems use multiple instruments and a variety of sources. To really locate those that provide the discriminating data, however, one must identify the

Exhibit 2.4

Major Features of Various TIP Models

Model	Feature Emphasis
Superior Teacher (Tennessee)	Promotion on CL High quality of overall performance, especially at highest levels High selectivity Large pay supplements Multiple data sources Multiple observations of teaching Eligibility of most teachers
Student Learning (South Carolina)	Student measures and outcome data Small pay supplements Eligibility of most teachers Annual bonuses
Staff Development (Orange County)	Limited focus Extra pay/extra duty Small pay supplements Low selectivity/high participation
Area Incentives	Extra pay for teaching particular subjects Extra pay for accepting assignments in particular schools or neighborhoods
High Participation (Hanover County)	Small pay supplements Low selectivity/high participation Limited measures/data sources Eligibility of most teachers
Full Career (Utah)	Extended contact/job enlargement Extra duty/extra pay Eligibility of most teachers Moderate participation

particular criteria and ratings (scores) on which persons fail. For an individual the failure may be indicated by the number of superior ratings on a classroom observation instrument below a stipulated standard. It may mean average gain scores in reading or math below target goals. It may mean more teacher absences than stipulated in the performance criteria. Or it may mean a combination of several failing scores or ratings. It is necessary to review the specific record of failures of persons considered to determine which instruments, criteria, and data sources were responsible for the decisions.

Consider again the six kinds of programs making up the taxonomy in relation to the several structural dimensions and see how they compare (see Exhibit 2.4). A clear understanding of what features are most desired is an essential prerequisite to the design of a good program, the subject of the next chapter.

Planning: Issues and Procedures

In this chapter I will examine the planning of incentive pay programs and the issues that typically arise during that process. How these issues are resolved determines in great part what will be featured and how they will operate. Each of the six types of programs represents a different resolution of the several dozen major issues confronted in the design of an incentive pay program.

A case history of one school district's planning and implementation of a career ladder program will be used to identify the issues that can be expected to arise in developing such a program. As issues are discussed, program features from other localities will be cited to illustrate different resolutions of the issues.

The great diversity I found among plans was no accident. Each program reflects a unique history of planning and design. Persons involved had their own agenda and saw somewhat different possibilities in the incentive pay notion than others in their communities or than those designing programs elsewhere.

It is noteworthy that incentive pay plans developed in one community or state are almost never adopted elsewhere. While program planners usually look at what others are doing and often borrow ideas liberally, they always generate their own product by considering what will and will not work in their own community.

Behind every plan, therefore, is a local history of intention and design. Who is involved, what they think about education, what kind of planning takes place, and who makes decisions about what features to include and exclude together determine what the program looks like and how it works. The study of school district planning in Virginia showed that, although the initiative to start programs came primarily from the school board and community, many other constituencies were involved before a green or red light decision was made. Planning was an involved process. Many people were consulted, much study undertaken, and many factors considered. Overall, a great deal of time and energy was required to initiate, design, and install a teacher incentive pay program (Brandt and Gansneder, 1987; Gansneder and Brandt, 1988).

STAGES OF PROGRAM DEVELOPMENT

The whole process can be divided into several stages. Stage one, *enactment*, establishes the general policy. A need for such a program is recognized and after considerable discussion and debate by governing bodies (legislatures, community councils, and school boards), the decision is made to design a plan and the general guidelines are prescribed. If it is to be a state program, special legislation is enacted and extra money set aside to fund the planning effort. If it is a local district initiative, school board action is taken and specific funding may also be allocated.

In stage two, *design*, detailed planning takes place. Operational procedures are prescribed, working documents prepared, and decisions reached about the many details that must be addressed before a program can actually be launched. Whereas the key persons involved in stage one are in the governing bodies, educators themselves do most of the planning in the design stage. The results of their efforts are then returned for approval and continued monitoring by the governing bodies.

Stage three consists of *initial implementation* on some scale. Quite often, the program is pilot tested for a year or so in one or more schools, or school districts, prior to full-scale implementation in all schools in a district or all districts in a state. In Campbell County, Virginia, for example, a student learning program was piloted in four elementary schools in 1984–86 and expanded to the middle school level in 1987–88. Four years after its introduction it was still not implemented at the secondary level; it was operational in all other schools. In both Arizona and North Carolina, career ladder programs were piloted in 8 to 10 percent of the districts for at least four years before deciding whether to continue or expand programs to other districts, or to modify or eliminate them. In South Carolina, the number of pilot districts was increased over a four-year period also until all districts were involved in 1988–89.

One advantage to piloting programs before full implementation is the opportunity it provides to improve procedures before they are adopted for everybody. This allows both governing bodies and administrators to reconsider how well programs are operating and take formal corrective action if needed. It also stimulates the need for close scrutiny of how programs operate and what effect they are having. Outside evaluation studies have been conducted on most state-initiated incentive pay pilot programs. They provide much of the information currently available about how well this movement is doing.

Stage four is *full implementation* throughout districts or states and, in the case of career ladders, at all levels. Of the several state plans under development, only California, South Carolina, Tennessee, and Utah were operating teacher incentive pay programs statewide at all levels in 1988–89. Of these, only Tennessee was functioning full-scale prior to that year. The Florida master-teacher program was fully operational in 1984–85, but subsequently put on hold and later withdrawn due, in part, to being implemented full-scale too quickly and without the chance to correct operational procedures. In 1988–89 North Carolina was completing its fourth year of a pilot program in sixteen districts. In Arizona, some pilot districts were in their fourth year of a pilot program, others in their second and third. Texas was operating three levels of a four-level career ladder across the state.[1]

Stage five is called *institutionalization* (Fullan, 1982). It occurs when an innovation, in this case teacher incentive pay, has been fully implemented for a sufficiently long time that its features and practices have become accepted as "standard operating procedure." People no longer question whether it is going to last or be eliminated. They have made whatever psychological adjustments they needed to make to learn to live with it. If they are interested in participating in the program, they know what procedures to follow and what standards they must meet. Perhaps the best indication that a program has reached stage five is its surviving a change of leadership—of governors and legislators for state programs and superintendents and school board members for districts. New leadership often establishes new programs and new priorities. If incentive pay survives a major leadership change relatively unscathed, it is likely to last a long time.

One should not infer that all educational reforms must necessarily proceed from stage one through stage five. This is the typical sequence for a reform that is initiated in the community at large. One initiated by educators themselves, however, might very well begin with design and pilot activity and eventually achieve enactment and institutionalization at later times.

The establishment of teacher incentive pay is a lengthy, complicated, multistage process. It should not be taken lightly. Many factors have to be considered. Many issues arise during the early and even later stages that need to be debated and resolved. How they are resolved and by whom determine what kind of plan is implemented and the impact it has. The various kinds of plans described in chapter 2 indicate how differently issues can be resolved by different individuals in different places.

Before discussing the issues, a capsule version of the Danville, Virginia, career ladder program is in order. This program did not become fully implemented until 1989 when the first master teachers were selected and began functioning in their new roles. Under the administration of a new superintendent, furthermore, a special committee was established that same year to review procedures and to improve the operation of the plan. Thus, it was not yet institutionalized.

Case History: Danville Career Ladder (1984–89)

In spring 1984, the Danville School Board charged the school administration with developing an incentive pay system that would recognize and reward superior teaching. A special task force designed a new teacher evaluation system and operational procedures for a career ladder program during the following summer. The new teacher evaluation system was installed during 1984–85 as plans for the career ladder were being completed. A special group of *teacher evaluators* was also selected from a pool of teachers nominated by their peers. The first group of candidates for career teacher status was reviewed during 1985–86 and individuals were chosen in July 1986.

The career ladder has four teacher status steps: *probationary, teacher, career,* and *master*. Advancement beyond the *teacher* level is limited to those who have taught in the district a specified number of years, have received favorable ratings from their principals in their summative evaluations for two successive years,[2] apply to become a candidate for promotion, and undergo a yearlong evaluation process involving administrators and teacher evaluators. Eligibility requirements include three years at the teacher level before one can be promoted to career teacher level and three years at the career teacher level before one can make master teacher. Partly because of this requirement, the first master teachers were selected in July 1989, at the end of the fourth year of operation.

Annual salary supplements above base salary were originally $2,500 for career teachers and $4,000 for master teachers. In addition, teachers in these ranks have priority for assuming extra responsibilities during the summer months on an extended contract basis. Teacher evaluators also receive a $2,500 supplement.

Interest and participation rates over the first three years were as follows:

- One of six eligible teachers applied: 67/405[3]
- Six of seven applicants were promoted: 57/67
- One of every seven eligible teachers was promoted: 57/405
- One of every nine teachers in the whole system held career teacher status in 1988–89: 52/470
- One of every seven eligible teachers was participating on the career ladder as a career teacher or teacher evaluator: 63/420. Of this group, twelve were candidates for promotion to master teacher. Another fifteen were career teacher candidates and undergoing review for promotion in July 1989.

The primary purpose of the Danville career ladder program is "to reward outstanding teaching and improve the quality of instruction." It is designed also "to enhance the professional stature of teachers in the system and attract and retain the best teaching talent in the future."

It is still early for passing final judgment on the success of the plan. The first master teachers were only recently selected. What new responsibilities they would assume and what impact they would have on the system was still to be determined. Participation rates, even at the career teacher level, have been quite modest, despite indications from interviews during summer 1987 that up to half the teachers would eventually apply for candidacy as they became eligible.

Most Danville educators agree that a vastly improved evaluation system has been installed. Higher and more precisely defined standards reflect not only increased expectations but the possibility of greater assistance and improved instruction. Undoubtedly, however, the costs in administrator time and teacher stress must also be acknowledged. When given the option of not being formally evaluated every year, unless they were interested in volunteering for the career ladder, most teachers chose not to be evaluated annually. As will be reported later, many felt that promotion on the career ladder was not worth the extra work or stress. Some may also have felt they would not succeed if they tried. The career ladder is clearly designed for teachers willing to undergo increased scrutiny as one price to pay for higher status and salary.

The plan contains several special features that distinguish it from many others:

- There is no initial rung, as with the Tennessee, Utah, and several other Virginia plans, where the vast majority of the teachers will participate in a salary supplement. The rungs above basic salary levels on the Danville ladder are clearly for those who are above average in overall performance.
- The quality of teaching performance is the primary basis for promotion and extra pay, not qualification for extra responsibilities nor willingness to work longer hours or extra days.
- Performance assessment data are derived from a variety of sources: observations by administrators and teacher evaluators, conferences with career ladder selection committees, student performance data collected early and late in the year, parent and student surveys, and teacher records.

Other special features include:

- teacher selection of one of three members of the review team
- clear specification of forty-five performance criteria and instructional variables
- special training for all evaluators
- a coordinating committee of teachers and administrators to enhance procedural and judgmental consistency across schools, grade levels and classes, review teams, and candidates
- evidence that significant student learning occurs
- inclusion of librarians and speech therapists.

Finally, the cost of pay supplements ($157,500 in 1988–89) is considerably less than one percent of the operating budget. Even with two or three times the number of participants, the program would seem to be operable without excessive direct expenditures. The trade-off in improved instruction and greater learning, assuming the primary goals are met, should be well worth it.

EMERGENT ISSUES

During the development of incentive pay plans, many issues are confronted. Exhibit 3.1 lists those with which the Danville task force grappled. Current operating procedures specified in the plan reflect how the group settled the issues. The issues will be discussed under the four general headings along with not only how they were resolved in Danville but in other programs as well.

Rewarding Teachers Differentially

Great differences prevail in how people think about even the general notion of providing incentive pay for teachers. Is it a good idea? Are workable systems possible? Can teachers be readily distinguished on the basis of the quality of their performance? What benefits and what drawbacks are likely? On what basis should extra pay be given? These and other questions related to the whole idea of paying some teachers more than others because of what they do need to be addressed in the early planning stages. How they are answered determines whether a plan emerges or does not; if so, what it looks like. In Virginia, for example, only a dozen school districts have decided to proceed with some kind of a differential pay plan so far; many of the others apparently answered such questions differently (Brandt and Gansneder, 1987).

In Danville, the general notion of merit pay and whether or not workable systems are possible were early topics for task force discussions. Published histories of merit pay systems were not encouraging nor was one consultant presentation during the first week of planning. The board had directed that some kind of a plan be drawn up, however, so to have or not have a plan was not an option. The most fundamental issue then became what the basis for extra pay should be: for performing better than others in the same work, or for doing extra work, putting in longer hours, having greater responsibility, and being paid on extended contracts. In resolving this issue, the task force also followed one of the school board's original guidelines. It designed a plan in which teachers would be promoted primarily on the high quality of their performance and the number of outstanding ratings they received.

The issue was not easily settled, however, and remained somewhat ambiguous for at least another year, because leadership roles and extended contract expectancies were included in role descriptions for career and master teachers. For the latter, leadership qualities were even included among the criteria for promotion. An

Exhibit 3.1

Emergent Issues During Career Ladder Planning in Danville

General Notion of Rewarding Teachers Differentially

1. Worthwhileness and workability of merit pay*
2. Basis of promotion
3. Extent of differences in the quality of teaching performance
4. The number of teachers less than outstanding

Likely Effects of Career Ladder Plan

5. Instructional improvement
6. Attracting and retaining teachers
7. Motivational value of merit pay
8. Competition or cooperation
9. Collegial relationships
10. Teacher-administrator relationships
11. Cost factors
12. Accountability and control
13. Threat to job security

Career Ladder Procedures

14. Workability of the evaluation/measurement system
15. Equal treatment
16. Increased expectations
17. Role and competence of the principal
18. Size and kind of reward
19. Ways to include student outcomes
20. Publicity
21. Amount of paperwork
22. Random drawing
23. Tenure or not on the career ladder
24. Credibility of career ladder selections

Planning Procedures

25. Representativeness of the task force
26. Which side are you on—union or management?
27. Planning too fast, not complete
28. Minority representation
29. Amount of understanding of the plan

---

* In this list of issues the term merit pay is meant to include all forms of extra pay for superior teaching, including promotion on a career ladder.

extensive array of performance criteria outside the classroom instruction section also conveyed the impression that extra work and responsibility counted heavily in the promotion assessment. Overall, however, incentive pay, the task force concluded, was to be given only to those who were clearly outstanding teachers.

Similar answers to what should be the basis for incentive pay are reflected in other superior teacher programs and in the student learning models as well, at least those in which awards are restricted to those with above-average productivity, that is, highly selective programs. Plans like Hanover's in which all but a few weak performers are rewarded clearly reflect a different answer to the question of whether identifying outstanding performance or productivity is workable and worthwhile. Obviously, staff development and full career programs as well are based on the notion that paying teachers to do extra things is a worthwhile venture. Even in Orange County, Virginia, where teachers are observed during regular classroom instruction, the emphasis is on doing something extra: selecting a set of generic teaching skills to work on, allowing peer evaluators to observe one teach and provide feedback, and trying to demonstrate competency or mastery of one skill at a time. One's overall performance or productivity is not the determining factor for incentive pay.

Early discussion typically focuses also on the kind of plan that is needed: what its purposes should be, whether incentive pay should be a bonus to be given annually to those who meet specified goals but without affecting one's base salary, or whether a career ladder is established and incentive pay amounts to a significant jump on the salary scale. An internal survey of the Danville task force taken immediately after several days of briefing by outside consultants revealed that almost everyone preferred a career ladder rather than a pay-for-performance format. Teachers should be promoted to a higher status with higher pay rather than receive a bonus for exceptional performance on an annual basis. To this group the career ladder format seemed more promising.

Other early issues had to do with whether mandatory participation was needed and quotas should be established. Neither required lengthy debate. The program should be voluntary for those who wished to apply. Teachers should not be coerced into participating. Although the group rejected the establishment of specific quotas as too arbitrary and restrictive, its consensus opinion was that superior performance meant better than average and something less than half of the teachers making the upper steps on a ladder.

Although this particular task force achieved general agreement rather easily, no issue divides the proponents and opponents of merit pay more fundamentally than this one. The public, by and large, believes that, no matter how hard teachers try to improve their teaching, some will always be better than others. Part of this belief stems from the notion that great teachers are born not made, and no amount of effort can turn a poor or mediocre teacher into an outstanding one. In most other walks of life, furthermore, great differences in performance are usually observable and readily taken for granted. Why should teaching be different?

The proponents of merit pay want the best practitioners identified and rewarded. They expect the worst to leave the profession and others to work toward improvement as best they can. Although the actual percentage of the population they would consider outstanding undoubtedly may vary from one person to the next, few would consider more than a minority of all teachers to be in that category or even potentially capable of being in it. After all, how many youthful aspirants ever make it into the big leagues of the athletic, political, or executive worlds? And it is the "big league teachers" they have in mind for merit pay.

The opponents, on the other hand, believe that most teachers are good despite obvious differences in teaching style and personality. Research is not yet definitive in showing what great teaching is, and until it is, they claim, the basis for giving merit pay will remain uncertain and controversial.

In keeping with this latter attitude, teachers often demand of merit pay programs that the criteria for successful teaching be precisely described and any shortcomings in the assessment of their own teaching fully explained, so they can make an effort to overcome them. The school system has a responsibility to tell them precisely why they failed to receive top ranking and to assist them in achieving it. The ultimate goal of all this effort is for everyone to achieve near-perfection and be included among "the best." In one survey of South Carolina teachers, half the teachers considered themselves among the best 10 percent of the teachers in their district (MGT, 1988). Clearly not a minority but the great majority of teachers think they should receive extra recognition and pay.

Superior teacher programs and other highly selective plans in which above average performance or productivity is the primary standard for extra pay reflect substantial differences in the way this issue was resolved from the other programs in the taxonomy.

In summary of its general position on these matters, the

Danville task force, with later endorsement by the school board, decided on a career ladder rather than a bonus plan. It felt the primary basis for promotion should be the quality of one's overall performance as a teacher. The extra duties that career teachers might assume were to be accomplished within the general confines of an ordinary week and to be no different from those many teachers were already performing. Little, if any, extra time would be required beyond what a good and fully functioning teacher typically puts into her job, only some reordering of responsibilities. No specific new tasks were designated for all career teachers. Although they would have priority for summer duties, they would not be pressed to extend their regular contract into the summer except perhaps to attend training workshops for career ladder evaluators. The latter was a new role they would be expected to assume. For master teachers, however, leadership potential was listed among the promotion criteria but not emphasized to the point of lessening the importance of the caliber of one's performance as a career teacher as the primary criterion. The standards should be set high enough, furthermore, that promotion to the upper levels is achieved by less than half the teachers.

Some resistance to the career ladder should be expected, furthermore, on the basis that some very good teachers are already overworked and do not want any more responsibilities. Whether or not a sizable number of outstanding teachers choose not to apply for this reason should become one measure of how well the plan is understood and accepted. The extra responsibility feature, on the other hand, does provide a legitimate excuse for teachers not choosing to apply and thereby serves a valuable function.

Likely Effects of Incentive Pay Programs

Initial discussions of incentive pay inevitably focus on reasons why they are needed and what effects they will have if they are installed. Will instruction be improved? Will the best teachers be attracted to the district and remain in teaching positions over the years? To what extent will incentive pay motivate teachers to teach better? Will competition among teachers undermine collegial relationships? How will relationships between teachers and principals be affected? How much will programs cost and from where will the money to pay for them come? To whom and for what are teachers to be held accountable? And will teacher morale be jeopardized or even job security threatened under the close scrutiny and high expectations of such systems?

All these questions represent issues for planners to debate and discuss. In each instance, how they are answered will determine the kind of plan that results. After plans have become operational, furthermore, they will serve as questions to be answered in judging how well they are working. Typically, the presumed purposes for incentive pay are to improve teaching and learning. But more intermediate goals have to do with attracting and retaining good teachers, encouraging teachers to improve, improving or at least not diminishing their pride in their job and overall morale, and strengthening the role of principals as instructional leaders.

No analysis will be presented at this point of the likely effects issues as they were discussed during the planning process in Danville or elsewhere. Later in this volume the evidence will be reviewed about the actual impact these programs are having on teacher morale, teacher-principal relationships, and student learning. How resolution of these issues led to particular program characteristics, furthermore, will be included when the next set of issues is presented, that is, those issues dealing with incentive pay procedures.

Operational Procedures

Many issues arose and were resolved by the Danville task force as its members wrestled with the procedural details of both the career ladder and a new evaluation system. What criteria should be considered? How could the impact on students best be measured and included in the assessment of teaching? How could teachers receive fair and equal consideration with vast differences in teaching assignments, grade levels, and subjects? How much should principals' judgments count in relation to those of others involved in the review process? How capable some principals were to evaluate instruction was an early concern of teachers in the group, although no specific names were mentioned. Another major concern was what kind of training would be needed to ensure similar consideration and treatment in the evaluation process from one school to another.

Early decisions that prompted considerable deliberation also were the sizes of rewards; three-year and five-year renewable terms, rather than permanent tenure in career teacher and master teacher ranks; minimal publicity for those promoted; and the necessity of solid documentation in out-of-class performance areas. The primary issues considered in specifying operational procedures will be discussed one at a time.

Workability of a Teacher Evaluation System. For performance-based incentive pay plans, the bases on which awards will be given need to be clearly specified. Who is eligible to compete, what they must do to be considered, on what criteria will they be judged, what standards will be used, and who will do the judging all have to be decided and included in program descriptions.

For highly selective systems, such as the upper levels of career ladders, higher standards are needed and perhaps more elaborate appraisal techniques than for those in which greater numbers are expected to participate successfully. For level I of the Tennessee career ladder, for example, one's own principal is primarily responsible for determining who is promoted, and 90 percent of the tenured teachers succeed. To be considered for levels II or III, however, one has to be observed by outside peer evaluators six times during the year, be interviewed on three occasions, take a subject matter test, and submit planning and evaluation materials—a much more elaborate and costly process. In the South Carolina program or the bonus component of the Utah plans, student learning targets must be specified along with the measurement instruments that will be used to determine whether they have been reached. Even with staff development, full career, and high participation programs, specification is needed of who is eligible to participate and what one has to do to receive incentive pay.

In Danville, the original evaluation system was obviously inadequate. Summative ratings had consistently placed most teachers at the highest performance level. In developing the new evaluation system several weeks were spent deciding on the criteria, setting the standards and determining the procedures for their assessment. Schedules were established for applicants and evaluators, forms developed for recording and evaluating data. Procedures were designed for selecting peer evaluators and administering the program.

Underlying all this planning was the desire to establish a fair, objective system that would distinguish between "the many teachers who were generally conscientious and doing a good job" and a lesser number who were "truly outstanding." Four rating categories were established for judging performance on the various criteria: outstanding, professionally competent, needs improvement, and unsatisfactory. The difference between "outstanding" and "professionally competent" was defined as follows:

(Outstanding)   The evaluatee is performing at
                                 an exemplary level, exceptionally

| | above what is expected of very capable and effective teachers in the (district). |
| (Professionally Competent) | The evaluatee is performing at a level that demonstrates a high degree of competence that meets the (district's) expectations. |

Several procedures were especially designed to strengthen the rating process and to establish "professionally competent" ratings as the norm for most teachers. All evaluators would be trained to write narrative script tapes while they were making classroom observations. Ratings of the eleven teaching variables would be done immediately after observations using the script tapes to recall and rate what they had seen. If a variable was rated as other than professionally competent, the reasons were to be noted on the rating form. Behavioral descriptors were also available to the rater for each level for each of the eleven classroom instruction criteria. Finally, for twenty of the forty-five criteria, no rating above professionally competent was permitted. These typically were variables where outstanding performance was not easily discernible or considered especially important (e.g., attends and participates in staff meetings and serves on staff committees; takes all necessary precautions to protect and maintain facilities, equipment, and materials).

Underlying all this effort was general acceptance of the notion that teachers differ considerably in the quality of their teaching and less than the majority should be considered outstanding. In general, however, the task force rejected comparative yardsticks—rankings, nominations, and test comparisons among teachers—even though these measurement techniques were recognized as adding objectivity and rigor to selection procedures. Instead they tried to establish sufficiently high standards that many teachers would either not try or, if they did try, would not easily pass the various hurdles.

A workable method is clearly needed for distinguishing between good and superior teaching if the best teachers are to be identified and rewarded as Governor Alexander, among others, would like to see happen. Asking individuals to rank, rather than rate, their peers, subordinates, teachers, or children's teachers is not acceptable to most teachers. When the Danville task force discussed various measurement instruments and procedures, the idea of comparing one teacher directly with another to enhance discriminative validity was rejected. It was considered too threatening and divisive, even though it might increase the power and objectivity of teaching effectiveness assessment. Ranking and nominating techniques in particular were considered and rejected because they might increase competition between teachers. In Lynchburg, Virginia, too, where teachers are asked to list on secret ballots those they consider the best teachers, only one-third of them typically respond and on some ballots everybody in the school is listed. Although this is not a career ladder nominations process, results are used in reviewing applications.

One of the primary deterrents to a valid system for measuring the quality of teaching is the taboo against comparing one teacher directly with others. Among the eleven Virginia districts with incentive pay plans, none used data that compared teachers with each other (Brandt and Gansneder, 1987). The closest practice to direct comparison was reported by one system in which principals were asked, in recommending career candidate applicants, to indicate if they were among the best, second-best, and so on, 10 percent of all the teachers they had ever seen with respect to particular variables. Even this judgment was submitted in private and not communicated to the applicants themselves. They had waived their rights to inspect such data when they first applied to be a career ladder candidate.

One of the issues complicating the development of a valid teacher appraisal system is a philosophical difference over what are considered acceptable standards. The public calls for a relative standard, that is, reward the best, for an institution in which only absolute standards are acceptable.

Therefore, in order to achieve some discriminatory capability at the positive end of the performance continuum, raters are sometimes instructed to specify teaching behaviors that cause them to assign above-average ratings. Special documentation of this sort is required for many variables of the Texas Teacher Appraisal System (TTAS) instrument. Precise descriptors of exceptional teaching patterns, as contrasted with good and poor teaching patterns, are also included in many plans. Objective running notes are to be made of classroom observations and used in filling out rating forms. In a few places (Florida and Alabama), low inference coding systems were developed so teaching behaviors could be tallied and counted as a basis for scoring how well teachers taught. All of these practices are designed to minimize the halo and ceiling effects of traditional rating scales, and to encourage valid identification of those who perform better than average. If these more sophisticated evaluation schemes do not seem satisfactory in selecting "the best teachers" as the public desires, it may be partly the fault of a tradition that prevents the use of better assessment methods.

One means of dealing with the assessment of teaching problem is to increase the number of judges and sources of data on which judgments are based. In Danville, for example, a team of three persons (including one's principal or assistant principal and someone selected by the candidate from a list of trained evaluators) monitors a candidate throughout a year, conducting six individual observations, conferring with her several times, approving student performance goals, and reviewing various teacher and student records and parent and student ratings. Recommendations of this team are further scrutinized by a systemwide committee that reviews and further approves or rejects all team recommendations before final action is taken by the superintendent and school board. In Tennessee and for many other highly selective career ladder programs, equally elaborate measurement and evaluation procedures serve to base final decisions on multiple data and judgments.

The complexity of such a system is an obvious drawback. It can be costly to administer in time and effort as well as in dollars. It is also difficult to understand and, therefore, to be easily accepted. This is one reason why not many highly selective, superior teacher or learner programs can be found. In most cases, where they exist, they are combined with more easily administered, less selective programs, such as the lower rungs of a career ladder (North Carolina, Tennessee, and Texas, for example) or the horizontal dimensions of the Utah programs. The difficulty of designing and administering a sound teacher appraisal system is a major reason why other incentive pay models are often more popular.

Equal Treatment. In schools, as in other organizations, principles of fairness apply. People expect to be treated consistently from one situation to the next, to be judged on the same standards, and be given equal opportunities to succeed or advance. These expectations are heightened by the introduction of incentive pay. People become extra sensitive that they receive similar treatment and opportunity when both pay and status are involved.

Teachers may be even more sensitive than other groups because of long established egalitarian traditions in education. When one Danville teacher was asked in a private conversation if teachers shouldn't be paid on more than education and experience, she replied: "They all ought to get the same; forget education and experience too." Another was heard to say: "I hope evaluators will know the difference between a teacher who struggles through a schedule of tough classes and hard-to-teach students, where I's [needs improvement] are easy to spot, and some government teacher who sails through his schedule with a bunch of O's [outstanding]."

Many task force members were surprised to find out during the initial planning period that the forms used to rate teachers and the number of expected classroom visits by principals and assistant principals differed in elementary and secondary schools. These differences reflected, in part, separate administrators' patterns at the central office level as well as local school leadership. A more important reason was the sheer difference in size of the various schools and the ratio of administrators to teachers. It is much easier for an elementary principal with twenty-four teachers and five grade levels to cover them all than a high school with 110 teachers and a great diversity of subjects as well as grade levels, even with the assistance of two assistant principals and department chairpersons.

Considerable discussion took place about these differences and whether similar scales and requirements were appropriate. In general, task force members felt that equal treatment was essential. They replaced the separate scales with a districtwide statement of criteria to be met and a single observation scale focused on generic teaching variables. They actually reduced the number of formal classroom visits in elementary classrooms to the two per year that seemed feasible in the high school. After much debate it was decided that department heads were not to be used for formal evaluation purposes and career ladder data-gathering although they could continue to make informal observations and provide instructional assistance.

With few exceptions (librarians, speech therapists, adult educators, teachers of the preschool handicapped, counselors, psychologists, and administrators themselves), all professional personnel were to be judged in the same way and with the same basic measurement tools. Several of the specialist groups did eventually propose separate yet parallel guidelines (criteria and scales) so they could participate in the career ladder program; several did not.

Within these general procedural guidelines, of course, differences in teaching assignment were to be considered and specialists used to judge teaching plans, processes, and products wherever they seemed especially needed to help evaluation panels make final judgments. For the most part, task force sentiments on the matter of equal treatment for all teachers not only prevailed in shaping the final plan but in gaining the confidence of teachers about it. Little direct complaint on this matter suggests it is only a minor bone of contention among those who tend to reject the plan. Being fair to everyone by specifying similar evaluation practices is apparently more important.

Increased Expectations. Underlying the whole movement is the notion that schools can do a better job than they have been doing. When this notion is dealt with by an educational planning group, it becomes a problem of specifying criteria and setting standards that increase expectations about how well teachers should teach and students should learn.

Early in the planning period it became clear that those on the Danville task force, teachers among others, perceived a need to upgrade expectations. Many discussions focused on slackness here and there in the way teachers conducted themselves outside the classroom especially—in relating to parents, in contributing to hearsay and making demeaning comments about school practices and personnel, among other things. Slackness in attendance and abuse of sick leave policies were two other items that drew a lot of attention. The fact that two-thirds of the teacher ratings each year were in the ceiling category and almost all the rest only one step below meant that evaluation procedures were not sufficiently rigorous. Almost every item on the forty-five-item criterion instrument was derived from discussion about its importance in a general statement of expectations, and instances were cited of inappropriate teacher behavior that damaged the schools in one way or another.

Many of the specific criteria included on the Danville instrument are contained on similar instruments elsewhere. In South Carolina, for example, teacher absence was apparently so widespread that very firm limits were set for those who would receive year-end bonuses—no more than ten days for whatever reason other than military or court-ordered absences.

There is little doubt that some teachers take offense at the fact that all these matters are spelled out. It infers that teachers cannot be trusted to use their own good judgment about how to conduct themselves. The real objection, however, is undoubtedly to the increased expectations overall and the implication that teachers are not doing their jobs as well as they could.

In the past, summative ratings have typically told teachers they were meeting district expectations in superior fashion. As new summative systems convey higher expectations and fewer top-of-the-scale ratings, teachers are initially upset. Whereas they have been accustomed to being told they were outstanding, they are now evaluated as something less than that. The almost universal reaction is: "Tell me specifically what I have to do to get an outstanding rating." An evaluator cannot always say, however, because the circumstances in another observation situation may be different. More importantly, the ceiling on the evaluation scale has been lifted. It is a different kind of scale, one which almost always indicates room for improvement. Most teachers are not expected to be judged outstanding on most of the variables. Much of the stress and hostility they feel, as modern summative systems are imposed on them, derives from these changed expectations.

Role and Competence of the Principal. Considerable concern was expressed in early meetings of the Danville task force over principals' abilities to recognize good instruction and to provide fair and objective ratings of classroom performance. Concerns were greater in some schools than others. These concerns led directly to the development of a multijudge, multisource evaluation system with built-in checks and balances against arbitrary judgment. It also led to the mandate that all principals and other evaluators must receive intensive training in the use of the new system.

The failure of many early merit pay programs has often been attributed to a tendency of principals to play favorites and make arbitrary judgments on the basis of little systematic evaluation (ERS, 1979; Hatry and Greiner, 1985). In more recent times the teaching experience and training they receive for their administrative roles, in many instances, simply does not prepare them for instructional leadership in the schools to which they are assigned. Some elementary principals have taught only at the high school level. Many who were former coaches have never taught traditional academic subjects. Some principals may appreciate good instruction, but they vary in how effectively they work with teachers to induce it. As one administrator himself stated:

> There's been tremendous pressure put on principals [by the new evaluation system] . . . great pressure on them to prove everything they put down. They're basically nice people. They don't want to hurt feelings.

Incentive pay programs often create a role conflict for principals and assistant principals. On the one hand they are to help teachers develop their skills and improve their teaching. On the other, they are the primary individual, or one of two or three primary individuals, responsible for passing judgment on how good teachers are and determining whether or not they receive incentive pay.

It is a complicated and important role. Planning decisions about the role of the principal need to be carefully made and clearly understood. If they are to be primary evaluators, they need to be thoroughly trained in the summative evaluation system, as should any other evaluators. They need to know the precise meaning of the various criteria. They must be able to collect and pass judgment on appropriate data according to established procedures. They may need training in scripting or in clinical supervision skills. Even their basic observation skills may need to be improved. After reviewing the North Carolina Teacher Performance Appraisal system, an outside evaluation team recommended that principals and other evaluators pass tests showing they rate classroom observation segments in the same way as others and be formally certified as an evaluator before being allowed to serve that function (Brandt et al., 1988). Such a procedure was pursued during 1984 with the Florida Performance Measurement System. Approximately nine thousand individuals were trained to serve as outside evaluators and record classroom observation data on those being reviewed for master teacher status. Of all who participated in the training programs, more than a few failed the criterion tests and were prevented from serving as official observers for this program (MGT of America, 1985).

Trained observers from outside the school district are also used for reviewing candidates for levels II and III in Tennessee. They make all the visits. The principal's judgments along with several other kinds of data are considered, but those responsible for collecting, analyzing, and scoring the data are all from outside the system.[4] Both Orange County and Lynchburg, Virginia, as well as the North Carolina career development pilot districts, have selected teachers to serve as peer observers to visit classrooms and write low-inference narrative records of teaching practices that are then rated by principals or their designates. In North Carolina, peer evaluators themselves, not just their records, are being increasingly involved directly in the final judgment process.

The role of the principal is different in different systems. In Orange County, Virginia, a peer teacher records teaching behavior that exemplifies the targeted teaching practices, but the principal judges whether this record includes a sufficient number and kinds of behavior to meet competency or proficiency requirements. If he visits the classroom, it is to assist a teacher, not to collect data to be used in evaluating her. In the North Carolina pilot districts, the principal divides the four observation visits with the observer evaluators, each making two. With each visit the observer scripts a narrative record of happenings and completes an analysis which is shared with the teacher. The four sets of records, along with other documentation available to the principal, including whatever the teacher supplies, serve as the basis of the year-end summative evaluation for career status determination.

An underlying concern wherever summative evaluation is used for pay or promotion purposes is how much consistency there is in the evaluation process from teacher to teacher, school to school, and district to district. The North Carolina State Department publishes the rating distributions by school district and teaching functions each year, so those involved can monitor how similar or different they are from others who use the same system. Within districts too, administrators can monitor and question differences between schools or even between individuals as a means of upgrading understanding of the system and improving the consistency of evaluations.

Summative evaluation for incentive pay purposes requires not only good instruments and procedures but people who are well trained in their use and some means to monitor how consistently they are used from school to school and district to district. Where human judgment is involved, some inconsistency will always be found from one situation to another. For individuals to have confidence in incentive pay programs, however, they must feel that such inconsistency is minimal and, where it exists, someone in authority is trying to do something about it.

The Size and Kind of Award. Various considerations underlie final decisions about the amount of pay for recipients and whether it comes in the form of a yearly bonus or a longer term jump to a new salary level. Even questions about the rate of pay for extended contracts during the summer months or job enlargement activities during the school year need to be answered. In some cases, summer activities are paid on a daily rate that is different from what the regular teaching year provides. In Tennessee, a total supplement is specified for those reaching level II or III with the requirement that recipients work an extra month or two.

As indicated in chapter 2, the size of the award often depends on how many are expected to be given and how much the school system estimates it can budget for this item. It varies also with the purpose of the award. If it is to serve primarily as a symbolic pat on the back for a job well done it can be much smaller than if it is intended to attract and retain outstanding teachers with a living income.

In Danville, the general sentiment of the task force was for substantial enough sums to make the struggle for promotion worthwhile. Yearly supplements of $2,500 and $4,000 above regular salary levels were chosen for those promoted to career teacher and master teacher ranks. Additional money would be paid as well for those whose contracts were extended into the summer. It was recognized and discussed briefly that master teachers with extended contracts, a master's degree, considerable longevity, and this career ladder supplement would undoubtedly earn more than some principals. No task force member objected to that possibility even though it violated one of the Secondary Principals' Association principles. In fact, it seemed entirely congruent with the central purpose of career ladder planning, namely, to keep excellent teachers in the classroom rather than forcing them to become administrators.

The other cost concern that required discussion was where the money would eventually come from once the extra funds to start the project were used up. A board member stated early in the planning:

> The plan is no substitute for our continuing effort to raise basic pay. . . . Merit payments would represent additional money (22 June 1984).

A teacher member of the task force commented later:

> Are we going to rob basic salary to pay for career and master teachers? It would be awful if we only get five percent in our basic salary increase next year (20 July 1984).

Increased costs to implement the plan will have to come from somewhere. The larger the number of teachers who are promoted, the greater the cost. An initial sum of $150,000 was put away by the City Council specifically to help launch a merit pay program once one was designed and ready to be put into effect. Across-the-board increases in teachers' salaries had averaged 10 percent over each of the previous three years, above statewide averages during that period. With the number of candidates being considered for promotion during the first year limited to twenty-four for management reasons, costs did not seem particularly troubling during the planning period.

Looking into the future, however, both the administration and teachers expressed concern. With the former, it was how much extra expense would ultimately be added to school budgets and where would it come from. If other Virginia school systems did not have such programs and the state did not provide financial assistance specifically for such programs, the locality would be faced with either raising more money for teachers' salaries than other school districts or including the incentive money some teachers would receive as part of the overall salary package. If this overall package were no greater than those of school districts without an incentive plan, the across-the-board raises most local teachers would receive would be less than teacher raises elsewhere. It is relatively common in industry for a certain percentage of wage increases to be based on merit; but, as yet, merit pay for teachers has not been regarded as part of the overall wage increase. School districts with such plans have an extra financial burden to assume unless they are ready to tell all those teachers who do not receive merit pay that they cannot expect the same raises as teachers elsewhere.

Teachers feel generally at this time that the extra money some teachers should receive because they are promoted must not affect what others receive. That can only happen, however, if there is an extra outside funding source. In Danville, initial extra funds had been set aside. At some future time, more would be needed or the expectations would have to change. That is one of the major dilemmas to be faced in launching merit pay plans today. Some of the resistance to this new plan resulted from a clear recognition of this long-range dilemma. The school board, too, was concerned about potential long-range costs.

The Use of Student Outcomes. Among the primary data sources for judging teaching effectiveness, the last to have guidelines developed and accepted by the Danville task force was student learning and improvement. Even though the school board had urged its inclusion as one of the original charges, the group was very aware of the difficulties inherent in the use of student data for judging how well teachers do. Too many intervening variables affect a teacher's impact or lack of impact on students.

Until recently, very few examples could be found of school

systems trying to use student outcome data for this purpose. Glass tried to review such programs for the *The New Handbook of Teacher Evaluation* (Millman and Darling-Hammond, 1989) and found none that had survived very long.

The technical and logistic problems are substantial in finding appropriate measures; and in administering, scoring, and interpreting them properly. A massive amount of information has to be handled efficiently and fairly. Vast differences in the ability levels of students, in curricular content, in grade levels, and teaching purposes need to be considered in setting standards which teachers have an equal opportunity to achieve.

For these reasons, the student learning incentive pay programs currently being implemented in South Carolina and Arizona particularly may well be the most substantial efforts to date to use student outcome data as a measure of teacher productivity. The idea that great teachers have a lasting influence on their students has not yet been translated into a simple system for measuring how good teachers are by how much their students learn.

What emerged from the long discussions in Danville was a decision to include student outcomes, as the school board had suggested, but to leave it to teachers to decide the instructional goals to be assessed and the means for doing so. Measurement plans would have to be approved against a series of guidelines designed to ensure fairness and objectivity in the collection and scoring of data.

The task force emphasized that student outcome data should be only one kind of information to be considered, not the primary source, in making final judgments about promotion. While evidence of student learning was to be gathered and reviewed, the amount of learning did not have to appear exceptionally great for a teacher to be considered promotable. Too many other factors than excellent teaching could affect the results.

The Texas Teacher Appraisal System instrument contains a Teacher Self-Appraisal section on which teachers are to state their student performance goals at the beginning of the year and report performance accomplishments later in the year. Other questions ask for information about their classes (student abilities and other characteristics), the measures they used, and whether their goals have been achieved. A content analysis of teacher responses indicated too little information about student performance measurement or results to determine anything about the quality of teaching. Without some system for scoring at least the quality of information reported, this self-appraisal section was considered to have very limited value even for staff development purposes (MGT, 1987). It is clear that while teachers may need to be involved in selecting student goals on which they will be assessed, self-report alone of how well those goals are met is not a sound basis for granting incentive pay. More valid measures of student performance would be needed, which would be administered and scored by neutral parties in fair and objective ways.

Publicity. One question encountered in putting incentive pay plans into operation is how much to publicize the names of recipients and those under consideration. The recognition of outstanding teachers is a major reason for such programs. A strong argument can be made that their accomplishments ought to be featured as a model for others and to enhance community awareness of the high-quality teaching that goes on in the schools. Downplaying the publicity, on the other hand, even to the point of no public announcements of individuals by name, may ease jealousies and protect collegial relationships. Pay, after all, would seem to be a private matter, and personnel actions can legitimately be handled in executive session. Many teachers do not want the extra attention publicity would bring. They will not volunteer for such programs unless they are assured some protection from it.

Questions were raised during the Danville planning sessions about what could and should be kept confidential. The general preference was not to publicize the names of applicants in order to maintain normal relationships during the review period and reduce potential "humiliation" for those who did not make it. The decision was also reached not to publicize those who were promoted, in part, to minimize parental pressure for their children to have those teachers.

Discussion on this latter matter, which is often brought up as an excuse for not having merit pay, indicated that such parental preferences for particular teachers had always been requested and were seldom a problem. Where parents express choices among teachers, it is typically for a great variety of reasons. This tendency is not expected to change if there is not a great deal of extra publicity over those promoted. Danville administrators could also stress that there are many outstanding teachers who do not choose to apply for promotion for all kinds of good reasons. It was clearly recognized, of course, that despite this "low profile" approach those who were under consideration or promoted could be detected if someone were sufficiently snoopy, public employee salaries being open to public scrutiny.

Paperwork. One original intent of the task force was to keep the plan simple and operationally straightforward. Members knew that to be fair and equitable, however, procedures, criteria, and measurement devices had to be clearly and precisely specified. To reassure candidates that promotions judgments would be based on information about performance rather than hearsay or self-serving teacher reports, they would be asked to furnish documentary evidence about their various activities. At first, this documentation was to take the form of a written dossier which contained sample lesson plans, goal statements, logs of extra duties and parent contacts, among other items—any and all materials that they felt would provide a record of their overall teaching performance.

Proposed guidelines for the dossier contained a wide assortment of illustrative suggestions of what might be included. To allow for differences in teaching fields and assignments, however, very little was universally required and it was unclear just how much or what specific information was really needed.

To many teachers the preparation of the written dossier seemed extraordinarily burdensome. It was seen as a major deterrent to promotion rather than a means for building one's case. When it looked as if the care and attention one might give to preparing a written report might become the overriding basis for promotion, rather than the quality of one's teaching, the task force eliminated the submission of a dossier as a formal requirement for promotions consideration. Instead, career ladder selection committees were assigned the responsibility of asking candidates about out-of-class duties, parent contacts, lesson planning, and other activities that would not be seen directly during class observations. If they wished, however, teachers still had the option of providing their committees with documentary evidence rather than just talking about these matters.

Although the task force worked hard to streamline procedures and to clarify its descriptive documents wherever it could, the plan as a whole was probably much more complicated than the members originally thought it would be. To others, it undoubtedly looked more cumbersome than it would probably turn out to be after it was in effect for two or three years. In the attempt to be fair and equitable, it was more prescriptive than some people preferred; but assessment procedures were less standardized, in the interest of flexibility, than others liked.

The amount of additional paperwork for teachers created by the need to document performance on variables that are not observed directly during teaching is always a major issue. In Tennessee, complaints were so severe during the first year or two that teacher-constructed portfolio requirements were reduced substantially. The major portion of the portfolio was combined with the interview into a qualitatively scored dialogue. The program coordinator in one South Carolina district reported a great willingness of teachers to participate as long as someone else specified the instructional goals and collected the data to see if they had been reached. Texas teachers complained also over having to complete the self-appraisal section that was not scored or otherwise used in the assessment of teaching performance. An Arizona teacher said she had spent seventy hours documenting her activities and accomplishments, including what her students learned, but added insightfully: "That's about what you put into a three-credit course. What makes it seem so hard, however, is that for the career ladder, it's all diagnostic, self-reflective activity about yourself." Careful planning is obviously needed to design a system that will generate necessary documentation without overloading teachers with extra paperwork.

Random Drawing. Paperwork was one of the two issues most complained about during the first year of the Danville plan. The other was a random drawing taken to select the first set of candidates from among the applicant pool. Not knowing how many applications would be received and realizing that only a limited number of trained evaluators would be available the first year, the task force set a limit of twenty-four candidates to be reviewed in 1984–85. They decided that the fairest way to select the twenty-four out of however many applied would be by random drawing. They discussed and rejected other possible criteria, such as longevity, so as not to diminish the major purpose of the plan, that is, to reward outstanding teaching.

Non–task force members questioned this procedure heatedly as the excerpt from the plan presentation session below indicates:

> My only real concern is about the random sampling. Did you consider years of experience [when you had to limit the first year candidate list to twenty-four] and the fact that some teachers in their 50s may never get in on this?
>
> (non–task force teacher)

> It didn't seem right to penalize young, outstanding teachers.
> (Task force teacher, 23 August 1984,
> some clapping from audience)

The task force did not budge from its original notion that a random drawing was the only fair procedure. Random sampling was stratified according to the number of teachers at each teaching level (elementary, middle, junior high, senior high). After the drawing itself produced a concentration of candidates in certain departments and schools to the exclusion of candidates in other departments and schools, however, some thoughts were expressed that other sampling procedures might have worked better. One decision related to the issue was made early, namely, to give first priority the following year to those persons who had applied the first year but were not chosen.

Despite the explanation and decision to complete the review of first-year applicants before others would be considered, the issue was not quickly forgotten, as a committee excerpt more than a year later demonstrates:

> Teachers find repugnant the idea that even an infinitesimal part of salary is tied to the luck of the draw. Reply: This was a one-time thing and the only fair way to proceed.

> (16 October 1985)

The random drawing issue resulted from the procedure chosen for dealing with a more general problem, namely that of launching a plan rather than operating it once it is in place. Planning career ladders in particular necessitates looking ahead several years to the time when people will be located at different places on the ladder and procedures will be well established to continue to operate it successfully. During stage three, however, when implementation is just beginning, permanent structures are not yet in place. They too have to be set up simultaneously with the implementation.

In Danville, for example, a special group of peer evaluators had to be selected and a selection process established for choosing them until they could be replaced by teachers who had been promoted to top levels on the career ladder. The Lynchburg plan was similar. In both Charlotte-Mecklenburg, North Carolina, and Tennessee, a huge backlog of applicants for high levels on the career ladder was generated during the phase-in period which took several years to work through. Since all teachers who had met the experience requirements were eligible at the same time, there was no way that they could be reviewed in the same year under a system that was designed to function routinely after everyone was in place. So temporary procedures have to be established to get programs started that will not be used again once they are fully operational. Like the random drawing, they may be resented.

Tenure on a Career Ladder. One advantage of the bonus, student learning, and other plans where pay supplements are awarded on an annual basis is relatively little difficulty in discontinuing them. They do not affect basic salary. Teachers depend less on these extras than they would if they could expect them every year.

Career ladder promotions are usually more difficult to reverse. The stipends are typically larger, the performance evaluation more elaborate, and the expected term of office several years. Promotions often require official school board action. In Tennessee, one is even certificated by the state at particular levels, which facilitates job transfer from one district to another without loss of status or pay.

It was recognized early by the Danville task force that teachers promoted on the career ladder to career or master teacher ranks should not have indefinite status at these levels. The Virginia governor's task force guidelines had stipulated that a two-year period for the first promotion and another two years for the highest levels were appropriate before formal reapplication and review again (Governor's Special Advisory Committee, 1984). Three-year periods were endorsed without much discussion after parent and board members particularly indicated rather strong feelings against the possibility of tenuring people in at these higher ranks.

Some discussion ensued also over whether or not reapplicants would have priority over new applicants. No resolution of this question seemed needed since quotas were not anticipated by the time that might happen.

Although some sentiment for tenure in the new ranks was hinted at by other teachers after the initial presentation, it never became a vocally expressed issue that commanded much attention. Teachers themselves were probably divided on the matter. They undoubtedly realized how strong public sentiment was against tenure, and those who otherwise would have supported it did not feel it was a feature worth fighting for.

Typical comments on this issue follow: (from a teacher after hearing the plan presented for the first time, 23 August 1984) "The plan discourages participation—going through this process every three years." (From parents almost a year later, 14 March 1985, in a committee considering teacher complaints about having to reapply after three years on the career ladder):

I have strong feelings [against tenure].

Amen!

(Reply from a teacher task force member): "Now that the dossier [portfolio] has been toned down, reapplying should not be so tough."

Credibility of Recipients. Many teachers develop reputations among various constituencies—parents, students, peers, and administrators—as being demanding or easy, friendly or abrupt, good or not good, and so on. Such reputations may or may not be valid or deserved, and they may vary considerably from one member of a constituency to another. To the extent that consensus exists among constituency groups, especially teacher groups, that those who are promoted on the career ladder or otherwise identified as outstanding are indeed good teachers, the plan will have credibility. If teachers are promoted who are considered poor teachers by their colleagues, or by administrators, large numbers of students, or parents; and others who are generally recognized as good are not promoted, proponents of the plan will quickly lose confidence in it and opponents will crow, "We told you so."

The more selective a plan is presumed to be, furthermore, the more influential this reputation test becomes. Many such complaints were made about those selected during the first year of the Florida master teacher plan. A number of "teacher of the year" recipients in local communities were not selected, for example, and even those who were chosen felt it was possible for weak performers to make it. The plan was highly criticized for its failure both to select teachers whom others considered outstanding and to prevent mediocre teachers from being selected as master teachers (MGT, 1985).

Certainly, a significant difference exists between popularity and effectiveness. However, if the opinions of the clients, colleagues, or administrators differ substantially about who is and who is not a good teacher from what the incentive pay system rewards, the system itself will lack credibility. In addition, if the public is led to believe a system has been installed to reward the best and discourage the worst teachers and then finds out that more than 50 percent are considered best, including some "known to be weak," public confidence in school leadership will dissipate. Unfortunately perhaps, such perceptions, however valid, play a part in determining the success or failure of incentive pay plans. They are a reality that has to be recognized by those who plan and evaluate these programs.

Planning Processes

In Danville, stage one planning began with the school board charging the school administration to develop a plan for identifying and paying teachers who were "performing at a higher level in the classroom" more than other teachers. Operational procedures were drafted by a special committee the following summer. This planning task force presented the basic structure of a career ladder program to the entire teacher and administrator population at the opening of school six months after the school board's action. Along with the career ladder plan was a completely revised teacher evaluation system.

The original school board charge was preceded by several weeks of informal discussion both among its members and with the city council that controlled the overall budget. Later, when $154,000 became available from the underfunding of basic state aid, the council set aside this sum for the operation of such a plan.

The charge included revision of the evaluation system. It specified that principals should not have the complete responsibility for assessing teacher performance. It also stipulated that student achievement should be one criterion in awarding incentive pay and "classroom climate" and "relations with parents" were also to be considered.

The initial school board directive was the primary driving force behind the entire effort. Time and again, difficulties in constructing acceptable procedures and outside teacher resistance would have jeopardized the project were it not for the strength and specificity of the original charge. The board's later review and reaffirmation of members' intentions were also important in sustaining the effort.

A thirty-member task force was selected in the late spring of 1984, consisting of six administrators, twelve teachers, two school board members, and several parents and community representatives. The superintendent, an assistant superintendent, and the outside consultant were all regular members of the task force. Teacher members were selected from a larger pool of applicants who had expressed interest in participating. One of the bases for selection was a short written statement they were asked to submit with their application about how workable incentive pay plans might be constructed. Several but not all schools were represented on this original planning group. Teachers were paid at the regular summer salary rate for the days they worked.

Planning activities began with four days of presentations on teacher evaluation practices and merit pay and career ladder plans. Those presenting included teacher evaluation experts Donald Medley and George Redfern, personnel administrators from two major industrial concerns with plants in Danville, and school administrators from Dalton, Georgia; Charlotte Mecklenburg, North Carolina; and King William County, Virginia. Later, presentations were made by a Hopewell, Virginia, school administrator and by a Virginia Department of Public Instruction staff member.

On the first day after this period of extensive briefing, task force members were each asked to construct two lists in response to the ideas they had heard or thought about: one to consist of ideas or practices they would like to see incorporated in a Danville plan; the other to consist of ideas or practices that should not be included in it. Over the weekend, a Likert-type rating scale was developed that contained the items that had been submitted. Individual ratings were obtained from task force members on Monday, summarized that evening, and results reported to the group on Tuesday morning.

The outcome of this activity was the discovery of near-consensus about many items. Many more favorable attitudes were expressed toward career ladder than merit pay plans, for example. There was little need to discuss the advantages or disadvantages of this or other near-consensus items. Main features for a Danville plan were clearly indicated as well as starting points for further discussion and planning. The process not only saved time and provided the preliminary notions of what a plan ought to contain; it also stimulated enthusiasm for the task ahead as people realized how much they thought alike.

By the end of the second week of planning, the outline of Danville's career ladder plan was in place. The number and names of steps on the ladder had been decided as well as the general criteria for promotion and the kinds of extra responsibilities one might expect after being promoted. Discussion had covered which educational personnel would be included, what kinds of reviewing teams would conduct the evaluations, what kinds of evaluation procedures ought to be considered, and what amounts and kinds of awards should be given to those who were promoted. One decision reached easily and unanimously was to make participation in the plan a voluntary matter. No teacher should feel coerced into applying for promotion on the career ladder.

Progress was fast and thorough over the next month as the task force addressed evaluation criteria and operating procedures one after another. Long debates ensued on the many controversial matters discussed earlier, such as: what sources of information to include, what classroom variables were most important, what procedures would ensure fair and equal treatment, among others.

Led by its two cochairs, the task force debated issues, considered alternatives, and finally achieved near-consensus decisions about what to include or not include. Consensus was usually determined by nods of heads and occasionally by a show of hands. Too close a "vote" was typically followed by more debate.

Minutes were kept of main points of discussion and agreement. The first point of order each day was to review the minutes of the previous day to see if corrections were needed. More important to the emergence of a full-blown plan, however, were the drafts of various documents in preparation. They too were regularly submitted for group review and amendment.

As planning became more focused on operational details and the descriptive products that would be needed to run the system, the rather sizable task force broke down into subgroups to draft specific documents describing operational processes which would later be presented to the entire group for amendment, if desired, and final approval.

In this way a comprehensive manual was developed during the six-week planning period that had the full endorsement of the task force membership. The manual contained the following: the PCT (Performance Criteria for Teachers), a fifty-six-item (later amended to forty-five items) list of specific behavior patterns expected of good teachers; a new set of materials and procedures for observing teachers in the classroom, recording and assessing their teaching; and a full-blown description of a career ladder and the requirements and procedures for being promoted on it. Included also were descriptions of the kinds of documentary evidence that would be needed by committees reviewing one's performance. The accomplishments of this initial planning effort were substantial.

Before proceeding with this chronicle, several comments need to be made regarding the nature of the leaders and how they acted. The cochairs (one an elementary principal, the other a junior high language arts teacher, both women) took responsibility for keeping the group going. They saw to it that topics were announced ahead of time, useful minutes taken and reviewed, issues addressed fully without wasting time or getting bogged down in endless debate, consensus judgment achieved on important items, and steady progress made toward the necessary end products. They saw to it that materials were ready when needed and members felt comfortable in expressing their opinions.

The role of the consultant was important and deserves comment, because he was allowed to contribute when and how he could without dominating the process. He was used in the following ways:

- to stimulate full and open discussion of the ideas of other consultants
- to construct and administer a useful measurement tool, i.e., the post-consultant survey of group sentiments mentioned above
- to lead the review of state guidelines for the purpose of adapting them to a local plan
- to overview evaluation instruments and lead a discussion of what might be appropriate locally
- to provide outside encouragement to a local planning effort when it was making real progress
- to help redirect discussion toward those areas where decisions were needed
- to present special materials and provide technical assistance, usually about measurement procedures
- to write drafts of various documents for modification and adoption by a group, e.g., the preparing of a proposal for a block grant from the State and, later, an RFP for trainers of the new evaluation system
- to express opinions about what is or is not a good approach (the consultant held back on doing this until others had indicated a willingness to disagree openly with him)
- to allow him to conduct research designed to understand and perhaps enhance the planning effort.

The role of the superintendent was considerably more important to the success of the project. It deserves description. A review of the minutes shows that he contributed to the group's progress by:

- bringing up issues that needed to be addressed, such as excessive absenteeism or abuse of the sick leave policy
- finding extra sources of potential funding, i.e., the State block grant program
- reminding the group of the original intent of the school board and city council
- drafting a list of items that needed to be dealt with if the program were to function successfully
- expressing his own opinions about particular issues or approaches that he considered important.

Most importantly, he remained open to ideas from any source, flexible in making adjustments that would enhance the program's success, dedicated to steady progress toward launching a useful, beneficial system. He took the initiative on many occasions and often manned the word processor himself to draft a statement that expressed the sentiments of a group. A hard-working model of someone determined to make steady progress on the plan, he attended all but one or two of the summer planning sessions and participated often and well; yet he did not insist that his own ideas be adopted. At times he even let notions counter to his own carry the day if they represented the consensus. When he knew he could not support a given idea, he said so quickly and nonthreateningly so alternatives could be advanced and considered.

By the end of the first summer, several items had been produced with strong support and commitment from the entire task force: a new evaluation system complete with observational variables specified and separate descriptors for observers to use to distinguish "outstanding teaching" from "professionally competent," "needs improvement," and "unsatisfactory" teaching. Forms had been designed for recording and rating observational data and procedures established for conducting observations and pre- and post-observation conferences. Also, a career ladder plan was fully designed with operational procedures stating how teachers would participate and be judged.

Completion of these materials and presentation of the plan to the school board did not end the planning process. It was carried on in one way or another by various groups, including members of the original task force, for another two years.

Many issues discussed earlier about the evaluation system and career ladder procedures had to be addressed again when the task force presented the plan and distributed the manual and other materials that would guide its operation. A few new issues were raised about the planning process itself.

One was how representative the task force was of the Danville teachers and administrators. A teacher member replied to a newspaper reporter's question (24 July 1984):

> We're pretty representative . . . have had a lot of feedback from teachers . . . have considered their suggestions and incorporated them.

It is true that teachers and principals came from all levels of the system, but not all schools. Minorities were well represented on the task force.

A potential problem had been discussed earlier (26 July 1984) of the possibility that no blacks might be elected to the evaluator pool since black teachers were in the minority in all schools. The task force decided that administrative appointments could be made of black teachers as long as they met the same qualifications as other teachers, if this were to occur, so the final selection of evaluators would be "representative of the system." This procedure was not used, however, because the elections did result in the election of several minority teachers.

Attention was given to appropriate representation of minority teachers in each phase of the planning: inclusion on the task force, the evaluator pool (see above), and the Central Selection Committee that was to make final recommendations to the board about who should be promoted. As it turned out, the two teacher members of this five-member committee were both black. Some concern was expressed by white teachers, following their election, that block voting had occurred which resulted in the exclusion of the majority group. The amount of real concern expressed was limited, however, because of considerable respect among the whites as well as blacks for those who had been elected.

In one respect the task force may not have been representative of all teachers. Teacher members had been selected from a pool of volunteers. Their ideas about how incentive pay might work were considered during the selection process. Those who were most violently opposed to incentive pay were most certainly not included.

A teacher survey the following spring indicated people were divided on the question. A total of 35 percent agreed or strongly agreed with the statement: "The task force that has designed and revised the career ladder program has been representative of the teachers in the system." However, 40 percent disagreed or strongly disagreed.

Whatever differences may have existed at the beginning of summer 1984 between teacher members and other task force members had certainly diminished by the time it was presented to the school board and the whole staff in late July and August. A real sense of ownership had emerged. Teacher, parent, and administrator members felt it was a fair yet rigorous plan, and would be recognized as such once it was thoroughly explained and understood. The typical gap between administrator and teacher perspective on various issues had virtually disappeared. When challenged by a reporter to explain why the teachers in the group, who were all VEA members, were going against the NEA position in endorsing a career ladder plan, they indicated that the NEA had not clearly opposed all such plans and was willing to investigate them to see if they could work, the plan followed the NEA guidelines for such plans and included all those features that had been recommended, and the teachers in this community make up their own minds and do not necessarily follow association recommendations on all matters anyway.

Later in the year, as early resistance to the plan persisted, strong peer pressure to amend or even scrap it was clearly felt by at least several teacher members of the task force. One of them announced in the late fall that she herself did not intend to apply for promotion. Others indicated a lot of nasty comments had been heard in one of the secondary schools about those twelve teachers and the consultant and wanted the teachers polled about their feelings on the matter. Such pressure dampened the spirit of unanimous enthusiasm among task force members for what they were engaged in. With some new members and a few dropouts, however, they continued to meet during the year to address the complaints and complete the plan. Progress during the year was much slower, however, and it took another several weeks of full-time planning during summer 1985 to finalize procedural documents and complete stage two. The core of the original task force was still intact, however, and continued to stay involved either as evaluators or on one committee or another during the second year.

Was planning done too fast and without sufficient involvement of others? Was the program launched too soon, before the evaluation system was tested and all procedures fully worked out? In retrospect, it may have been. Yet others would say that dragging out the planning of something controversial only gives those who will try to sabotage it more time to do so.

Although the task force had given some thought to testing and perfecting the new evaluation system the first year and not accepting CL applications until the end of the second year, an almost unanimous feeling that the plan was workable and could be fine-tuned along with the evaluation system led to the decision to put it into effect as soon as possible. The number of years it would take before the first master teacher would be selected (five) was a major reason for wanting to launch the overall plan as quickly as possible.

Part of the resistance by other teachers, however, was undoubtedly brought about by a seemingly hasty start. Although general guidelines, procedures, and criteria had been specified by the end of the first summer, non–task force teachers had not been involved in the six weeks of day-long discussion and decision-making on these matters. When first presented in two half-day sessions at the beginning of school, it seemed both complicated in its prescriptive detail and incomplete because much still remained to be decided. It is quite likely that the comprehensive nature of the plan and the amount of procedural detail that had already been decided caught the majority of teachers by surprise.

Many questions were asked about underlying reasons for various procedures and possible alternatives both during the preschool presentation sessions and at briefing meetings task force members conducted in the schools throughout the fall semester. Negative sentiments actually seemed to increase despite continuing efforts to explain and promote the plan. Some revisions were made in line with teacher suggestions. Others were considered but changes were not made because the task force felt the original plan was better.

It became apparent that the basis of complaint by some persons was to the whole notion of merit pay, career ladder, and heightened evaluation, and that no amount of revision would be acceptable to a certain percentage of teachers. Those teachers who had served on the original task force had all expressed both an interest in the general task beforehand and some notions about how it might work. Many teachers undoubtedly felt differently, that the whole notion of identifying and rewarding outstanding teachers was a bad idea. No amount of explaining would convince them otherwise.

Another perhaps unexpressed basis of resistance was the discomfort that typically accompanies change itself. As teachers, and principals too, came to realize the scope and extensiveness of change in the teaching culture that the new evaluation system and career ladder program would induce, uneasiness mounted. It was very apparent that all teachers would come under greater scrutiny than ever before and principals would be more directly involved with instruction as well. Major change was in the offing.

It is difficult to ascertain how much teacher rejection of the plan was based initially on a clear understanding and sound analysis of the plan, or a misunderstanding and irrational reaction to the potential threats it imposed on the teaching culture. The teacher members of the task force assumed the primary burden of explaining the plan to their colleagues not only at the initial presentations (22–23 August 1984) but throughout the following semester. They met with teachers in their own schools to explain procedures and the reasons behind their inclusion and to solicit suggestions for change. With expanded teacher representation so someone was present from each school, the task force systematically listed and discussed all the complaints and suggestions they received. A number of changes were made such as eliminating the dossier requirement. Many suggestions were rejected either because they had only mixed support or because they were considered less workable than the original procedures.

Task force members truly felt they had developed a fair and objective plan that would accomplish what the school board wanted. They thought that as soon as people understood it and had a chance to amend it and assist in its completion, it would be widely endorsed.

What happened instead was the expression of a great deal of negative reaction to one feature after another. What the task force cited as reasons and rationale for the various planning decisions that had been incorporated into the draft documents was interpreted as rigidity and unwillingness to accept suggestions for real improvement. Task force members became frustrated as the fall went on and teacher questions continued to indicate lack of clear understanding of what the documents prescribed and how the plan would work.

Undoubtedly, during this period, those who were violently opposed to the whole idea were complaining about anything they could and communicating their strong objections to their colleagues. What teachers as a whole were hearing, therefore, was a mixture of clarifying information from task force members and a wide variety of opinion and reaction from other colleagues. What seemed originally to be an easy communication task became a long, difficult effort to revise and fine-tune documents so as to ease as much dissatisfaction as possible. It was a full year later before all documents were in final form. Task force members were less enthusiastic about the whole effort than a year earlier, being a bit battle-scarred from the controversy. Teacher surveys still showed widespread rejection of the plan on the surface, but a reasonably good interest in participation.

Several new task force members, incidentally, and specialist representatives, after planning their own participation procedures with help from the task force, did express considerably greater acceptance as they came to understand the complexities of developing a fair plan.

A closer examination of reactions to the plan and changing sentiments as additional planning and implementation occurred will be pursued in the next chapter.

Changing Sentiments and Procedures

In this chapter, the attitudes and procedures that emerged from the planning stage will be traced through the later stages of partial and full implementation to note whatever changes took place. Developments will be traced not only in Danville but in Utah and Arizona as well, so the similarities and differences can be highlighted. The data for this review come from various surveys, evaluation reports, interviews, program documents, and ethnographic materials. A close examination of how programs were initiated and developed in various states and localities reveals some interesting similarities and differences. Among the former are the stages they go through. Five stages can be identified from enactment to institutionalization. It is in how planning is conducted and what results from it that one finds great differences.

The initial planning of teacher incentive pay programs is conducted in two stages: program enactment and program design. During the first, policymakers (governors, legislators, superintendents, school boards) interact with lobbyists for various stakeholders in the educational enterprise (business leaders, teacher association officers, government officials) and debate the need for such a program and its general design. They eventually decide that teacher incentive pay is a good idea and enact the legislation and policies needed to start planning a program. For stage two, some group or individual is charged with designing the program and providing progress reports from time to time. Funds are budgeted to support this activity. General guidelines about the kind of plan desired are often contained in the charge as well.

The strength and direction of the mandate depends on the relative influence of various parties and the extent to which consensus is reached. It is no accident that many of the current programs were instigated at the same time (1983–85). *A Nation at Risk* vocalized the widespread sentiment that something was seriously wrong with public education, and fundamental changes were needed. Respect for traditional educational leadership was at an all-time low. New leadership was needed; new ideas about how schools should be run. In Texas, billionaire businessman H. Ross Perot chaired the key reform committee. In Tennessee and Florida, Governors Lamar Alexander and Bob Graham spotlighted educational reform as the top priority of their terms in office. They competed furiously to put the first statewide teacher incentive pay plan into operation. Management practices from the private sector were in vogue. Included among them was incentive pay.

Despite large constituencies in the educational community, the educator's voice was temporarily subdued in all the clamor for something new. Even though merit pay and differentiated staffing had been tried before, with only limited success, this time it might be different. Even a majority of teachers themselves, when polled in the abstract about the merits of paying teachers on the basis of performance, approved the idea (Rist, 1983).

When such programs were to be part of a total reform effort with such attractive components as increased revenues for schools, they were hard to resist. This was especially true when taxes were actually raised to finance educational reform legislation, as in Tennessee and South Carolina. In any number of communities the trade-off for accepting an incentive pay program was a substantial increase in the basic pay for teachers. In Danville, teachers had received several consecutive 10 percent pay increases prior to the decision to launch its program. In Fairfax County, Virginia, a 30 percent increment over three years was promised before the unions agreed to help develop a new incentive plan.

Where the leadership was strong and consensus achieved early in the policy-making body regarding the kind of program needed (for example, Danville, Lynchburg, Florida, and Tennessee), the charge to the phase two design groups was clear and progress could be made rapidly. Committees and planning staffs established procedures to implement policies, and full-scale programs were launched within a year or two.

Where greater debate and more compromise occurred within the policy-making body, incentive pay guidelines suggested more eclectic programs and pilot efforts before the launching of full-scale programs. In Utah, for example, heavy legislative debate about the kind of program needed led to the inclusion of the several components described earlier and the requirement that at least 10 percent should go to bonus pay and no more than 50 percent for extra work days. Local districts were given extra funds for the incentive awards and the task of developing their own programs within general guidelines. Thus, the phase two planning occurred at the district level.

In North Carolina, the State Board of Education was charged with program development and pilot testing a four-year implementation in sixteen districts. In South Carolina, three general models were designed under state leadership and pilot tested in an expanding number of districts over a four-year period. Much of the phase two planning took place at the local level, but under coordinated state leadership. Most of these state efforts have been subject to one or more third-party evaluations as a means of assessing their effectiveness and improving procedures.

Obvious advantages accrue to individuals and districts that volunteer and are selected to participate in the stage two planning and stage three pilot testing and early implementation. One is more money and resources to operate programs and extra pay for individuals who participate. Those involved can also enjoy whatever satisfaction is derived from helping shape a program. Those districts and people that become involved later, at stage four, have the advantage in seeing how others have benefited and smoother operational procedures. A disadvantage is having to adjust to whatever others have worked out. Presumably at stage five, the latter advantages and disadvantages will be even more pronounced.

One reason for discussing who is involved at various stages is to establish an appropriate context for reviewing program and attitude changes from stage one into stages two, three, and four. How people feel about programs and various specific issues depends a great deal on what stage a program is in, how they have been involved with the program, what constituencies they represent, and how issues have already been settled. For the members of the Danville task force, for example, most of the procedural issues had been settled by the end of the summer planning period in July 1984. For the majority of the Danville teachers, however, many of the same issues were raised again and again over the next year and reasons requested about why particular procedures had been chosen over other options.

The remainder of this chapter, therefore, will be devoted to reviewing attitude and procedure changes over the several stages, that is, from the time planning begins until they are fully implemented if not yet institutionalized. Although Danville will again be used as a primary case study because of its rich, in-depth data, two state programs and another local one will also be tracked.

SENTIMENTS (DANVILLE)

During Planning

The attitudes of Danville teachers were first solicited following the task force presentation of a new evaluation system and a career ladder plan on 22 and 23 August 1984. This was approximately nine months after the school board began discussing the need for a new evaluation system and incentive pay, four months after its charge was formulated, two months after planning by the task force was started, and three weeks after the board adopted what had been developed. The decision was made to install the evaluation system during the coming year while plans were being completed on the career ladder. Selection of peer evaluators would be accomplished through a nominating process in spring 1985, and they along with administrators would receive two weeks of training in the evaluation system and review process in summer 1985. The first applicants would be accepted in July 1985, and reviewed for promotion to the career teacher level during the 1985–86 year. Selection of the first career teachers would be completed in July 1986.

Official planning of the career ladder ended in summer 1985 with the completion of the manual and other operating documents and formal training of those who would be operating the system. During this year and a half of planning, teachers were represented in substantial numbers (twelve of thirty) on the task force during the first summer and in majority proportions during the school year and the second summer. The written reactions of all teachers were solicited three times while planning was going on: by written reactions to the task force proposal in fall 1984, and by two surveys conducted in April 1985.

For the first of these, teachers were asked to indicate their feelings by listing what they liked best and least about both the proposed evaluation system and career ladder plan and what suggestions they had for improving them. The task force developed categories for coding and tallying responses. The five most frequently mentioned best liked and least liked aspects of the two proposals are shown in Exhibits 4.1 and 4.2.

These initial reactions indicate a mixture of pro and con sentiment. The specificity of the evaluation system was its most

Exhibit 4.1

Aspects of the Danville Evaluation System Liked Best and Least
(August 1984)

Like Best	f
1. The plan is specific; expectations and requirements are clear	96
2. It will improve instruction	48
3. Requirement that evaluators communicate concerns/suggestions	47
4. Documentation	46
5. Fair; applies to everyone in the same way	33
Like Least	
1. Paper work and time consuming	36
2. Still subjective	27
3. Administrators may not interpret consistently	23
4. There is no average rating	17
5. It is disturbing—too long, complicated, and detailed	14

frequently mentioned good feature. Expectations and requirements were judged to be clear, and many people thought that it would improve instruction. Although documentation requirements were viewed favorably by several dozen teachers, the amount of

Exhibit 4.2

Aspects of the Danville Career Ladder Plan Liked Best and Least
(August 1984)

Like Best	f
1. It rewards good teachers	77
2. Clear, details, well presented	43
3. It is voluntary	42
4. Incentive and opportunity for advancement without having to leave the classroom	32
5. It is fair	29
Like Least	
1. Extra duties will spread teachers too "thin"	41
2. Question of fairness	40
3. Too detailed and lengthy	39
4. Paperwork involved in the dossier	32
5. Documentation is over emphasized	31

paperwork connected with it was cited more often than any other feature among its least liked characteristics. Overall, best liked features were more frequently mentioned than least liked features.

Reactions to the career ladder were less favorable, on balance. Almost as many negative as positive remarks were tallied. The notion that good teachers would be rewarded was cited most often. The fact that it was clear, detailed, and well presented was considered an asset by quite a few people. Also mentioned frequently was the fact that it provided a voluntary means of advancement for people who did not want to leave the classroom.

Although more than a few teachers considered it a fair system, its fairness was questioned by a few more. Its length and extensive details were viewed negatively by a good many teachers, and dossier paperwork and documentation seemed unnecessarily burdensome.

At best, supporters of the career ladder at this early stage in its development did not outnumber opponents and may well have been in the minority. The evaluation system seemed more acceptable.

Realizing that the plan was not particularly well accepted or even thoroughly understood, the task force, then expanded to include teachers from every school, set out in small groups to explain the plan and answer questions school by school. A long list of questions was compiled from these briefing sessions as the task force continued to finalize operational procedures. Questions that had not been fully addressed at the time included:[1]

How much weight will be given to parent and student surveys?

How will situations be handled where teachers 'fudge' test results?

How many teachers can be accommodated in future years?

What assurance do I have that principal-bias will not keep me from qualifying for the career ladder?

Meanwhile principals were using the new evaluation materials, visiting classrooms, filling out the rating forms, and sharing the ratings they had made in post-observation conferences. Principals and assistant principals themselves spent several meetings discussing evaluation procedures and the experiences they were having during the first use of the new system.

The more questions were asked and explanations given during all this activity, the more uneasy many people seemed to become. A survey was planned for the spring semester to be conducted by an outside evaluator to assess teacher sentiment and obtain specific suggestions for improving the plan and making it more acceptable.

In April 1985, teachers were surveyed twice, once by the Danville Education Association using a form developed by the NEA research unit. The other survey was conducted by Wayne Willis of Averett College. Both survey reports confirmed predominantly negative feelings about the career ladder. Although some reservations were expressed about the evaluation system, reactions were much more positive overall toward it than the career ladder. Major findings from these surveys follow:

Willis Survey

- The new teacher evaluation procedure is better than the previous one.
  17% strongly agree, 40% agree vs. 15% disagree, 10% strongly disagree
- Teachers need performance-based awards in addition to across-the-board raises.
  20% strongly agree, 31% agree vs. 18% disagree, 17% strongly disagree
- I approve of the career ladder program.
  3% strongly agree, 13% agree vs. 26% disagree, 38% strongly disagree
- Do you plan to apply for promotion on the career ladder during the next two years?
  18% yes   82% no
- Do you expect to apply for promotion on the career ladder later?
  24% yes   76% no
- The best feature of the career ladder program is
  a. extra rewards for outstanding teaching   17%
  b. the new evaluation procedure   23%
  c. the opportunity for promotion without going into administration   14%
  d. increased motivation of teachers to excel   4%
  e. teachers' increased awareness of the quality of their instructional performance   21%
  f. competitiveness among teachers   3%
  g. the involvement of promoted teachers in leadership roles   3%
  h. other (specify)   14%

- The worst feature of the career ladder program is
  a. the difficulty of evaluating teachers fairly   41%
  b. the funding of it   2%
  c. potential morale problems among teachers   24%
  d. potential problems with parents who want the children only in classes of career ladder teachers   6%
  e. competitiveness among teachers   4%
  f. the paperwork involved in applying for promotion   4%
  g. the work load of career ladder teachers   9%
  h. other (specify) _____   9%

DEA Survey

- 88% indicated that continued general increases in the level of teacher salaries would do more to attract and retain highly qualified teachers than the career ladder plan
- 82% disagreed that the career ladder plan would encourage them to do a better job of teaching
- 73% indicated that evaluation practices were not consistent from one school to the next
- 81% supported the statement "My evaluator [principal, assistant principal] seems competent to evaluate."

Perhaps the most important finding from these two surveys taken eight months after the plans had first been presented was the very small percentage of teachers who expressed approval of the career ladder program that was about to be implemented. Four times as many teachers indicated disapproval. Much time and effort had gone into its planning and dissemination. Those most involved were clearly disappointed that there was not more favorable reaction to what had been drawn up. The evaluation system, however, was apparently appreciated, with 57 percent indicating it was an improvement over the old one versus only 25 percent saying it was not. Teachers did express a moderate amount of support of the need for performance-based pay (51 percent versus 35 percent), however, so the basic notion apparently was not rejected in principle. Even more puzzling perhaps was an expressed interest on the part of two out of five teachers (42 percent) in applying for promotion either in the next two years or later.

One hypothesis for this early rejection of the career ladder plan is that many of the issues the task force had resolved among its members the previous summer, as they considered various alternatives and selected what they thought would be appropriate operational procedures, left very little for others to work on. The task force had dealt with issues they had to resolve in one way or another if more than a skeleton of a plan was to be generated. For many other teachers, there was no appropriate forum in which to work on and resolve such issues. The key decisions had already been made by the task force; they remained for others merely as points of controversy. Perhaps the best example of a carefully considered task force decision that others blatantly rejected was the random drawing.

Teachers "second-guessed" the task force throughout this period by raising questions about why other procedures would not be better. They complained about why it was being put into operation before the evaluation system had been perfected and administrators and other evaluators fully trained. They asked for a delay in implementation until planning was complete and their suggestions for revisions had been incorporated, or at least considered. Many teachers felt "bull-dozed" by a planning effort that had gone too far too fast without sufficient involvement of others.

Others, based on candid remarks indicating their rejection of the whole idea of incentive pay and career ladders, were unhappy that they had too little time or opportunity to force the board to withdraw the directive. Unlike the teacher members of the task force, whose motivation was to design the best program possible given the board's mandate, some teachers never accepted the mandate as "irreversible." They just did not have time to organize sufficient opposition to force the program's withdrawal during this first year. Things were moving too fast, and the teacher ranks were divided. Some of the school system's strongest leaders and most respected teachers were the very people who had designed it.

Consequently, despite considerable opposition of many teachers, the board had endorsed it, the administration was committed to making it work, some teachers were interested in applying; so implementation proceeded on schedule in the summer of 1985. Although the plan had been refined and revised in a few places, incorporating some of the recommendations others had made, it was basically what the task force had designed. The major revision was the elimination of the dossier by allowing candidates to provide their committees with needed documentation more informally during conferences.

During Initial Implementation

This section will draw heavily on three documents. The first is a report of still another survey of the Danville teachers. This survey was conducted by the consultant and a colleague in April 1986, one year after the DEA and Willis surveys. Several questions included in the Willis survey were repeated to permit direct comparisons of teacher attitudes over the interim.

The other two documents are research papers prepared by the consultant in 1986 and 1987 in which he identified and described ethnographic documentation of twenty-nine issues that had stimulated major controversy and debate during the development of the plan (see Exhibit 3.1; Brandt, 1986a; Brandt, 1987). These issues were discussed in the previous chapter. They will be discussed again briefly later in this chapter along with any other issues that remained or emerged.

In April 1986, questionnaires for obtaining reactions to the career ladder plan were mailed to all Danville teachers. A total of 318 were returned, a two-thirds response rate. Five of the seventeen questions had been used in a previous survey permitting direct comparison of year earlier results. Interjudge coding agreement averaged 84 percent in the categorizing of responses to the five open-ended questions the questionnaire included.

Overall findings of the April 1986 poll of teachers suggested little change in the negative sentiment reported in the 1985 surveys. Approximately two-thirds of the teachers did not approve of the plan for one or more reasons. Relatively few expressed a belief that it would improve instruction (14 percent) or enhance the attraction or retention of outstanding teachers (9 percent). Quite the contrary, many indicated that it would cause dissension and distract teachers from good teaching. Responses to the five questions that had been asked a year earlier produced only one significant change, that is, from almost no teachers to 10 percent indicating that other teachers would encourage them to apply for the career ladder if they wanted to do so. As in the earlier Willis poll, attitudes toward the summative teacher evaluation system, now in its third year of use, were quite positive.

Two other major findings of the April 1986 poll were a considerably greater amount of support for the plan among teachers new to the system, and among those who expressed some interest in applying for the career ladder themselves or some belief that it might improve instruction. Approximately one-third of the teachers were grouped in the latter category by not expressing a categorical "no" to all three opening questions: "Did you apply, do you intend to apply at the next opportunity, and do you think it will improve instruction?" Teachers new to the system, incidentally, were not beginning teachers. Almost all of them had taught elsewhere a number of years, so their significantly more positive attitudes were not a function of age or experience. More likely, they reflected their relative lack of full assimilation into the peer culture of the majority of teachers.

The lack of change in overall teacher attitudes from April 1985 to April 1986 is not surprising given the fact that not much had taken place during that year which could be expected to induce change. Candidates had been selected out of the first pool of applicants, review teams had been appointed and were busy performing their year-long review; but the results would not be in until summer 1986, so no one was yet able to see the whole process completed. Earlier reactions would be expected to prevail because the structure of both the career ladder and the teacher evaluation system was unchanged from what had been described twenty months earlier. The intensive effort to communicate a full understanding of the plan which had been attempted in the fall and winter 1984–85, and to address the complaints made in the communications committee meetings a year later (see section below) was apparently unsuccessful in winning new converts. Many teachers expected the plan to be dropped if enough teacher hostility could be expressed for a long enough time. Others adopted a "wait and see" attitude until the process was completed and they could see who was promoted and how they fared.

A communications committee was formed in fall 1985, consisting of representatives from each school, to meet with the superintendent, his assistants, and two board members from the task force. The teachers were specifically asked to represent those opposed to what had been developed so that changes might be made to increase teacher acceptance.

A summary of concerns raised by committee members in October 1985 indicates that many of the issues identified during the planning stages earlier were far from resolved among other teachers. Many had to do with the evaluation system, furthermore, not just the career ladder. Several are listed below, along with the numbers of the issues they reflect (see Exhibit 3.1).

1,5   —Career ladder is not doing what teachers thought it would, strengthening the profession by working with the weak teachers. Emphasis is on the strong teachers.

7   —Identification of master teachers will keep others from volunteering.

8   —Teachers aren't willing to share—ladder will breed
          in-house competition.

12   —Teachers may have to alter their approach to
          teaching . . . to please the evaluator.

14   —Teachers feel that evaluators are looking for little
          things.

14   —How can someone from the outside show up three
          times and know what I'm doing in my classes?

14,15,17 —The consistency of evaluations and the role and
          competence of principals are major concerns (cited
          by six teachers).

16   —There is a general feeling that evaluations are going
          to be tougher.

16   —Some teachers feel as though they are doing all they
          can right now. They fear that being on the ladder
          will be more demanding.

22   —The lottery was ill-conceived. Perhaps consideration
          should have been given to teachers with long
          records, especially those nearing retirement.

24   —Opposition is coming from the very best teachers.
          They don't want to have anything to do with it.

Although the agenda for this committee was problems with the
plan, presumably so improvements could be made, few constructive
recommendations were forthcoming. Most of the time was taken up
during the half-dozen meetings by four or five vocal individuals
reiterating these complaints and citing examples of their manifesta-
tion.

Several teachers who tended to say little in the meetings had
actually applied for the ladder the previous June but had not been
selected in the random drawing. One of them volunteered privately
to the consultant: "I always favored the career ladder idea and even
applied for the original task force; I wished I had been on it; and I
know that the committee did a splendid job." She said further that
the plan had done a lot of good. She also indicated that she and other
teachers had talked about one teacher in particular who had worked
much harder to be a good teacher because of it.

So most of the issues were still unresolved as the first year of the plan's operation came to a close. A majority of the teachers reacted negatively to the career ladder and quite a few had concerns about specific features of the evaluation system, even though most teachers felt it was a major improvement over what had existed before. A minority, on the other hand, were interested in the career ladder and felt much about the evaluation system was commendable.

During Later Implementation

In July 1987, after the second group of career teachers had been selected (although the results were not yet generally known), a final assessment was made of teacher sentiment toward the career ladder. A year earlier, teachers had indicated little interest in being surveyed again; and the administration, ever since, had adopted a "low profile" approach to the career ladder. Its previous "center stage" status was apparently resented.

Therefore, the consultant requested permission to interview two to four teachers from each school, depending on its size. He selected names by random number from the school directory, called teachers at home to invite their participation and establish a schedule, and promised not to identify them or their schools in connection with any comments or analyses that might appear in later reports. Teachers were told that the superintendent had granted permission for the interviews to be conducted with the understanding that the names of teachers interviewed would not be revealed by the investigator to him or anyone else, and individual comments would be depersonalized so teachers or schools could not be identified. For the most part, they would be aggregated with statements of other teachers in summary fashion in later reports. They were also told that the superintendent wanted them to feel perfectly free to turn down the interview request; they were under no obligation to participate if they chose not to. Three or four did so, saying they were teaching summer school, taking classes, going on vacation or otherwise involved. Another half dozen could not be reached. But, when this happened, randomly drawn alternatives were found from all but two relatively small elementary schools. The final sample included twenty-three individuals from twelve schools, approximately 5 percent of the teacher population.

The hour-long interviews were structured around a dozen open-ended questions designed to elicit complete and candid reactions toward the plan and evaluation system. Probing questions were also asked to find out why teachers felt as they did. Several key questions were essentially the same as those used in previous polls.

(For instance, "Are you interested or do you expect to be interested in applying? . . . Why? Why not?") Two were identical in wording to questions asked in the April 1986 survey:

> If you were to apply for promotion on the career ladder, would most other teachers in your school respond to you enthusiastically with encouragement? . . . Why? Why not?
>
> In your estimation will the career ladder program improve the quality of education for Danville's young people? (If yes) In what way? (If no) Why not?

These latter, tightly phrased questions were asked near the end of the interview after most attitudes had been fully revealed. Interviews were not tape recorded. The investigator took handwritten notes, using scripting procedures, to provide a running account of what teachers said. Occasionally, he read back a statement a teacher had just made, partly to check on the accuracy of recording but also to show the interviewee how specifically and accurately his statements were being taken down.

Later, copies of the interview notes were coded and filed in the appropriate issues folders along with other ethnographic material. Attitudes to several of the general questions were summarized as follows:

Question: "Have you been involved with the career ladder? How?" Seven said yes; sixteen, no. The seven included three evaluators, three career teachers, and one current candidate. Two of the seven had also served on the original task force, and one had served on the 1984–86 communications committee. By this time, 21 percent of the teachers in the division had been officially involved in one or more of the above capacities. Thus, this interview sample had two teachers more in it who had been so involved than the general population of Danville teachers (30 percent versus 21 percent). This slightly larger proportion of teachers for the interview sample needs to be considered in the interpretation of findings. In other demographic respects the sample was representative of the full range of subjects, schools, and grade levels. One or two of the group, furthermore, were in their first three years of teaching in Danville, another two or three nearing retirement and the remainder well spread out across the experience spectrum.

Question: "Do you expect to be interested? Why? Why not?" Answers from the 19 who were not already career teachers or candidates were: yes –6; probably–2; perhaps–3; probably not–2; no–6. This evenly divided sentiment between those interested versus those not interested in applying for career ladder promotion is in considerable contrast to survey results fifteen months earlier. Then, 10 percent had already applied and only another 13 percent said they intended to apply during the next two years.

When the three career teachers and one candidate in the sample are added to the eight who indicated they would or probably would apply, the increased interest in the career ladder is even more obvious; approximately half the sample appeared interested in applying versus less than a quarter of the teachers earlier.

Reasons for being interested or not were similar to those of a year earlier. Typical comments were:

> Purely money. I'm the sole breadwinner with a child going to college soon.

> . . . interested in the money and being set apart from colleagues.

> . . . not many administrative positions. It's a chance to upgrade myself.

> . . . too busy now.

> . . . definitely not . . . lots of complaints . . . Experience and degrees alone should count.

Question: "Given the fact that the board and city council wanted a system for identifying and rewarding outstanding teachers, what is your overall impression of the system that has been developed?" Although this was asked as a closing question near the end of the interview and the question about their interest in trying for the career ladder was used early, responses to both questions were read together as a basis for judging each teacher's overall attitude toward it. Results are shown in Exhibit 4.3.

Interjudge reliability was calculated by reading responses of nine teachers to five other persons. Kendall's Contingency coefficient was .71. There was unanimous concurrence about three teachers and consensus on the rest.

One of those who was positive but, until then, had not decided to participate said:

> I like the career ladder. Those who have made it are all

Exhibit 4.3

Later Attitudes of Teachers Toward the Career Ladder Plan (July 1987)

General Sentiment	f
Enthusiastic toward CL and am participating or intending to participate	9
Favorable to CL but am not participating or intending to	4
Neutral or mixed feelings; may participate	3
Still against CL but am participating or intending to	0
Strongly negative toward CL; will not participate	7

outstanding. They deserve merit pay. I hope the career ladder is here to stay.

One teacher who advised dropping the career ladder, because "too many people are involved and favoritism keeps it from being administered accurately," said about the evaluation system:

The instrument is fine . . . has more advantages (than the old evaluation scale), is more quantifiable, more detailed.

At least two others among the seven who expressed strongly negative feelings toward the career ladder also reacted positively to the new evaluation system.

In addition to the 5 percent random sample of teachers, eight teacher members (including two in the random sample) from the original task force were also interviewed in the same manner. Although all of them were judged as still positive toward the career ladder, and several as very positive and glad to be involved, several cited problems with it. Among the concerns they expressed were the lack of significance of some student outcome goals, insufficient training of one or two career ladder selection committee (CLSC) members, changes in the way third members of CLSCs were chosen, possible discontinuance of needed central administration oversight with changes in the superintendency, documentation demands still too great for some excellent teachers, and uncertainties about long-term funding. One complained that a few career teachers "just squeaked by" while some other "truly outstanding teachers" did not choose to apply.

Each of these task force teachers had played key leadership

roles in drafting the requirements and writing the directives for the plan. They knew how it was intended to work. Six of them had been selected as evaluators and had served on several CLSCs by the time they expressed these comments. The other two had become candidates, experienced the year-long scrutiny, and been promoted to career teacher status. One was appointed chairman of a high school academic department during this period. Another was elected and served as President of the Danville Education Association.

A primary desire of several of these teachers, perhaps all, both when they first applied to be on the task force and later when it was made operational, was this: If they were going to have a system for recognizing and rewarding outstanding teachers, it should be as fair a system as possible, one that improves the education of young people, and one they can be proud of. At the end of the 1984 summer planning, this group was proud of its accomplishments. Over the next three years these teachers, along with administrators and others, worked hard to address the initial concerns of their colleagues and to perfect the operational procedures. They undoubtedly absorbed some direct flak from their colleagues, although I have little direct evidence of that happening. The fact that most of them were nominated by their colleagues to be evaluators in March 1985 shows the high regard others had for them.

It is noteworthy that these teachers, who probably understood the system better than anyone else, remained enthusiastic, not as blatantly so perhaps as they once had been. At the same time, they still saw the need for its improvement. The responsibility they assumed so well for so long and the concerns they still had for improving the system reflect the essence of teacher professionalism.

As noted in the comparisons above between summer 1987 and spring 1986, rather sharp changes in teacher attitudes toward the career ladder took place, from a large majority being hostile to the plan to at least as much interest and positive feeling as negative feeling on average. Some teachers, but unfortunately not all, were asked directly if teacher attitudes had changed. Of those who were asked, all twelve who expressed a clear opinion said they had changed:

Question: "Have attitudes changed this past year?"

It's more and more supported. I was negative; I've changed my mind.

Totally negative feelings have moved to apathetic ones.

The first year, if you showed interest, you were 'crazy.' Not so now.

Three people from another school asked me how to go about (getting on) it.

I still hear many concerns. It's more accepted as being here.

Several who are now applying originally said 'No.' (Why?) Money.

As noted earlier, two questions asked near the end of the interviews were worded exactly as they had been on the survey questionnaire fifteen months earlier. On the question of peers responding enthusiastically and with respect if they applied for the current ladder, "Yes" responses outnumbered "No" responses eleven to eight in 1987 (four were uncertain). In 1986, only 10 percent indicated peers would respond in a supportive manner while 24 percent would be neutral, and 65 percent would be nonsupportive. Even greater nonsupport was indicated in 1985, comparable figures being five, thirteen, and eighty-two. A significant change had clearly taken place from one year to the next in the perceived peer pressure against participation in the plan. To express interest had once been considered tabu by almost everyone. By 1987, most teachers were no longer hesitant to indicate an interest. Negative remarks, however, would still be expected by several teachers. Comments made by interviewees included the following:

. . . not personally rude; just wonder what's wrong with me.

. . . hard to say. Some who are downing candidates would support me.

I believe so. I've had seven subjects. They know I've had a big load.

Some teachers told me to apply. I'd be encouraged.

Most would, but they also know I never would; they would expect some explanation.

Oh, yes. Our's is a small school. We care about each other.

To the question of whether the career ladder would improve the quality of education in Danville, twelve said "yes," five were not sure, and six said "no." Fifteen months earlier, on the survey, only

14 percent said "yes" and a year earlier, 18 percent. The rest said "no" in each instance. Of the task force members who were asked this question, six of seven said "yes"; the other expressed uncertainty.

Typical reasons cited for "yes" responses:

The evaluation tool is much better. It's spelled out in writing what's expected.

New, younger teachers should find this appealing.

Unquestionably yes. Already has. Everybody is working harder than before whether they like it or not.

I think so. Standards will be raised.

Some "no" reasons:

Seeing other people doing a good job is not what incites me.

No bad teachers are removed; none improved by the evaluation system.

Poor on morale.

Two examples of uncertain responses:

I don't know. It's most important to get rid of poor teachers. The evaluation has helped improve the weak.

Not much difference. Teachers who are lazy put on a show. Teachers who are conscientious do it anyway.

It is clear from the summaries of all the questions and responses above that a major change occurred in feelings about the career ladder between spring 1986 and summer 1987. While sentiment overall was predominantly negative in 1986, it was actually more positive than negative on most items in 1987. I do not imply that everyone enthusiastically endorsed the career ladder. Rather, there was a wide range of feelings toward it from great interest and enthusiasm through cautiously mixed, perhaps ambivalent attitudes, to apathy for some who did not like it but had not been able to scuttle it and a few who were still hostile over it. The comments above suggest there are many reasons why people feel as they do. While certain themes were occasionally recurrent, many were not, reflecting the full range of reaction that then existed among Danville teachers.

ISSUE AND PROCEDURE UPDATE (DANVILLE, SUMMER 1987)

The three issues related to paying teachers differentially according to how well they teach continued to be important, debatable matters. A major shift had taken place in attitudes toward the career ladder. Up to half the teachers expressed an interest in it, for a variety of reasons; a majority were favorable or actually enthusiastic about it. That was quite different from feelings expressed fifteen months earlier. While up to half of the teachers still did not favor the notion, the school board and community at large continued to believe it was a good idea.

There was little debate, however, over the Danville plan being workable, the other half of issue #1.[2] The system was in place and had been implemented twice over its full cycle. Several adjustments had been made in how it operated at first, but it was well into a third cycle. Whether the benefits matched or exceeded the trade-offs in teacher stress and extra administrative time to make it function may still have been debatable, but the system was obviously workable.

The basis of the promotion (#2)—that is, whether extra pay was for extra work or for doing the same work better—took on heightened meaning in July 1986 with the promotion of nineteen teachers to the new rank of career teacher. In interviews conducted at the time, principals expressed a great deal of concern about what these teachers were to do in their new roles. Both the board and the central administration asked questions or made suggestions about how career teachers should be used, and other teachers watched as well to see how their own situations might be affected. Would they be expected to observe career teachers teach, as part of staff development? Would they be relieved of curriculum committee assignments which career teachers would take on? Principals were especially concerned that career teachers might be given new responsibilities for which they were not prepared. For example, a kindergarten teacher might be asked to direct a staff workshop on reading. Board members wanted to know what extra duties would be carried out to justify the extra salaries.

Concerns were eased when people were reminded that the primary reason for promotion was to reward good teaching, not to require more work. In most cases, the newly promoted teachers were among those who typically took whatever action was needed to do their jobs professionally and well regardless of the time and energy involved. New responsibilities for career teachers, if any, were not expected to take more time, only a reordering of priorities, unless one accepted an extended contract.

The issue would undoubtedly arise again in fall 1989, after the promotion of the first master teachers. Although the quality of one's teaching was still supposed to be the primary basis for promotion, leadership characteristics were to be considered as well. Master teachers would be expected to serve other functions than classroom teaching alone. What those functions would be would most certainly have to be considered eventually.

Likely Effects of the Plan

With the school board reviewing and making minor adjustments to the plan in the face of back-to-back polls showing considerable teacher opposition and the superintendent projecting costs into the 1990s, a message was clearly conveyed that the plan was here to stay. People were more likely to take a "wait and see" attitude rather than to make quick and perhaps superficial judgments that teacher morale would deteriorate (#7) and teacher-administrator relationships would be damaged (#10). For some issues, it was still early to judge the full impact.

Although the early polls had indicated that the majority of teachers did not think the plan would improve instruction (#5), teachers interviewed in summer 1987 felt otherwise by a two to one margin. One teacher raved about several useful teaching techniques the evaluation process had taught her, such as how to ask probing questions and to call on all children every day, even the quiet ones. "This tool" she said, "is the first time I've ever been given real help on my teaching."

One parent reported his child wishing the evaluator, who had been to his class that day, would come every day because they had such a good lesson. "Usually we just read," the child had said.

Several comments of principals the previous summer also described improved teaching which they attributed to the plan, the performance criteria, and the evaluation process. The vast majority of task force members, too, felt teaching had improved.

It was still too early to tell how many teachers would be attracted to teaching in Danville (#6) because of the plan. In the April 1986 survey, teachers who had been in Danville three years or less expressed significantly more positive attitudes toward the plan than other teachers and greater interest in applying for promotion when they became eligible. These teachers were more positive than negative, on average, on most of the survey items. With few exceptions, furthermore, they were experienced, not beginning, teachers because a relatively low turnover rate in recent years had not exhausted the pool of experienced applicants available. One of the telling arguments behind the board's continued support of the project was that the enhanced career and salary opportunities the plan offered would place Danville in a good position to attract some of the best teaching recruits a few years hence when large numbers of teachers would retire and the supply of new prospects would be quite limited.

How and how much the plan affected teacher motivation (#7) was a sufficiently complex issue so as not to attempt a summary here. Suffice it to say that teachers reacted differently to it. For some, it represented a challenge and something worth striving for. For others, the extra money was enticing and the sole basis for participation or interest. For still others, it was threatening and the source of great discomfort. Still others objected on principle. Greater analysis will be attempted in the next chapter.

There was no direct evidence that teachers had become more competitive (#8) and less willing to share ideas or offer assistance because of the plan. None of the teachers interviewed cited examples they had observed themselves of teachers withholding assistance to others. In a number of instances, career ladder candidates actually received help from their colleagues when they served as neutral third parties in administering or scoring student outcome measures. Again, it would seem, actions speak more loudly than words. Despite initial peer pressure not to participate, teachers who made the attempt received considerable help from other teachers in their efforts to be promoted.

One teacher said her colleagues urged her to postpone a scheduled formal observation by her review team because she was sick: "They wanted me to do well."

Another teacher, who was not interested in the career ladder herself, replied, when asked if she had noticed any holding back on the sharing of ideas: "Not at our school, but I've heard comments about it happening elsewhere." The few comments related to this issue in the data base indicate that teachers remained as cooperative as ever with each other.

Evidence of changed collegial relationships (#9) was also sparse. In one school, teachers were at least mildly upset over "an affected air" on the part of their promoted colleague. In other instances, teachers serving as evaluators on career ladder selection committees were considered "more rigorous and discriminating" than administrators in their use of performance measures and their judgments about the quality of teaching. There certainly was no indication that teachers, properly selected and trained, could not serve as effectively as administrators on review teams established to identify outstanding teachers. The strong peer pressure that was directed against anyone expressing an interest in the career ladder had clearly subsided in most schools. Several of those who had initially voiced strong opposition to the career ladder were now participating. A number of persons who still did not intend to participate said: "There was nothing wrong with anyone who did."

Teacher-administrator relationships remained a touchy issue (#10), more in some schools than others. Where administrators had a solid teaching background themselves in the grades and subjects they were assigned to administer, teachers tended to respect instructional leadership and evaluation by their principals. Where principals lacked such backgrounds, teachers were more uneasy. In indicating on the 1986 survey why they did not intend to apply, twenty-eight teachers specifically cited "inconsistency between schools" or "incompetency of principals as instructional evaluators." A year later, more than a few had the same concern.

The fact that during the first year no teachers from two schools applied for career ladder candidacy may have reflected the quality of trust between administrators and teachers in those buildings. On the other hand, as several teacher remarks suggested, it more likely was a product of the attitudes of the individual educators and the particular working cultures in those schools. Traditional trade-offs between building principals and teachers, for example, "I won't bother you if you don't bother me with problems and complaints," do not occur so easily in a system where rigorous evaluation is expected and administrators as well as teachers are held accountable. Participation in the career ladder could jeopardize such relationships and understandings.

Teacher comments in several schools indicated improvement in principals' evaluation practices following workshop training in the new system. Teachers who had seldom been observed in any formal way were now reporting systematic observation and conferencing in effect. In most places teachers were expressing greater confidence than earlier in principals' ability to evaluate teaching and provide assistance. More will be said later about principals' role conflicts (#17) brought on by the plan.

As with most career ladder or merit pay plans, how the system would operate if budgets became tight and salary reductions were needed was a major concern, not just for board members but teachers as well (#11). In the 1987 interviews it was brought up by most of the teachers, task force members, and administrators as a basic long-term concern. In the 1987 budget, money to pay for the career ladder supplements had to come out of other priority items so as to honor the board's commitment that it not reduce regular pay increases for all teachers.

Considerable teacher resistance to the installation of teacher incentive structures has come from the feeling that basic salaries must be raised substantially in most school districts before any consideration should be given to a differential reward structure. Opinions differ, from locality to locality and individual to individual, about how much they should be raised first. The target is always moving so it is hard to tell when it might be reached. Compared to employee gains in many other fields during the past six years, teachers' salaries have typically progressed much faster. What the basic salary level should be before incentive pay becomes acceptable is always debatable.

To finesse this issue and reduce one source of likely resistance, two Virginia school systems included the highest across-the-board salary raises ever (16 percent and 12 percent) as part of their proposals for career ladder plans (Brandt and Gansneder, 1987). In Danville, budget figures were projected to cover the supplements for career and master teachers through the 1990–91 school year. Estimates were made that as many as 121 of the teachers might be on the ladder by then earning $2,500 and $4,000 supplements per year, exclusive of extended contract activities in which they might also engage. A total of 1.4 million dollars would be needed to cover the five years of supplements between 1986 and 1991, 1.7 percent of what the basic instructional salaries alone would total.[3] By that time, several things might have occurred to resolve issues related to the financing of such plans:

(a) Most Virginia school systems would have installed some form of incentive pay, thus increasing the acceptance of career ladders as common practice.

(b) Virginia would have provided special funding for such programs, in keeping with many other states.

(c)   The city council would continue to provide extra support specifically for this program. One administrator suggested that any unspent school funds that must be returned to the city each year should be set aside for this purpose.

(d)   Improvements would have occurred in the way schools were organized and instruction delivered under a partially differentiated staffing plan, so the separation of basic salary and incentive pay line items would not longer seem necessary. Teaching personnel would be paid according to the ranks they held and responsibilities they carried. The latter would be determined by the needs of the school system.

Until one or more of the above happened, it was important to keep pay supplements separate from basic salary components, so teachers who were promoted would not feel their extra pay came from the salaries of other teachers. In the eleven Virginia school systems that were then operating pay-for-performance or career ladder programs, most superintendents indicated the overall cost of teacher salaries, including incentive supplements, was greater than it probably would have been if they did not have such a plan. In other words, greater raises in across-the-board salaries were unlikely, in the judgment of the chief administrators. The supplements were add-ons that would probably not have been distributed as further basic pay increases if there were no incentive system (Brandt and Gansneder, 1987). Taxpayer resistance to across-the-board raises strengthened even more during the late 1980s as teacher salaries in Virginia approached the national average. One editorial commented (Charlottesville *Daily Progress*, 7 December 1989):

> Teachers must accept the necessity of tying pay to performance if they ever are to convince taxpayers that higher salaries and greater respect are justified.

The extent to which schools are, and should be, responsive to parents and the community as a whole is a part of the accountability and control issue (#12). Teachers and administrators often feel parents and other members of the community cannot be expected to know what goes on at school, nor are they able to provide much useful direction. How much weight should be assigned to parent survey data, for example, in determining whether or not a candidate should be promoted to career teacher rank? "Parent opinions," it was argued in connection with interpreting the results of a candidate's survey, "merely parrot what their children say."

Many parents, however, are not only highly interested in what the school is trying to do but have strong opinions about the quality of teaching of particular individuals. Whether their judgments are accurate or not, parents and other taxpayers are the ultimate consumers who must be at least moderately satisfied if schools are to be allowed to function. Although they are not expected to have a major role in the operation of the career ladder, their collective judgment is considered in the evaluation process. In at least one Danville case, parent surveys provided the most critical data affecting a final promotions decision. How effectively teachers communicate with parents is one of several performance patterns that is almost always examined. Because of this assessment, a high school teacher remarked that he was making much more effort than before the program to contact parents and stay in touch with them.

Job security (#13) was still not threatened directly by how, or even whether, one participated in the program. Nevertheless, to the extent that increased scrutiny of teacher behavior leads to greater detection of performance deficiencies, job security of teachers who regularly perform poorly may ultimately be placed in jeopardy. To the extent that teachers try and fail to be promoted, furthermore, disappointment could lead to disillusionment with teaching and ultimately to withdrawal from the profession. However, none of the first two sets of candidates who had dropped out of candidacy or ultimately failed to be promoted on their first try resigned from teaching the following year. There is little reason to believe that job security should be threatened or become a major issue because of the career ladder.

Still a major issue (#4), most teachers saw themselves as outstanding and rejected the notion that others might be significantly better than they. This perception underlies much of the fault-finding with the career ladder.

Who actually made it and who did not also affected the general acceptance of the plan by teachers and administrators. Administrators and teachers involved in the evaluation process were supposed to treat the review process very confidentially, not revealing to others outside their career ladder selection teams what they observed and learned about candidates or, presumably, even who they were. In most schools, however, the "grapevine" worked fast and teachers learned rather quickly, often from remarks candidates themselves made, who had applied. With such an intense and prolonged review process the candidates' identities could not be hidden from those who worked near them.

Many comments of teachers as well as principals alluded to the fact that teachers had established reputations as especially good teachers or, in other instances, as rather poor ones. The extent of consensus varied from one colleague to another. How valid were these judgments was less important than how much conviction and agreement existed about who the especially good and especially weak teachers were.

A career ladder tends to gain favor with teachers if a number of "especially good" teachers apply and make it. It loses credibility as a system to the extent that "weak teachers" apply and are promoted.

In Danville, this informal "grapevine jury" was still out. Not enough "especially good" teachers were considered in the first set of candidates. Because of the luck of the draw, no high school teachers of regular academic subjects were chosen from the first pool of applicants; vocational, business, and resource specialists were selected instead. Acceptance of the plan increased after the second year when several teachers of traditional academic subjects were reviewed and promoted. Informal consensus comments then indicated that, although some of the first candidates were not outstanding, relatively few poor teachers had applied; and of those who had completed the process successfully, none were considered really poor teachers.

Career Ladder Procedures

Many of the original issues related to procedural details about the plan or the planning process itself. How would candidates be selected and reviewed? Who would be involved in the process? What criteria, standards, and measurement processes would be used? How could fair and equal treatment be assured, paperwork kept manageable, minorities appropriately represented, and a realistic time schedule for all the conferences and observations worked out?

For the most part, the debates on these and other planning issues subsided as the plan was put into operation and found functional. Planning decisions had taken the form of specific procedures, standards, and guidelines that together constitute the Danville career ladder plan. Although occasional comments were still made that some alternative ways of doing things might have been better, the major features of the plan were no longer issues that demanded further reflection and debate. For the most part these issues had been resolved through consensus decision-making of the original task force with relatively minor adjustments made later in the process of securing final board action and endorsement.

Brief comments will be made about each of these former issues, how they were resolved and how a relatively few lingered on as areas of continuing concern.

Because of the heavy burden the new evaluation system (#14) imposes on administrators, the administration no longer requires teachers who are not interested in career ladder promotion to be formally evaluated annually; every other year is sufficient. Career ladder candidates, however, must still be formally evaluated in two successive years to be eligible for candidacy the following year.

Principals are still expected to make informal, drop-in visits in all classrooms and provide feedback to teachers on what they observe. In response to an open-ended question on how to improve the system, thirty-six teachers suggested "unannounced, unscheduled observations," which tied with "outside evaluators" as the most frequently mentioned recommendation in the 1986 survey. Nevertheless, several complaints were heard after the alternative year evaluation schedule was adopted from teachers who found these informal visits as much of a nuisance as formal evaluation would have created.

It is still important for teachers to receive equal treatment (#15). The importance of this principle was evident in at least three ways after the plan became operational: First, in reviewing student outcome plans and results, the central selection committee had to judge whether stated teaching goals were important and data collected would really indicate that solid learning had occurred. On numerous occasions, questions were raised about the consistency of this committee's judgments from one candidate to another. Second, similar charges were also heard of inconsistency from one school to another in how principals applied the evaluation procedures and criteria even though a number of teachers indicated improvement had occurred as a result of the training workshops. Third, when the standards were increased following the August 1986 board meeting, the new standards were not to be applied until the remainder of the first pool of applicants had been reviewed for promotion. The new standards eventually went into effect for everyone, including those already on the career ladder. The equal treatment principle may be hard to apply in all situations, but if it is not practiced, personnel troubles are likely.

Vocal complaint over increased expectations (#16) in the initial specification of the many factors that teachers were to be judged on, that is, the PCT, and the presumed rigor of the assessment procedures for career ladder candidates, was reduced as teachers and principals conferred over how well teaching was being conducted. Feedback teachers received from principals after observing, scripting, and then rating instructional variables was usually informative, and expectations were communicated much more precisely than ever before. On average, ratings improved from fall to spring in 1984–85. Still higher ratings resulted during the second year of use (1985–86) as teachers became even more accustomed to how they were being judged and tried to meet these more precise expectations.

The distribution of final ratings that second year was about the same as it had been under the old system. When an analysis showed that more than half the teachers received high enough ratings to qualify for career ladder promotion, a decision was made, based on the consultant's and superintendent's recommendations, to increase the number of O's needed to qualify as a career teacher and to increase even more the number needed to become a master teacher. The amount of increase was relatively modest in both instances but designed to restrict advancement to those whose teaching was clearly above average. This action was justified by reference to the arbitrary establishment of the original standards. Based on a two-year experience with the new system, an increase seemed in order. Later interviews of principals and evaluators contained a number of comments that the higher standards were needed if only outstanding teachers were to be promoted.

Representatives of the local teachers' association informed the superintendent in fall 1986 that the lack of descriptors for noninstructional criteria was the biggest remaining weakness of the plan. (The original task force had developed descriptors for only the eleven instructional variables.) With advice from a committee of building administrators, he prepared and distributed a draft of descriptors covering the other areas. After viewing these proposed descriptors, which stated rather explicitly what outstanding, as contrasted with competent, performance ought to look like, teachers complained about unfairly changing the rules in midstream; and some of the current candidates threatened to withdraw from the program. In response, the superintendent indicated that the proposed descriptors would not be used, as they had been designed to help, not hurt, the evaluation process. He invited teachers again to suggest descriptors for these areas. None were submitted, however, nor was there further teacher pressure for the plan to contain them. It would seem as if the adjusted standards and procedures were firmly entrenched and unlikely to change much in the future. Also, in judging performance in lesson planning and out-of-class activities, administrators continue to have some discretion because no precise descriptors are available for use.

As indicated earlier (#10, #15), principals' ability to evaluate consistently improved as a result of training and increased familiarity with the new system. Some concerns about the competence of both principals and teacher evaluators were raised in the 1986 survey, but the number of teachers making such complaints was less than 12 percent of the responders. With two or three exceptions, teachers interviewed in 1987 spoke positively about the competency of those doing the evaluations.

It is clear that the principal has a dual function to perform (#17). He is supposed to provide an objective, neutrally toned rating of the quality of instruction as an outside observer might do. At the same time, he is employed to assist in the improvement of instruction and to do whatever he can to help teachers improve. He obviously has a vested interest in the ratings, which complicates his task of making an objective assessment for the institution. Teacher interviewees reported some inconsistency from one school to another in how principals resolved this dilemma, some providing more assistance to candidates than others. Several teachers indicated the influence of principals who encouraged certain teachers to apply for the career ladder. In other cases, teachers interested in applying could not do so because their principal's summative evaluation was not sufficiently positive. The principal remains a key person in this system. In addition, the role of assistant principals has been strengthened because they serve also as evaluators and chair candidate review teams.

The system provides one safeguard for the principal by letting him share the responsibility with two other people for the ratings career ladder candidates receive. Thus, the decision is a team judgment, and individual ratings are not communicated. They are used instead to work out a final team judgment. This practice should help the principal keep his two roles separate. Several principals spoke favorably of this feature.

Little was said and certainly no concentrated effort made to amend the amount of money that accompanies promotion or to develop other specific rewards (#18). A year after the program was installed, however, a state budget directive required salaries, including career ladder supplements, to be increased a specific percentage, so they actually were raised somewhat.

Some teachers suggested that the amount of money involved was too little to interest them in applying. Some of those who applied, however, were more negative than positive about the plan themselves; so the reward was obviously big enough to serve as an inducement for them. To the extent that the kinds of and numbers of people the board would like to attract do indeed participate, the present rewards will probably be maintained. So far, there seems little reason to change them.

Considerable effort is expended in developing and using appropriate measures to gather, score, and interpret valid student outcome data (#19) (Brandt, 1987b). Despite early misgivings about the inclusion of such data, teachers chose student outcome data out of several alternatives as the second most relevant source of data for determining teaching effectiveness. As a good data source only the principal received a higher rating on the 1985 survey that posed this question.

The relatively high ranking for student data undoubtedly stems in part from the fact that candidates have a great deal to say about what instructional objectives are to be assessed and how student attainment of these objectives is to be determined. They propose the objectives, the assessment instruments, and a plan for collecting, scoring, and interpreting relevant information. Their career ladder selection committees review and approve, after modification if needed, these proposals. So does a central selection committee. Recent interview comments indicate that the focus on what children learn is a most constructive feature even though it is not always easy to assess.

Controversy arose during the first two years when the central committee did not approve the vast majority of plans when they were first submitted but after they had been approved by the individual candidate committees. In some cases, more operational details were requested before a final judgment would be rendered: Who was going to score a test? What steps were being taken to prevent direct teaching of a test? In several cases, the significance of target objectives or passing standards was questioned, that is, whether proposed objectives really indicated significant learning or whether, instead, most children could be expected to reach them regardless of the teaching. The central committee was attempting to enhance the collection and use of valid data and ensure consistency in what candidates were expected to provide despite vast differences in teaching objectives, grade levels, and subject matter. The lack of common measures and local norms for many tests exacerbated scoring and interpretation problems. Two indications of cheating by teaching specific items or potential cheating by duplicating a supposedly secure standardized test were reported.

Complaints emanating from principals chairing career ladder selection committees suggested that the central selection committee needed to provide better directives ahead of time rather than reject the combined judgment of three professionals closer to the situation. To help reduce such controversy, 1987–88 candidates were briefed directly by the central committee at the beginning of school on how to develop good student outcome plans.

What might once have been an issue no longer seems to be one (#20). Although the names of candidates under review were not announced officially in any way, almost everyone in a building knew who they were. It was left to principals to decide how those who were actually promoted in their schools would first be announced. Even the press did not insist on knowing the names of the new career teachers when the board acted in executive session. They were told of the complications such publicity might create at the school level, especially with parents, and did not pursue the matter. When the names of the career teachers appeared later in the school system's newsletter, "School Talk," no strong complaints or extra publicity resulted from the announcement. In brief, a decision was made by the original task force to minimize the fanfare and keep the names of teachers involved as much out of the limelight as possible. Publicity is still minimal. There have been few instances of parents asking for career ladder teachers for their children, which was one of the fears about public announcements. The public has been told on a number of occasions that many excellent teachers chose not to go on the ladder.

Although the original paperwork requirements were reduced when the dossier was eliminated (#21), a lot of information does have to be collected and analyzed about each candidate. What data and how they are collected are up to the candidate and principal particularly to decide, along with the other committee members. The main difference between the former dossier requirement and current procedures is the expectation that considerable information about the candidate's activities will be conveyed orally during several conferences with the committee rather than in written form. Some candidates keep written records, anyway, to be sure their committees have what they consider important.

The amount of information gathered and assessed on each candidate is considerable. People realize that a comprehensive, fair assessment system requires record keeping. The elimination of the formal dossier, however, did result in less controversy over "too much paperwork."

The great random drawing controversy (#22) seemed to be over. What had been chosen by the task force as the fairest way to ensure unbiased selection of the first candidates from a pool that was too large for the number of trained evaluators available became a major symbol of all that was wrong with the plan. That some teachers would receive a $2,500 promotion one year earlier than other teachers because of a random drawing seemed wrong to many teachers. The negative emotion expressed over this matter was far greater than that displayed toward almost any other issue. It was singled out in the 1987 interviews as the most negative feature of the plan when it was first presented and the reason for much initial hostility.

To ease tension over this issue the superintendent announced in August 1986 that after all of the remaining first-year candidates were reviewed that year, the promotion review process would be open to all teachers who met initial requirements and chose to participate as career ladder candidates. He stated publicly: "We hope we'll never have to use a random drawing again."

Despite subsequent rumors that teachers would try to flood the system by everyone applying, only a very manageable number (seventeen) actually did so the following summer. According to several interviewees, the chance to opt out of summative evaluation and the increased standards were the major reasons behind so few applications.

The task force's decision to require persons on the career ladder to reapply and undergo periodic review every few years to keep their advanced status has never been seriously questioned. Indefinite promotion to advanced rank is no longer under consideration, and, therefore, not an issue (#23).

One of the adjustments made in August 1986 was increasing time in the career teacher rank from two to three years before one could become a master teacher. The change was made to help synchronize promotion schedules for the two advanced ranks and to increase the availability of trained evaluators. Career teachers cannot serve as evaluators during a year when they are under review themselves. No serious objections were made to this change, presumably because of the reasons cited but also because no one had yet reached the stage when she would be directly affected. Again the wisdom of fine-tuning such plans as early as possible is clear.

By 1987, both teacher evaluators and those who had been

promoted were generally considered either good or outstanding by those who knew them best, that is, principals and teachers in particular (#24). At the same time more than a few teachers who were thought to be outstanding did not seem interested in the career ladder. Although some comments were recorded that the quality of some of the first candidates was not impressive, specific complaints that "weak" teachers had really made it came only from two or three of those most hostile to the entire plan. In fact, seeing some make it who were not considered outstanding apparently encouraged others who were originally not interested to become so.

With the main task force disbanded by September 1985, how representative it was of all teachers (#25) had become a moot point. During the 1984–85 school year while the plan was being completed, members were added to the initial task force from schools not originally represented. In addition, a communications committee was established in 1985–86, composed in part of active dissenters, to continue to review procedures and hopefully to resolve whatever issues remained. Thus, all schools and many individuals were directly involved in the planning process before it was finished.

The special quality of the original task force members was formally recognized by the superintendent when he proposed to the board in August 1986 that because some of them had become evaluators, thus postponing the opportunity to go on the career ladder for three years, and because "they were among the best teachers in the system," they should be allowed to apply directly for master teacher status so as to be included in the first group to reach this step on the ladder. The board supported this fast-tracking recommendation. Subsequently, few complaints were heard about fast-tracking the evaluators, presumably because their teaching competence was widely recognized. Two relevant teacher comments follow:

> The school board did a great job of selecting the evaluators.

> I have the utmost respect for the evaluators who were chosen.

Locally as well as nationally, teacher association leadership was cautious about, if not firmly opposed to, career ladder and merit pay plans to the extent that they might promote elitism and divide the membership ranks (#26). In Danville, a former president of the DEA was quite critical. Following the August 1986 board meeting, she was quoted: "I hope this will be the last effort to save this poor thing."

Her successor, however, a member of the original task force, stated publicly after the same meeting:

It's now a working plan; it's not a proposal. We have to deal with it since it is here. If it fails, it'll fail because people won't apply to it. If they apply, it'll work.

It is certain that career ladders, which have typically been established in response to board or legislative actions rather than teacher demands, present a challenge to teacher association leadership. The local leadership is likely to play an important part in helping or resisting the development of a successful plan.

The speed of planning and implementation issue (#27) was mainly history by fall 1987. Despite the plan's complexity and considerable resistance to it, two cycles had been completed on schedule with forty-three teachers promoted and a third cycle was well underway. Substantial annual salary supplements had already been paid to more than 12 percent of the teachers (career teachers and evaluators). The numbers of participants and corresponding budget commitments were projected to more than double in the next three years. What changes had been made were relatively minor in relation to the many criteria, standards, procedures, and schedule details that together constitute the plan. In hindsight, more planning time might have permitted more involvement and greater initial support from teachers. It is also possible that more time would have given the forces opposing the plan more opportunity to resist its development and perhaps succeed in scuttling it.

Proper representation (#28), too, was no longer an issue. Minorities were fully involved in all aspects of the program—as evaluators, candidates, career teachers, and operational committee members—in numbers approximately proportionate to their population. No special actions were needed to produce these results.

The April 1986 survey produced a number of teacher comments suggesting a certain degree of resentment of the hard sell effort that had been made in the communications committee meetings, in school briefings, and in much repeated explanation of how the plan would work. Several teachers expressed strong displeasure at being surveyed several times, when their previous complaints to get rid of the plan were not heeded.

Despite the complaints of "explanation overload," numerous statements or questions recorded in the ethnographic data base as late as 1987 indicated the plan was still not fully and accurately understood by all teachers (#29). Some early complaints were clearly based on misconceptions of how the plan works and were not justified. Overall, however, increased understanding seemed to be occurring as more and more people went through the review process.

DEVELOPMENTS IN UTAH[4]

The Utah career ladder program was the state's primary reform initiative of the eighties. It was not enacted as part of a larger, comprehensive reform package.

As the major legislative vehicle for improving public education, it was the subject of great debate and controversy at its very inception. The statute that launched the program in 1984 had three (now four) components, each quite different from the others and each backed by different political factions. Governor Matheson, a number of school superintendents, and key legislators on the Utah Education Reform Steering Committee wanted a career ladder that promoted teachers to higher ranks with greater pay and responsibility. Teacher work patterns would be redesigned and staff differentiation encouraged. Factions within the Republican Caucus of the legislature argued for merit pay based on classroom teaching. Not surprisingly, the Utah Education Association (UEA) opted for some way of giving all teachers a uniform salary increase. No group alone could get its preferred option through the legislature. What resulted then was an eclectic, multicomponent program established and maintained through political compromise. Arguments have continued through the years over the minimum and maximum amounts of money to be spent on particular components. Overall, however, the several factions that constitute the public school lobby continue to support the policy and have made no move to replace the career ladder (Malen and Hart, 1987).

Teachers and administrators have been surveyed or interviewed several times to assess their reactions to programs and how they were being implemented in their districts. While the state established the program and provided funds, the districts were responsible for designing their own programs within very general guidelines and state appoval. A statewide survey early in the second year revealed considerable support overall for the programs underway. Specific reactions to various features included the following (Nelson, 1986):

- Twice as many teachers thought than did not think that if it was continued for a minimum of five years, the program would encourage good teachers to remain in the classroom.
- Three times as many teachers felt the career ladder system would make the profession more attractive for both current and prospective teachers.
- Two of every three teachers indicated that the program had enabled them personally to improve the quality of their instruction.
- Almost three of every four teachers indicated that it was having a positive influence on student achievement.
- The extended contract component was viewed as the most effective one for enhancing the teaching profession, 80 percent rating it as either very effective or extremely effective. Similar ratings for the extra-pay-for-extra-work components and the performance bonus were given by 44 percent and 28 percent respectively.

A study of teachers' reactions early in the second year of one district's career ladder program is quite revealing (Hart, 1987). The program had three major components: *Teacher leaders* (approximately 10 percent of all teachers) were selected on a competitive basis after being evaluated through a multisource, multijudge process as comprehensive as Danville's system. They received a special stipend plus additional days of pay for an extended period at their regular contract rate. They served two years in these positions but could reapply for additional terms in competition with new applicants. They worked primarily at the school level supervising and assisting colleagues, developing curriculum, and providing other instructional and school improvement help.

A second group (approximately 40 percent of all teachers) was selected competitively through evaluation for more narrowly defined roles as *teacher specialists*. They too received a stipend and a few extra days of pay. The term of appointment was one year.

The third component consisted of additional contract days without students at school for all teachers.

Among the findings were the following:

- Teachers were positive, though not overwhelmingly so, about most aspects of the career ladder.
- Attitudes toward career ladder teachers differed significantly according to the number of years of teaching

experience. As with the Danville teachers, those in their first three years of teaching were most positive and most likely to seek their assistance. Those with more than ten years of experience were less positive about the work career ladder teachers did and perceived less of it going on than did other teachers.

- Those on the career ladder, especially *teacher leaders*, were more positive in their overall assessment of it than other teachers.
- *Teacher leaders'* feelings about conducting peer observation and supervision were somewhat ambivalent: pride in the accuracy and fairness of their observations, but moderately uneasy about the new responsibilities they had.
- Secondary teachers were significantly less convinced than elementary teachers that the career ladder was an important influence on their schools.

Some changes can be noted in general sentiments of teachers and others toward the program over the next two years. In a statewide survey of 1500 randomly selected teachers in fall 1987, ratings indicated slightly more agreement than disagreement that the program had improved the instructional program, attention to student academic progress, the teacher evaluation process, and teacher leadership. Principals agreed in substantially greater proportions that the program had induced these good effects. They were more positive than teachers toward the program on almost all survey questions (Amsler et al., 1988).

As with the earlier survey, teachers assigned their highest ratings to the extended contract feature among the four components. Job enlargement was the second most highly rated incentive, to be followed by career ladder levels and performance bonuses. Although the latter component had the poorest ratings, as many or more teachers said it was effective in improving instruction and morale as those who indicated it was not.

There were apparently considerable differences in how this particular component was implemented in the various districts, and significantly lower ratings were given in those where it was not implemented well. Case studies in twelve districts showed considerable variation in how closely they followed state guidelines. Outside evaluators reported four kinds of implementation strategies: "managerial," "programmatic," "procedural," and "proforma."

In "managerial" districts, the focus is on individual and

institutional goals. Teachers and administrators view career ladders "as both an attractive teacher professional growth and compensation system and a valuable school improvement tool." In "programmatic" districts, the program is seen primarily as an administrative tool. Emphasis is on achieving the right results, regardless of formal procedures. "Teachers perceive currying favor, not improving professionally, as the driving force of the system." In districts that emphasize "procedural" implementation strategies, the focus is on adherence to fair rules and regulations rather than achieving organizational improvement and professional development of educators. Teachers often speak of career ladder activities as "hoop-jumping" rather than acknowledge their relationship to the achievement of important school or district goals for staff or program improvement. In "proforma" districts, local needs and interests take precedence and there is minimal compliance with state goals and guidelines. Much confusion typically exists about how programs are supposed to work. Severe criticism is heard from both principals and teachers who are unclear about the program's purposes and the regulations that are suppose to govern its operation.

The Far West Lab teams categorized the twelve districts they studied as follows (Amsler et al., 1988):

Managerial/Professional	2
Programmatic	4
Procedural	2
Proforma	4

Case study records indicated a tendency for districts to move over time from proforma to both procedural and programmatic implementation as they gained experience in tailoring the various components to district needs and goals. Thus, one of the main features of the Utah career ladder's evolution was considerable diversity during the implementation stage. Sentiments tended to vary as well, in accordance with both how and how well programs were functioning at the district and even school level.

Overall, however, the career ladder was launched as the primary state vehicle for educational reform. Funding was increased from $15 million in 1984 to $30 million in 1985, $35 million in 1986, and $41 million in each of the next two years, despite some reduction in state revenues and fiscal cutbacks in other areas. Implementation has varied somewhat from one locality to another. A substantial reallocation of teacher salaries has occurred in ways consistent with the purposes of a performance-based system. The majority sentiment is moderately favorable to what has happened so far, more so toward some features than others and in some districts than others.

At the same time, some of the original intended effects have been reduced through implementation and may in time give way altogether to traditional practice. Legislation in 1985 left the required minimum for performance bonus at 10 percent, rather than 25 percent as originally set. Many districts established teaching experience minimums as eligibility requirements for promotion on the career ladder, thereby reinforcing seniority traditions. In many places performance standards were set sufficiently low that almost all who applied for merit bonuses received them. Less than one percent of the applicants were denied bonuses in some districts. In plans where projects and short-term assignments were subject to extra pay, teachers sometimes agreed informally among themselves to take turns signing up for them. Even for promotions to advanced levels which were subject to being reopened every one to three years, sentiment was expressed that one should not necessarily reapply as others deserved a chance. How many early effects will be sustained in the years ahead rather than vanish and be replaced by familiar practice will determine how much structural reform has really occurred (Malen and Hart, 1987).

The Salt Lake City career ladder model illustrates how the several components included in the Utah legislation provide a variety of incentives and career options. Almost all teachers choose the six-day extended contract option, which provides them paid planning time without children around. A four-level career ladder permits those who want extra responsibilities, further contract extensions, or additional money for teaching well, to compete for such incentives. After the first two years of successful teaching in the system at the provisional teacher level, one is advanced to the second level (career educator) and becomes eligible to apply for level three (teacher specialist) or level four (teacher leader), or a performance bonus.

We summarize how teachers fare in relation to the several incentive or award possibilities:

(a)   Virtually all teachers have six additional paid days at school without children around for planning and inservice.

(b)   One in ten are teacher leaders with three-year renewable terms. They assume substantially greater instructional leadership responsibilities in the summer (twenty additional paid days) and during the school year, substitutes providing them with up to four days of released time from their own teaching. Extra pay includes a $1,500 stipend and averages $4,360.

(c)   One in four are teacher specialists (one-year renewable terms) in one or another aspect of curriculum and instruction in their building with three additional paid days. Extra pay includes a $1,200 stipend and averages $1,629.

(d)   About three in ten receive a performance bonus ($620 in 1987–88) for being evaluated as good teachers. They assume no extra responsibilities but do undergo a more rigorous evaluation process than other career educators who do not apply for career ladder status.

(e)   Almost two of every three teachers in the district achieve career ladder status and with it extra remuneration as well.

Superintendent John Bennion reports two major impacts of the Salt Lake City career ladder: first, the evaluation process, with its heavy emphasis on instruction and student learning, has been considerably strengthened, and second, the role of teacher leader has taken shape and become an important factor in the improvement of instruction in the school system. A cadre of more than one hundred outstanding teachers have joined principals to help with formative peer evaluation and assist in the dissemination of effective teaching practices throughout the district. Job descriptions have been developed and teachers selected for such positions as:

- Teacher leader: alternative curriculum
- Teacher leader: cooperative learning
- Teacher leader: career ladder coordinator
- Teacher leader: writing across the curriculum
- Teacher specialist: English
- Teacher specialist: fine arts
- Teacher specialist: math

Weber school district has also implemented a differentiated staffing plan which provides upper-level career ladder teachers with such extra responsibilities as:

- elementary curriculum coordinator
- secondary department head
- gifted education facilitator
- core curriculum facilitator
- summer curriculum development
- tutoring
- mentoring of teachers
- homework hot line teacher
- career ladder committee
- evaluation committee

The amounts of extra compensation for assuming these extra responsibilities range from $100 to several hundred dollars.

ARIZONA PROGRAMS

In this section, program developments in Arizona will be described in order to identify similarities and differences with career ladders in Danville, Utah, and other places. Many similarities exist from one place to the other including the number of years programs have been in operation. Major differences between the Arizona and Danville programs include the originating source and the amount of state control and funding. In Danville, it was a local initiative; state funding was limited to short-term consulting assistance and the use of outside trainers to help launch the program in stage three. Money for evaluators and career ladder participants as well as other operational expenses came from local sources. Direction of the project came from the administration under local school board guidelines.

The initiative in Arizona, including the funding of a multiyear pilot effort, began in the legislature. Continued monitoring from 1985 through 1989 [5] was provided by a joint legislative committee on career ladders. Included in this monitoring were extensive district reporting; annual approval or disapproval of local district plans; full funding of those that were approved, following site visitation by committee members; and support of third-party evaluation through-out the entire pilot project. The committee's recommendation to establish or not to establish the career ladder on a permanent basis would be made during the 1990 legislative session after a five-year research and development effort. Presumably, recommendations and data derived from the third-party evaluation center at Northern Arizona University would provide at least some of the information needed for the final recommendation of the committee. Control of this pilot program was retained by the legislature itself rather than being assigned to the board of education or another agency.

Legislative Actions and Guidelines (Arizona)

Planning grants were made to sixteen school districts in 1984, and a year later nine district plans were approved for funding of career ladder programs. Seven of these programs were continued throughout the five-year test period. A joint legislative committee was created to direct and monitor the project. In 1986, three more districts of the original sixteen with planning grants had their programs approved, and a third group of five districts was also alerted to start the following year to field test a slightly different career development model.

The purpose of the state pilot project was to test an alternative method for compensating teachers against the long-standing practice of basing salaries only on one's education and teaching experience. Legislative requirements indicated that, while a minimum number of years of experience might be specified for the various career ladder levels, remaining on levels a specified number of years was not acceptable. Advancement was to be based on advanced performance or expertise. More than one measure of teacher performance was to be used in evaluating teachers, including evidence of student academic progress and improved or advanced teaching skills. Plans were to indicate also how any higher level or additional teaching responsibilities would be incorporated into a teacher's placement on the ladder. The legislation indicated that the compensation system was to be

> based on a completely restructured salary schedule in which a salary range is set for each level on the career ladder and the salary for a teacher within the range is based on objective performance evaluation or other objective factors. The salary schedule shall not be the traditional schedule based on experience with additional stipends added on for higher levels.
> (Senate Bill 1336 introduced 11 February 1985)

Another basic distinction can be seen between the Arizona career ladders and the Danville plan as well as Tennessee's and most other career ladders. The notion of uniform basic salary schedule is completely replaced in the Arizona design with a fully restructured salary schedule tied specifically to performance. The argument that one's reward for outstanding teaching does not come out of someone else's wallet or purse seems less relevant under restructured salary schedules even though it may be completely so in fact. Certainly, the question of which pot of money takes priority when funds get tight, the basic schedule or career ladder bonus, is truly no longer relevant.

Funding over the pilot period for career ladder programs was set at 0.5 percent (first year), 2.5 percent (second year), 3.7 percent (third year) and 5.0 percent (fourth year and thereafter) above district base level budgets. A total of 14.5 million dollars was appropriated in 1988–89 for the pilot programs, most of which would be used for higher salaries for career ladder participants in the pilot districts than they would have received under the traditional salary schedules.

In all pilot districts, participation was voluntary for existing teachers and they had a choice of remaining on the traditional schedule or choosing the performance-based one.[6] Many experienced teachers were sufficiently high on the traditional schedule, due to extensive years in their district, that they did not apply for candidacy on the career ladder as they saw little chance to improve their salary under the performance-based system, or their contract offer based on their performance as a candidate was actually lower than what they would receive under the traditional schedule. They were allowed their choice. Thus, the potential was considerably greater for younger teachers to improve their salaries substantially by participating on the career ladder. There was less monetary incentive for senior teachers with many years in the district.

The incentive value of the program varied somewhat, therefore, from one individual to another according to how districts structured the new scale and the actual increments that were established for the various levels and steps on the career ladder. The amounts were restricted as well by the 5.0 percent (1988–89) district allocations. Caps[7] were set in many districts in which participation rates were high and the amount of money for individual salary increases was less than it would have been with less participation.

It is important to recognize these differences in incentive value. They help explain teacher reactions to the career ladder and why they choose or do not choose to participate. The program is structured so no one loses money because of it. One can only win or, at worst, stay even by choosing the traditional schedule. Some may and actually do earn much more than others, of course, so the monetary incentives and rewards vary greatly.

An incentive was provided for districts to participate as well. The program brought additional state funds beyond what nonparticipating districts would receive. Pilot districts would have 5 percent more (1988–89 and 1989–90) to use for teacher salaries than other districts. With better salaries and various opportunities to enhance them substantially over what they would be without the career ladder, perhaps the best teachers would be attracted and retained in those districts that had a career ladder. That was a guiding theme behind the career ladder legislation.

So incentives existed in 1985–90 both for Arizona school districts to have a career ladder pilot program and for many of their teachers to participate in it. It was all additional money. Not all persons would receive more, but none would receive less. In this respect, Arizona's program was like North Carolina's career ladder. Pilot districts in both states received extra state money, and teacher participants had higher salaries than they would have had without the program.

If these programs are not continued, these districts and their participants will no longer have extra salary funds over those of other districts. At least they will lose whatever competitive edge the programs have provided. It would be surprising, under these circumstances, for participating teachers in pilot districts not to support strongly continuation of the programs. The larger the number of participants, furthermore, the greater the support; at least to the point where reductions in the amount of extra pay because of heavy participation lessen the incentive value sufficiently that the costs of participation outweigh the benefits.

If decisions are made to continue the career ladder programs beyond the pilot stage and expand them to other districts as well, factors affecting these incentive values ought to be considered as well. Whether or not the 5 percent state supplement is sufficient, especially with high participation rates, is one concern. How many districts could be phased in at any one time without jeopardizing overall funding sources for career ladders in relation to other important components of school budgets, destroying the special district incentive value of having more state money than nonpartici-pating districts, or compromising the quality of existing programs? Much concern exists among career ladder districts that if expansion is too rapid, new programs will be poorly implemented and result in a negative image of the entire effort. As long as districts have a choice of whether to participate or not and extra funds are provided if they do so, a strong incentive will exist to develop and implement a career ladder. People will work to design and run such programs successfully. If this extra inducement is taken away by mandates that career ladders be established everywhere, some of the incentive value will undoubtedly be lost. The proverbial carrot will be gone and replaced by the equally proverbial stick with very different incentive characteristics.

An Arizona District Program (Amphitheater)

The Amphitheater school district in northwest Tucson began receiving state funds to launch a pilot program in 1985–86. Funding increased annually from approximately $118,000 that year when the first candidates were under review to 1.6 million dollars in 1988–89 and a similar amount in 1989–90.

Only a small number of persons were selected initially while program procedures were being developed. The percentages of eligible teachers, counselors, and librarians who participated and were successful in meeting performance requirements for placement on the ladder were 2 percent (1986–87), 12 percent (1987–88), and 40 percent (1988–89). Of 720 teachers in the district in 1988–89, 210 were placed on the career ladder.

The ladder itself consists of four levels, with eligibility requirements (number of years in the district) increasing as follows: career teacher–3, CT I–5, CT II–8, CT III–11. Within each level, six steps have also been established for movement upward or downward from year to year on the basis of annual teacher and student performance evaluations. Success in meeting performance criteria is based on the total number of points one receives on the several evaluation instruments. The number of points to be earned increases at each career ladder level and at each step within levels. Exhibit 4.4 shows the number of points to be earned and accompanying salaries for each place on the scale. It is easy to see how clearly salaries are tied to performance. A score of sixty-eight earned by a CT I in her fifth year of teaching would be paid $30,820, as compared to $30,440 for a CT III in her twelfth year of teaching.

For placement on the ladder and movement from one level to another, ten observations (three announced and seven unannounced) are made by an evaluation team consisting of one's building administrator and two peer evaluators. Professional duties and responsibilities are rated only by the principal. The teacher must also submit a student achievement plan in the fall covering five long-term objectives including two affective objectives. For each long-term objective she may also list one to four supporting objectives. Near the end of the year the teacher submits the results of her student achievement plan, which document how well each of the

Exhibit 4.4

Placement Scores and Related Compensation for the
Amphitheater Career Ladder

| | | Career Ladder Criteria | | | | | |
Position	Min Years	Step 1	Step 2	Step 3	Step 4	Step 5	Step 6
Career Teacher	3	38	43	48	53	58	63
Career Teacher I	5	44	50	56	62	68	74
Career Teacher II	8	53	59	65	71	77	83
Career Teacher III	11	64	71	78	85	92	99

| | Career Ladder Compensation System | | | | | |
Position	Step 1	Step 2	Step 3	Step 4	Step 5	Step 6
Career Teacher	$21,440	$23,092	$24,744	$26,396	$28,048	$29,700
Career Teacher I	$23,440	$25,285	$27,130	$28,975	$30,820	$32,665
Career Teacher II	$26,440	$28,591	$30,742	$32,893	$35,044	$37,195
Career Teacher III	$30,440	$32,928	$35,416	$37,904	$40,392	$42,880

Career Ladder Manual, Amphitheater Public Schools, 1988—89

objectives was met. A two-member career advancement committee (CAC), consisting of her administrator and a peer evaluator, reviews and evaluates both the plan and its results. This committee also reviews and evaluates the professional activities a teacher participates in during the year.

For the yearly performance assessment related to stepwise movement within levels, the system is somewhat less complicated. Only three observations are made, all unannounced but within a two-week prescheduled period. Professional responsibilities and duties are rated by one's principal, and student achievement plans and results for three rather than five long-term objectives are approved and evaluated by a two-member career advancement committee.

All career ladder teachers are also required to participate in a school or district project each year designed to improve their instructional and professional performance and to provide needed resources to operate various school and district programs. Such responsibilities might include serving as a peer evaluator, mentor, CAC member, or curriculum developer. Plans are reviewed and mutually agreed upon each year by career ladder teachers and their career advancement committees.

It is these committees that, at the end of the year, review the ratings of instructional skill made by the classroom observation teams, of principals' ratings of professional responsibilities and duties, and of their own judgments about the quality of performance of the extra responsibilities and the student achievement results; and then they assign the specific points to all these factors that determine career ladder placement and salary. Guidelines are specified in the manual about the number of units to be assigned according to the ratings of individual competencies and subfactors, but, "since the criteria for each subfactor are not all-inclusive, career advancement committees have the flexibility to make qualitative decisions based on these guidelines."

Although participation increased substantially in the latter two years of the pilot program, it appeared to be moderately selective. Of the 210 participants in 1988–89 (40 percent of those eligible), twenty-five were career teachers, seventy were at the CT I level, fifty-five at the CT II level, and sixty at CT III. In September 1987, seventy-two applied for the first time; forty-seven of them were placed on the ladder the following June. Sixteen had dropped out during the year for personal reasons or because they were dissatisfied with their evaluations. Nine completed the candidacy, but opted to accept a traditional contract when they learned what their performance-based salaries would be. Their salaries based on years of experience were either higher or almost as high and not worth the extra hassle of career ladder participation. Although the same teacher evaluation scale is used on participants and nonparticipants, the former have three times as many annual observations (ten times if they want to move to a higher level) plus the other career ladder and student achievement data-gathering responsibilities to assume. In the example cited earlier, for instance, the CT III individual would actually have received $31,520 on the traditional salary schedule, $1,060 more than the step one performance-based salary, by having taught twelve years and acquired thirty graduate credits. Major reasons for her accepting the career ladder contract were whatever additional status might be acquired by so doing and the possibility of stepwise movement the following year.

It can be seen, therefore, that the career ladder has considerably less financial incentive value for more experienced than younger teachers. The point system provides less room for salary improvement for those with twelve to fourteen years of experience than those with fewer years, unless one is exceptionally good and evaluated in the eighties or nineties. The ceiling on the traditional schedule in 1988–89 was $34,050 for those with fourteen years of teaching and a master's degree. A CT II person with only eight years of teaching could earn almost a thousand dollars more by receiving seventy-seven points (step five) and a fifth-year teacher could earn almost as much ($32,665) by receiving seventy-four points (step six).

The Amphitheater career ladder program is similar to the Danville program in several ways. Both are voluntary programs for experienced teachers. Teachers have to apply to be considered and then be reviewed closely during a yearlong candidacy. A three-person team consisting of both administrators and peers conducts a number of classroom observations (six or more in Danville, ten in Amphitheater) to evaluate instructional skills. Evaluators are carefully trained, especially in Amphitheater where they receive fifteen days of training and practice; final selection is based on their performance in this role. Script taping is done and consensus ratings made of candidates' performance on specified teaching variables. Some one individual or group is responsible for monitoring consistency across teams. Hurdles are sufficiently demanding, as in Danville, that not all teachers are choosing to apply and subject themselves to the extra scrutiny the evaluation system imposes. Student outcome data are required of all candidates with specific teaching objectives specified by candidates in the fall and results reviewed in the spring. While student learning is a major dimension of both programs, it has seldom provided sufficiently discriminating data to have much effect on final summative judgments about candidates or participants. The lack of valid measures and district norms for many variables and differences in objectives from one teacher to another preclude easy comparisons. Nevertheless, the student outcome component is considered important in both plans. In Amphitheater, it accounts for thirty-five of the one hundred points a teacher may receive. The focus on student outcomes is considered by many participants to be the best feature of the whole program. In fact, in Amphitheater, a separate track option is under consideration which would use student outcomes as the primary measure for determining teacher placement on the ladder.

The Amphitheater program differs from Danville's in several ways as well. The most obvious difference is the inclusion of six steps within career ladder levels, and a system for annual performance appraisal and performance-based salary change yearly. The primary theme of the Arizona legislation is "equal pay for equal performance." The variable pay changes up or down each year, based on a similar though less closely monitored evaluation process than that used in promotion across levels, reflect that theme much more precisely than basic pay with a fixed career ladder supplement, as in Danville and many other places.

Another major difference with Danville but a similar feature with Utah is the carefully prescribed job expansion track projects required of Amphitheater teachers. Over twenty-five additional assignments have been identified so far that the district needs teachers to tackle if its programs are to function well and the community be served effectively. Specific job descriptions have been designed for peer evaluators, mentor or peer coaches, CAC coordinators, staff development coordinators, research and development roles, and educational technology roles. Career ladder participants apply for roles and assignments they choose in fulfillment of the extra responsibility requirement and have their plan for participation approved by their CAC. Their performance in these activities is considered in their placement on the career ladder. In Danville, leadership criteria are included among the criteria for promotion to master teacher rank, but with the first group of candidates under review in 1988–89, the full scope of new roles and responsibilities had not yet been fully determined.

One other distinction should be noted. Whereas Danville peer evaluators are to serve in that capacity on a released time basis, that is, while they continue their regular teaching duties, in Amphitheater they serve part-time or full-time in that capacity for a year before returning to the classroom. They are much like North Carolina in this respect. Observer evaluators there serve full-time, usually for two or three years, before returning to the classroom. During 1988–89, Amphitheater had nine full-time observers to conduct the observations and help operate the career ladder.

In summary, then, the Amphitheater career ladder is a highly complex system designed "to provide opportunities to teachers for career advancement with the ultimate goal of improving the productivity and satisfaction of the students." Specific goals focus on providing effective instruction, attracting and retaining effective teachers, better utilization of the skills of good teachers, rewarding them for effective performance, and providing a variety of avenues for advancement within the teaching profession. It seems well on the way toward accomplishing these goals. Not only is participation considerable and increasing, but teachers and administrators feel the program is working quite well and has had a number of positive impacts.

Research and Evaluation (Arizona)

The Center for Excellence in Education at Northern Arizona University was selected to conduct evaluation studies of the pilot program and provide data to be used in deciding whether or not to continue supporting career ladder programs after the five-year trial. Among the data collected were the responses of participants and nonparticipants in the fifteen districts to the "Perception Assessment Scale." This instrument was designed to measure attitudes toward the program and several of its main components in particular, including general career ladder, staff development, teacher evaluation, and career ladder placement concepts. The organizational climate was also assessed along with peer evaluation concepts. Those surveyed were asked to rate the extent of their agreement or disagreement on a four-point scale with each of sixty-six concept statements and then answer four open-ended questions regarding strengths and areas needing improvement. Data were gathered annually beginning in 1986, permitting comparisons to be made across districts, years in the program, gender, career ladder participation, position held, ethnicity, teaching experience, degree earned, and level taught.

Among the findings from three years of data collection are the following:

- Participants were considerably more positive than nonparticipants in almost all comparisons— within each district, each phase group, and toward each of the components. With 2.5 the dividing point on the four-point scale, they typically averaged 0.5 scale points higher. This finding, of course, is not surprising. Individuals who are really hostile toward such a program are less likely to apply, and those who have applied and successfully made the ladder have already received awards; others have not.
- For phase I districts, sentiments typically were most negative in the first two years of operation and became more positive in the third year. Consistent with this finding is the comparison of phase I, II, and III districts' average sentiments for the four components in 1988. The older the programs, as indicated in Exhibit 4.5, the more positive the responses. Similar changes toward positive sentiments were found in several phase I districts, including Amphitheater, from the first through the third year of operation.

Exhibit 4.5

Range of Average Attitude Scores Toward Major Program Components
(Arizona, 1988)

	Teacher Participants	*Teacher Nonparticipants*
Phase I districts (3rd year in operation)	2.7–2.9	2.3–2.7
Phase II districts (2nd year in operation)	2.6–2.7	2.0–2.3
Phase III districts (1st year in operation)	2.3–2.6	1.9–2.0

Above 2.5 is positive
Below 2.5 is negative

This trend is the same, of course, as described earlier in the Danville case history. Sentiments after one year of operation in the five phase III Arizona districts tended to be more negative than positive, even for those participating on the ladder.

- In a related finding those who had received five or more hours of in-service development about the program were much more positive than those who had received zero to four hours. The survey revealed, unfortunately, that 70 percent were in the latter category. This minimal amount of involvement and understanding was probably one reason for the negative sentiment.
- There were great differences from one district to another in attitudes toward the program. Some were much more favorable than others. Programs themselves vary a great deal, of course, in structure and participation rates especially. Portfolio and observation requirements differ from one place to another as do the amounts received for movement up the ladder. Despite the wide salary range (up to $12,000) at each of the several levels of the Amphitheater program, for example, and only a moderate participation rate, most individuals were highly positive in 1988. The average ratings of those who were participants toward the four program components ranged between 3.3 and 3.5. Even nonparticipants were a bit more positive than

negative (2.7 to 2.8) and above the average for nonparticipants in all phase I districts (see Exhibit 4.5).

- Again as in Danville, those in their early years of teaching
were almost always more favorable toward career ladder
concepts, as rated on individual items, than those with
many years of teaching experience. In many districts, those
with many years of experience had to perform near the
highest levels to reach a salary better than one based on the
traditional schedule. Even then the extra salary might not
be enough to be worth the effort. Younger teachers, on the
other hand, would have a high jump in salary if they
performed so well.

- Among the greatest strengths of the programs, as indicated
by responses to the open-ended questions, were higher pay
(34 percent mentioned it) than the traditional schedule;
information about the recognition and definition of specific
skills, clear objectives, and portfolio guidelines (13 percent);
and the evaluation system, the instrument, and trained
evaluators (13 percent).

- Among the most frequently cited features needing improvement were inconsistency in the evaluations and the need
for better information about expectations and the system
itself; too much time and paperwork; and too little money
for the amount of effort required. Again, these are reactions
similar to those heard in Danville and many other
programs.

A Proposed Readiness Model

Exhibit 4.6 diagrams a readiness model for basing future
decisions to support local district career ladder programs on a
multidimensional assessment process. According to its developer,
Richard Packard, each of the eleven dimensions listed on the left side
of the diagram (Student Achievement, etc.) is a major contributor to
the success or failure of career ladder programs in a local district.
Adequate functioning and contribution from each of these areas is
essential for program success. Not all pilot programs have been
equally successful, as the varied sentiment data alone clearly
indicate. Two of the original phase I districts, in fact, actually failed
to operationalize their plans successfully by not complying with the
salary restructuring requirements and dropped out of the pilot study.
One phase III district also withdrew because three new members of a

Exhibit 4.6

A Readiness Model for Support of Local District Career Ladder Programs
(Packard, & Dereshiwsky, Center for Excellence in Education, Northern
Arizona University, 1989b)

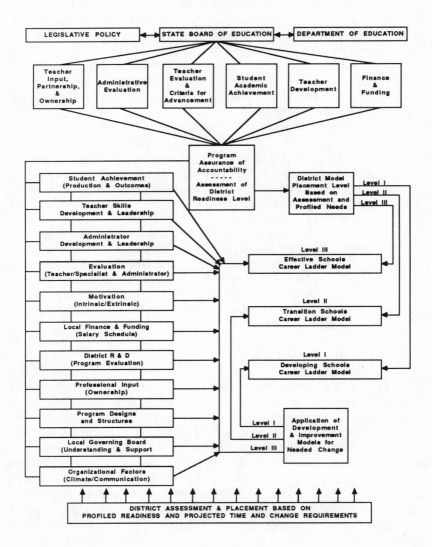

governing board felt the state's oversight on how to spend the career ladder money was too intrusive.

The model suggests the need to review and evaluate data covering each of these components as a basis for judging whether a district is adequately prepared to start or continue a career ladder program (Level III on the right side of the diagram). If not, any state career ladder appropriations should be used instead for development, research, and training activities (Levels I and II) that might improve the readiness conditions for such a program. The top half of the diagram obviously indicates the essential state components and the relationship they would have to the program review and approval process.

Summary of Arizona Pilot Study

Legislation beginning in 1984 led to a state pilot study in fifteen districts, containing approximately 25 percent of the state's teachers, of a career ladder program. District programs were highly diverse with respect to participation rates, the involvement of peers as well as administrators in teacher evaluation, the numbers of levels and steps, extra responsibilities, and many other operational features.

Although districts were given considerable freedom to design their own programs, several guidelines were specified that distinguish the Arizona effort. First, all programs were to contain a "plan for improving student progress." Second, "More than one measure of teacher performance" was to be used in the evaluation of teachers, including "performance in relation to student academic progress," "fair and objective" procedures, and "opportunities for improvement of teacher performance." Third, the basis for advancement was to be "improved or advanced teaching skills." Finally, "Criteria for advancement must be challenging enough that not all teachers shall be expected to advance to the highest level."

A most distinctive feature was the requirement for a complete restructuring of the salary schedule "in which a salary range is set for each level on the career ladder and the salary for a teacher within the range is based on objective performance evaluation or other objective factors." This feature led to steps on each rung of the ladder and changes in salary from one year to the next based on the points one received from the various evaluation sources, as in the Amphitheater plan. Districts were permitted to allow individuals to choose whether or not they wanted to be paid on the traditional schedule, based on teaching experience and education, or the restructured, performance-based one, and to make that choice after they saw the results of their evaluation. This option was made possible by districts receiving 5 percent more state money for salaries (1988–89 and 1989–90) than nonpilot districts.

Another special feature was the requirement that research and evaluation be conducted at both the district and state level for program improvement purposes and to provide data that would be used in determining what would happen after the pilot period was over.

Control throughout the pilot study remained with the legislature. A special joint committee was established to monitor the program and make recommendations for continued funding and changes in the legislation as needed. A network of pilot districts was formalized, and district program leaders met on a monthly basis to share information and coordinate activities.

COMPARISON SUMMARY

Exhibit 4.7. compares selected features of the three sets of programs. For further discussion of several of these dimensions, refer back to chapter 2, pages 44 to 49.

It should be understood that most programs combine features from several models. Most Arizona plans, for example, require advanced career ladder placement participants to assume extra responsibilities and be evaluated in part, as in Amphitheater, on how well they are performed. Student learning is also highly featured both in the Arizona legislative mandate and in school district assessment criteria. It is also included in the Danville teacher performance assessment system and emphasized in several Utah districts. Not yet, however, does student learning serve as the major criterion for teacher incentive pay or career ladder advancement in any of these programs.

There is one other caveat: The great variability among both Utah and Arizona school districts makes it difficult to characterize their career ladder programs on some of the dimensions listed in Exhibit 4.7. Even more diversity exists within these states on certain variables than across the three localities (one district and two states). Elements of both merit pay and additional pay for extra responsibility can be found in almost all plans. The distinctions indicated are estimates of the overall emphasis.

Common features (not shown) for most programs include more positive attitudes among participants rather than nonparticipants, administrators rather than teachers, and teachers who are relatively

Exhibit 4.7

Comparison of Selected Program Characteristics in Danville, Utah, and Arizona

	Danville	*Utah*	*Arizona*
Basic Model	Superior teacher	Full career	Superior teacher
Policy Guidelines	Local school board	Legislature Local school board	Legislature Local school board
Program Design	Special task force	Local planning groups	Local planning groups
Funding Source	Local city council	Legislature Local supplements (opt)	Legislature Special state legislation
Type of Program	Career ladder	Career ladder with bonus and other components	Career ladder
Selectivity	High (less than 50% on CL)	Considerable diversity	Considerable diversity
Emphasis (merit pay, extra duty)	Merit pay	Extra duty	Merit pay
Criteria Measures	Multimeasure multi- judge (observa- tion, outcomes, surveys)	Varies with component and district	Multimeasure (observations, outcomes, projects)
Teacher Role	Minimal change, teacher evaluator	Job enlargement mentoring	Job enlargement mentoring

new in their districts rather than those with considerable seniority. In addition, more negative reactions are typically found in the early stages of program development than later on after individuals have had a chance to see how they work and how they might relate to one's personal goals.

Teacher Motivation and Organizational Change

This chapter will explore likely reasons for the less-than-enthusiastic response of many teachers to career ladder programs, especially during the initial planning and early implementation stages. A number of reasons will be proposed and discussed about why teachers often react negatively at first. Relevant comments and actions from Danville and other case materials will be reported and summarized as a basis for judging their plausibility.

Teacher motivation will be examined next and a needs model used to analyze differences in teacher interest in such plans. Teacher comments will be organized around features that serve as incentives or disincentives to participation.

The next section will focus on the organizational change process and increased acceptance of the career ladder as an instrument to accommodate teacher needs. Finally, the power struggles among major stakeholders in this particular reform movement will be reviewed along with the positions they have taken on critical issues. First, let me review again the kind of change the plan introduced.

THE PRIMARY CHANGE

Career ladders and other types of teacher incentive plans vary greatly, not only in operational procedures but in the effects they have on school organization and the teaching culture. Some permit almost any teacher who desires extra pay to assume additional responsibilities and work a few hours longer each week or a few days more each year, that is, the job enlargement and extended contract provisions. Participation is open to all on a noncompetitive basis.

Other plans feature highly competitive merit pay or selective promotion on a career ladder, that is, superior teacher programs. They are based on presumed differences in the quality of teaching. Ways must be established to distinguish between poor, average, and good performance. Teachers must be compared either directly with each other or with some general performance standards which all teachers do not meet. The Arizona career ladder legislation, for example, actually specifies that criteria should "be challenging enough that not all teachers are expected to advance to the highest level."

Some teacher incentive programs induce more change than either extended contract or merit pay features alone produce by differentiating teacher roles and restructuring school organizational patterns. Mentor teachers in California and elsewhere and lead teachers, as proposed by the Carnegie Forum, are assigned greater responsibility than other teachers for assisting new or inexperienced teachers, conducting staff development activities, and performing other leadership functions. In restructured schools, teachers might be organized into teams responsible for larger clusters of students rather than single classes alone. Lead, mentor, head, or master teachers (whatever the label) would fulfill the primary leadership function; all teachers would provide the instruction.

Traditionally, schools have not been organized to highlight differences between teachers. Adjustments for individual differences in style and ability have been accommodated quite informally. The public mandate to select and reward the best runs completely counter to the egalitarian manner in which schools have traditionally operated. Therefore, it is not surprising to find strong resistance to the mandate when it is interpreted strictly as differential rewards for outstanding teaching. Such an interpretation was made by the Danville task force when it designed its plan. It was reinforced by the board when it tightened the standards in August 1986.

By way of contrast, at least four of eleven incentive pay programs in Virginia are barely selective at all, that is, extra pay is not restricted to those who teach best but is given instead to a relatively high percentage of all teachers (96 percent and 97 percent of all teachers in two systems who meet other eligibility requirements on other factors) (Brandt and Gansneder, 1987). The intent of these four plans is to encourage participation in staff development, to raise the pay of all teachers except a few who are performing poorly, and perhaps to participate nominally in the current incentive pay movement.

One relatively common response to merit pay mandates is to design plans that actually minimize the need for differential assessment of teaching by adding other requirements as the basis for extra pay. In Utah, for example, current legislation specifies that district plans might require that as little as 10 percent of a teacher's extra pay be based on meritorious performance. The rest could be tied to extended work days, extra duties, and/or other noncompetitive features (Malen and Hart, 1987).[1] In Iowa, where districts have the option of using state incentive pay money to reward high quality teaching, teachers' assumption of extra instructional responsibilities, or for both purposes, most programs fund job enlargement activities only and do not provide performance-based pay. Less than 2 percent of the districts use these funds for performance-based pay alone (Cornett, 1990).

Murnane and Cohen (1986) interviewed teachers and principals in six districts with long-standing "merit pay" plans. In each instance, the merit pay feature was played down or actually disguised by such practices as basing extra pay on teacher documentation of school activities outside the classroom, giving almost all teachers a special increment without publicizing the widespread distribution, or not identifying recipients by name. Most districts where lasting programs had been in effect were not in urban settings, but in small suburbs or communities that served homogeneous populations and used relatively small amounts of bonus money in addition to salaries that were already higher than those in nearby communities.

It should be clear, then, that the superior teacher programs established in the eighties constitute educational reform of an unprecedented magnitude that, if they last, would impose major change on the traditional egalitarian patterns found in most school systems. Their most fundamental feature is the identification of a minority of teachers who are outstanding or at least above average in overall teaching performance, and promotion of them to higher ranks with significantly higher pay than the majority of teachers.

Even in Danville, however, where the charge clearly called for a superior teacher program, egalitarian traditions were clearly in evidence as task force members labored over operational details. It was upsetting to the group, for example, to learn that elementary and secondary teachers had not been observed the same number of times each year or with the same rating instrument. The plan now calls for a similar schedule and instrument at both levels. The tendency not to treat people differently nor to compare one against the other limited the kinds of teacher performance measures that might be used. The task force considered but rejected any measure that ranked teachers or required other forced-choice, direct comparisons of one teacher with another. In the eleven Virginia incentive plans we studied, furthermore, none use rating forms that cause direct comparisons of teachers against each other. Only in Lynchburg, where a point system is applied to data derived from several sources, is it possible to rank candidates for final selection if the number meeting standards exceeds the projected budget.

REASONS FOR THE RESISTANCE

The Danville administration and original task force were clearly surprised by the amount and duration of negative teacher reaction to the plan. Although some hostility had been expected, almost no one thought that teachers would remain negative after clear explanations had been made of how it would work and why teachers could expect fair and equal treatment. After all it was a voluntary plan; nobody had to participate. Teachers had obviously been very involved in designing it and teachers would be among those serving on candidate review committees.

Special efforts were made to expand the number of teachers involved in further planning during the fall and winter of 1984–85, to explain operational procedures clearly and completely school by school, and even to consider various suggestions for change and improvement. A few modifications were made, the most notable being the elimination of a dossier.

Despite all this effort to explain and sell the plan, most teachers continued to reject it. The only change that some wanted was to scrap the whole idea, and this was not seriously considered. The board had carefully specified its original charge. The administration and task force had devoted a great deal of time and energy to developing a plan, and it was not to be dropped without at least a fair trial. Teacher sentiment, however, remained predominantly negative for two years. Strong resentment was even expressed toward being surveyed three times over this period, as a number of teachers complained that their suggestions to drop it had not been heeded. Almost one-fourth (24 percent) of the 318 respondents to the April 1986 survey gave as their primary suggestion for the career ladder, "Eliminate it," (Brandt and Kingston, 1986).

It was not until two particular events occurred that sentiment began to change. The first was completion of the review process for the initial group of candidates and seeing nineteen out of an original twenty-four achieve career teacher status. The process was not just on paper; it had become directly visible as colleagues were reviewed and promoted. The second and perhaps more important event was the board's review of the program in August 1986. By making procedural adjustments, increasing the standards, and projecting costs into the 1990s, the board clearly conveyed the notion that, despite a lot of negative teacher sentiment, the plan would be in effect for those who were interested during the foreseeable future.

In retrospect, the initial teacher reaction should not have been unexpected. Early teacher reactions to many of these programs have been negative on balance—seldom enthusiastic, often hostile. The history of educational change indicates clearly that considerable time is needed, as well as opportunity for teachers to interact with each other about new ideas, before they are likely to be viewed favorably.

> Yet even when the innovation is thoroughly "explained" at the beginning, it cannot be absorbed, for teachers like anybody else do not learn new ideas all at once. Change is a process, not an event. (Fullan, 1982, p. 115)

We propose several reasons and discuss relevant data about why the Danville plan was so strongly resisted at first.

The plan was much too complete before the vast majority of teachers had an opportunity to participate in the planning process. The task force had left little for other teachers to work on. Most how-to-do-it issues had already been resolved. Many early reactions of other teachers were suggestions for alternative ways for it to work that had already been discussed and rejected by the task force.

The planning task force had spent approximately 150 uninterrupted hours together in the summer of 1984 resolving the various issues outlined earlier, achieving consensus on the kind of plan they felt would work, and hammering out scores of operational details. Members represented several constituencies and expressed diverse positions on many matters. As decisions were reached, a strong sense of ownership of the plan emerged as well as a feeling that it probably represented the best compromise possible among the various stakeholders.

Although the task force recognized that some additional planning was needed (e.g., specific student outcome, parent and student survey measures were not yet spelled out), the interrelatedness of many procedural details made members particularly cautious about accepting suggestions for change. Because of the extensive deliberation it had taken to achieve agreement about specific procedures within the task force itself, members appeared hesitant, even defensive, to receive suggestions for change when the plan was first presented to the whole faculty.

One frequently stated reason teachers gave in later polls and interviews for rejecting the plan was an apparent unwillingness on the part of the task force, when they first presented it to their colleagues, to consider alternative procedures or major changes in what they had proposed. Their responses to most of the questions raised indicated how the plan already was designed to address each particular concern. There was no real opportunity, however, to explore all the options that had been considered or to explain the full rationale behind final procedural decisions. Many teachers saw the plan as a fait accompli. The basic decisions had been made and what suggestions or complaints they might offer would not lead to major alteration.

Some of the resentment may have come, in fact, from having a plan presented enthusiastically and in great detail by one's own peers without input from the larger constituency. It was undoubtedly assumed by those who had already rejected the whole idea that it would not get very far if teachers were involved in the planning. The teacher ranks were now clearly divided, and those most hostile to the plan would have to find appropriate rallying points around which opposition could be organized. It had happened so fast that an effective, organized, rational protest was difficult to muster. Some of the early questions and complaints were clearly efforts to discover issues around which legitimate concerns could be registered. The emotional intensity surrounding the dossier specifications and random drawing suggests that they served that function in part. They were not a sufficient basis for complaint, it turned out later, to mount a successful rebellion. The formal dossier requirement was dropped with no damage to the plan. The random drawing was a temporary expedient that would not have to be repeated.

The question of how long to plan and how much procedural detail needs to be finalized before starting a program is a difficult one. Those who like the idea are eager to proceed and will accept fine-tuning after it is underway. Those opposed to the basic need for such a program want every last detail clearly prescribed. In Tennessee and Florida, Governors Alexander and Graham were anxious "to capitalize on the wave of public support for improved education" that prevailed in 1984 by installing statewide programs as fast as possible (ASCD *Update*, November 1984). While most educators decried the haste, University of South Florida Professor

B. O. Smith said, "If we had another year, nobody would be ready. If we had another year after that, still no one would be ready," (p. 7)

By moving fast, one may be charged with insufficient involvement of those for whom the plan is designed. If procedures are installed that do not work, hasty planning will be blamed, and those who opposed the idea to begin with will have extra ammunition to fight it again.

This, in effect, is what happened in Florida. The plan was installed too fast. Subject matter tests had to be developed and administered; thousands of people trained to be classroom observers; program description, application, and scoring materials developed and disseminated; and more than 18,000 teachers reviewed, all within a year after the master teacher legislation was passed. The sheer logistics of such an effort were bound to create problems. There were indeed many legitimate individual complaints of people not being adequately briefed or of having to drive hundreds of miles rather than the prescribed fifty or less to test centers. The biggest problem, however, which caused only a relatively few of those being considered to actually be selected as master teachers, was one of design. The standards specified in the legislation required master teachers to be in the top quartile of both the subject matter test and the classroom observation instrument distributions. The low correlation between teaching behavior and subject matter knowledge is what caused only one in six applicants to make it.

The multiyear pilot testing of programs in North Carolina, South Carolina, and Arizona represents the other end of the planning time continuum. In these cases, early designs were field tested and subjected to third-party evaluations as legislators gave programs a chance to be studied thoroughly before long-term commitments were made.

Perhaps Graham and Alexander attempted end runs around the organized teacher resistance by moving too fast for the opposition to get organized. The slower pilot test efforts elsewhere circumvented early resistance tendencies somewhat by giving districts and teachers that were willing to participate certain advantages over those not participating. The opposition was fragmented and end runs not needed.

Task force teachers and other teachers had significantly different interests and concerns regarding the innovation. The process of selecting teacher members for the task force had produced a group that accepted the fact that some kind of a plan would be developed.

Either they had some notions of what it might look like, or they felt that some features would be better than others. In addition, they had worked intensively on equal footing for six weeks with another fifteen people representing other constituencies in the education community—parents, administrators, board members. Their orientation to the career ladder had to be strikingly different by the end of this process than that of other teachers.

To examine this difference, a level of concerns analysis, as prescribed by Hall and Hord (1987, pp. 60, 67), was done on the comments made by the two groups of teachers (task force and non–task force high school teachers) during the presentation and discussion of the new evaluation system and career ladder plan in late August 1984. Exhibits 5.1 and 5.2 categorize the comments and questions made by high school teachers that reflect their initial concern at this first presentation of these plans.[2] The relatively few comments of task force teachers were primarily asides. They made these comments as they presented the plans, which indicated their awareness of the concerns teachers might have about them. The heavy expression of self and task management concerns of the high school teachers is clearly evident, as well as the caustic nature of their remarks, especially about the career ladder. Task force teachers, on the other hand, were primarily concerned by this time with the impact of the plan they had designed and seeing it accepted and working.

An analysis of task force teacher comments made during the earlier planning sessions would also show a preponderance of items addressing task and impact concerns (levels 3 to 6) and relatively few focused on the personal and awareness levels (0 to 2). Among task force members throughout the planning process, expressions of personal concerns were rare, for example: "I would be utterly devastated to apply for promotion and not make it. It would cause me to consider getting out of teaching." Most task force teachers were confident of their own abilities, and concentrated their attention on designing a workable system.

In contrast, many other teachers indicated not only general opposition to the plan during the next two years but much specific objection to its various features. The thrust of most objections was how it would further complicate their already busy lives or otherwise affect them personally and negatively in some way.

The career ladder induced self-assessment and triggered uncertainty for many teachers about how good their teaching really was. The task force

Exhibit 5.1

Levels of Concern in Evaluation System Presentation and High School Discussion (22 August 1984)

	TF Presentation Comments	Discussion Comments and Questions
Impact Refocusing[6]		"Announced, formal observations don't tell you how Ts teach regularly. Ss know how you do & should have a say in this evaluation." (lots of clapping)
		"You are evaluated by P & dept H. I'd like to see other Ts evaluate me."
		"Will someone be watching to see if same rating inflation as in the past doesn't occur because this requires more effort?"
Collaborative[5]		
Consequence[4]	"Hopefully this will improve instruction."	"How many tenured Ts have been dismissed for incompetence?"
	"Hope it will provide consistency.	"How does this help dismiss the incompetent?"
Task Management[3]		"How does a T model time?"
Self Personal[2]		"I get feeling that O's are to be given infrequently. If so, how are you going to get the required number for CL?"
	"You will get written comments of any concerns."	"I like evaluation stuff that was done . . . may have questions tomorrow on CL."
	"You will know where you stand at all times—no surprises."	"Will evaluator recognize what tough classes I teach or will I get a bunch of Is?"
Informational[1]	"Evaluation is a necessary evil. We've tried to make it as fair and objective as possible."	
	"This will require documentation so you'll know why you received a particular rating."	"There's a big gap between Is & PCs." "Does PC mean adequate?" "What's included in extra or cocurricular? How evaluated?"
	"Not great change from what you've done before . . . greater specification of what you're doing."	"What is place for dept H. evaluation? Will principal take it into account in final evaluation?"
Awareness Unrelated[0]		

Exhibit 5.2

Levels of Concern in Career Ladder Presentation and High School
Discussion (23 August 1984)

	TF Presentation Comments	*Discussion Comments and Questions*
Impact Refocusing[6]		"Only real concern is about random sampling. Did you consider years of experience as an alternative for selecting first 24?" "Couldn't we choose the 24 from those with the highest ratings?" "Why the CL rather than some other plan?"
Collaborative[5]		
Consequence[4]		
Task Management[3]	Regarding CL procedures/responsibilities, you might be thinking "When do I teach?" "It's not as bad as it sounds. "Evaluators can't be on more than 3 com. so you're not taken out of classroom more than other Ts."	". . . unbelievably complicated." "Some excellent Ts will not put up with the hassle of climbing the CL and not get recognition they deserve." "English Ts work like crazy . . . none will apply." "Program discourages participation . . . going through this review every 3 years."
Self Personal[2]		"Dossier is most complicated . . . designed for elementary Ts." If one is chosen & doesn't apply, everyone knows." "Does debriefing (for unsuccessful candidates) prepare them for humilitation?"
Informational[1]	"We feel good about the plan. It'll work if Danville Ts feel good about it too."	"Any plan to increase supplements in years ahead?" "Will MTs teach more difficult Ss?" "What does satisfactory attendance mean?" "How much publicity over CT selection?" "Any redress (grievance procedure) if turned down?" "How handle a parent who asks for MT?" "Would the record of a team count for a coach?" "How much time is required of evaluators?" "How much weight for class observations & dossier?" "Who's looking at who gives consistently higher or lower ratings?"
Awareness Unrelated[0]		"Central selection committee sounds like Politburo."

had anticipated that teachers would have to face this fundamental question when it designed the plan. By accepting the board's dictum that above-average teachers were to be identified and rewarded, it established a system whereby the first assessment procedure after the principal's judgment of eligibility would be by self-selection. The hassle that candidacy entails or the extra responsibility for those on the career ladder was considered by the task force less of a burden and more of a challenge for someone who is already an outstanding teacher. One who teaches exceptionally well ought to be able to face the extra scrutiny of candidacy and extra responsibilities of promotion more easily than someone who is already struggling quite hard to do acceptably well.

It was no accident, therefore, that personal and management concerns were raised so often. The system was designed to trigger them as teachers made the personal decision to participate or not. If 80 percent believe they are in the top quartile of the performance distribution, something is needed to induce more realistic self-appraisal. Interviewing teachers in five Utah schools, Hart and Murphy (1989) found a heightened self-awareness and increased recognition that teacher improvement was an appropriate goal, even in schools where teachers and principals were negative toward the program. One teacher commented:

> The self-awareness is important. We haven't looked at it before. The efforts to improve instruction have made us grow. (p. 28)

As it became apparent that the Danville career ladder was designed for something less than 50 percent of the teachers, each one consciously or subconsciously faced two questions: "Should I subject myself to extra pressure and responsibility?" and "Am I really good enough to make it?" With the system raising both questions, however, rather than merely the latter, one had very acceptable reasons for not participating and ego defenses could generally be maintained. Programs in which almost everybody makes it (Hanover County, Virginia, and career ladder I levels in many programs) are less threatening but also induce less realistic self-assessment. The motivational impact of the plan will be examined more closely later in this chapter.

For many teachers, the notion of complicating an already burdensome, complicated job by being the recipient of an extensive review process and, if successful, assuming extra responsibilities, seemed overwhelming. "I'm already too busy," said many teachers. One second-grade teacher expressed it this way:

> There's very little interest in the career ladder at my grade level. We don't have time to cover all we are suppose to now. When I first came to Danville we were expected to teach reading, math, spelling, and art. Now, in addition, we have separate preparations for science, english, social studies, and health. So many moral things like saying "no" to drugs are also expected. There's lots of planning and preparation. You have to grade everything, reteach, and keep other children going at the same time. We have to send papers home to parents with notes attached. . . . If I could be sure that the workload would be no greater than what I have now, I would consider applying.

Another teacher commented more succinctly: "Teaching is tough. If you are at a school where discipline is difficult, you have a daily hassle."

Many teachers indicated that teaching was not easy and involving oneself on the career ladder meant extra work. This was a sufficient deterrent to prevent their participation. It is a primary reason why, throughout the country, many teachers do not choose to participate in these programs.

The increased accountability and extra scrutiny brought on by the new evaluation system added stress and discouraged career ladder participation for many teachers. Goodlad and Klein (1970), among many others, have highlighted a common tendency of teachers to shut the classroom door and teach the way they have always taught regardless of what might be prescribed by the front office. As reported earlier by several Danville teachers, overly busy principals had previously, on occasion, filled out summative rating forms on teachers whose classes they had seldom observed. In 1987, 45 percent of the teachers in the Arizona pilot districts indicated they had not been observed for the career ladder at all that year (Packard, 1987). In many schools across the country, teachers receive little or even no direct supervision if their classes seem to run smoothly and few complaints are made by pupils or parents. An informal truce is often struck between teachers and administrators, "If you don't bother me, I won't bother you."

Danville's new evaluation system clearly reduced teacher autonomy to conduct classes as one saw fit. Principals were now expected not just to visit classrooms but to take extensive running notes on what was going on, rate and document reasons for their ratings, conduct conferences with teachers before and after formal observations, do informal observing as well, review lesson plans and other records of teacher performance, and complete a highly specific forty-five-item PCT rating form on each teacher at the end of the year. Originally all teachers, not just those volunteering for the career ladder, were to be observed and evaluated in this manner annually. For many teachers this increased scrutiny caused them considerable concern over how well they would meet expectations. They interpreted the closer scrutiny and extra documentation demanded by the new evaluation system as meaning they were less trusted to decide how they would teach and conduct their classes.

Although the 1985 and 1986 surveys indicated that a solid majority of teachers thought the new evaluation procedure was an improvement over the previous one (see pp. 97-103), many commented from time to time how anxious they were whenever anyone, even their principal, was evaluating them. Beginning in fall 1986, teachers were given the option of being evaluated formally every other year rather than annually, unless they planned to apply for the career ladder. The majority chose the option. It eliminated the possibility of their applying for the career ladder the next year since eligibility requirements include two consecutive, successful annual evaluations by one's principal. As one teacher commented:

> Teachers really like the year off from summative evaluation. There's no pressure. They can just teach that year and not worry about the PCT at the end of the year.

In discussing recent changes in teachers' attitudes toward the career ladder, another teacher said:

> What really helped teachers' attitudes was going to alternate years for formal evaluation of most teachers but requiring annual evaluation for those on the career ladder. They do see formal evaluation as a hassle.

Added stress for teacher participants is a common complaint in many programs. For two years in a row the most negatively rated item on an organizational climate survey in the Arizona pilot districts was: "I work in an environment free from excessive stress" (Packard, 1987, p. 8). In one pilot district teachers said it was "too unsettling" to know only the week in which peer observers were going to observe, and so procedures were changed so all observations would be announced. After three years of trying, and in most cases succeeding, to meet increasingly high schoolwide student achievement gains in Campbell County, Virginia, teachers asked for a year free of the pressure to focus instead on less stressful process evaluation. In Flowing Wells school district, Arizona, the higher one goes on the career ladder, the fewer times one is observed. Less observation itself is apparently used as an incentive to pursue advancement.

It would appear that, for many teachers, the improved evaluation system increases the psychological burden of their teaching to the point where participation on the career ladder is discouraged. The extra scrutiny is a significant deterrent.

A relatively small number of outspoken, highly critical teachers served as early opinion makers and effectively restricted full consideration and favorable attitudes for many others. In at least two schools where no one applied for the career ladder, peer pressure was at least partly responsible. Strong pressure not to participate was put on anyone who expressed any interest whatsoever during the first year. Typical teachers' room comments were:

> Anyone is crazy to be interested in this plan.
> What makes you think you're any better than the rest of us?

In some settings, saying positive things about the new plan made one the butt of scornful remarks, so teachers who saw value in what had been done learned quickly to keep their opinions to themselves. For example, in the fall of 1985, the vast majority of communications committee members, several of whom had already applied but were not chosen as candidates in the drawing, said very little while allowing four or five others to rant and rave throughout the meetings about all the evils of the career ladder. The hostile spirit was so pervasive that, on the spring 1985 Willis poll, only 5 percent of the teachers indicated that other teachers would support them if they applied; 82 percent felt they would not be given any encouragement or respect for so doing. A year later, answers were modified somewhat, but still strongly negative (10 percent and 64 percent). It was not until the summer of 1987 that the majority opinion shifted to predominantly positive responses on this question.

Related to this opinion-shaping hypothesis is the fact that many teachers, including opinion leaders, continued to lack a full understanding of all the procedural details that had been worked out. Once the overall negative reaction set in as the predominant feeling, relatively little interest was evident in all the explanations and efforts to inform people. As late as summer 1987, teachers who were considering applying would call task force members to ask them how to go about applying or pose other questions about operational procedures. Even though procedures had been fully explained on many occasions and were clearly described in various manuals and documents, the plan was apparently not fully understood.

Elsewhere, too, teachers were very sensitive about what their peers thought. A Utah teacher remarked:

> I didn't apply. I know I'm a good teacher. In fact, my principal encouraged me to apply. But why should I risk the envy of my friends and colleagues for $200. For all I know, it will disappear anyway next year, but I'll still be working here with these people. (Amsler et al., p. 18)

The depth of egalitarianism and the sensitivity of people to its being challenged are revealed by a not unusual comment from a principal:

> I was told I could award five bonuses. Well, maybe not all my teachers deserved one this year, but far more than five did outstanding work. The tensions around who gets it are terrific. It has taken a toll on the morale of my staff. The ones who actually receive the money keep it quiet. That doesn't make it a reward. It's a punishment . . . all for $150. (ibid.)

At the same time, both teachers and principals believe that the evaluation systems installed in connection with incentive pay have generally resulted in better assessment of teaching and improved instruction (Amsler et al., 1987, p. 19; Brandt and Kingston, 1986; Hart, 1987).

In the face of strong public endorsement of the notion that those who perform best should receive special recognition and extra pay, educators are hesitant to attack the fundamental premise underlying merit pay and career ladder programs. They resort instead to criticizing and trying to alter the most objectionable features of whatever plans are actually proposed. Teach-

ers along with noneducators will often endorse the general notion that pay should reflect performance (Rist, 1983). The history of teacher merit pay, however, reveals almost no specific programs that were actually initiated by teachers and few that were warmly endorsed (ERS, 1979; Hatry and Greiner, 1985).

With the possible exception of the AFT, state and national teacher associations have typically proposed a long list of concerns that need to be addressed if such plans are to have their support. Before showing some support, for example, the Tennessee Education Association insisted on a much greater percentage of teachers participating on the career ladder than would have been allowed by the initial proposal. In Utah, too, the UEA endorsed the career ladder legislation only if all teachers were to receive extra pay for working several additional days at school within the regular nine-month period and without children. In Virginia, teachers served on the Governor's planning commission that developed guidelines for pay-for-performance and master teacher programs. In numbers they represented about one-third of the panel with school administrators, businessmen, legislators, and others making up the rest. Behind the scenes, the VEA gave teacher members specific procedural guidelines to argue for which would have watered down the basic notion of recognizing and rewarding the best. When sufficient compromise did not occur, the teacher members failed to support the final document and filed a minority report instead. In a separate survey of Virginia teachers at this time, Crews (1984) found significantly more negative feelings toward merit pay on the part of teachers who were VEA members than nonmembers.

In Danville, too, according to both the 1985 Willis and the 1986 Brandt and Kingston surveys, a somewhat greater percentage of teachers agreed than disagreed with the general statement, "Teachers need performance-based rewards in addition to across-the-board raises." Yet, only a small percentage indicated their approval, rather than disapproval (14 percent verses 70 percent), of the career ladder plan that had been so carefully developed to provide such rewards. It would seem that, as opinion leaders played up potential problems with particular procedures and downplayed any likely benefits for the majority of teachers, the predominantly negative sentiment quickly submerged any rational arguments in favor of such plans.

TEACHER MOTIVATION

Much has been written about the motivation of teachers and sources of their job satisfaction and dissatisfaction. Not all of it can be reviewed here. Nevertheless, some analysis of motivational factors is essential if the effect on teachers of such fundamental change is to be understood.

For this analysis, a needs model is employed. The long lists of variables that presumably influence teachers' attitudes toward their jobs are reduced to three kinds of needs: basic survival needs that relate to one's overall living standard and life-style; relationship needs of status and respect from others, especially one's supervisors and peers; and self-actualization needs including self-confidence, sense of accomplishment, and autonomy. This list is not unlike those proposed by Herzberg (1959) or Maslow (1954), although I do not consider the hierarchical order in which needs interrelate as a necessary construct for this analysis.

Under basic survival needs, one can include not only money and job security but the compatibility of work schedules with family and other nonwork life patterns, and mental as well as physical health factors related to teaching. Thus, teaching provides an opportunity for teachers who are also parents to be at home when their children are out of school. This feature was cited as the most satisfying ancillary reward by Dade County teachers recently in a replication of Lortie's research—(35 percent verses 23 percent two decades earlier) (Kottkamp et al., 1986). To the extent that job-related stress and frustration (from undisciplined pupils, misbehaving children, heavy teaching responsibilities, noise, and upsetting working conditions) disturb teachers' sleep, sap their energy, and upset their health, basic survival needs come into play.

To what extent money serves as a direct motivator of improved performance is debatable, however, even in business and industry where factory piecework and sales commission compensation plans are quite common. Arguments and supporting evidence can be found on both sides of the question, varying somewhat with the industry and the kind of work being discussed.

In education, there is little empirical evidence so far that teachers will teach better if they receive a bonus for doing so. In part, this lack of evidence is a function of insufficient research. In the past there have been few places with both teacher bonus plans and the research capability to test their effectiveness. Perhaps some of the current interest in incentive pay will endure long enough for decent research to be done in this area. Lortie (1975) considers insufficient money a primary source of dissatisfaction among teachers. Improving teachers' salaries substantially, he claims, would reduce a basic source of dissatisfaction with teaching, but it would not necessarily improve the teaching itself. Rosenholtz (1984) indicates that teachers are more strongly motivated by intrinsic rewards, such as working with young children and feeling that they have learned, and the organizational conditions of their work.

On the other hand, when former Georgia teachers were asked why they left teaching and what it would take to get them back, the most frequently cited factor was money. More than one-fourth of the teachers surveyed gave low salary as the single reason most responsible for leaving teaching. More than half of them cited more pay and benefits as the major item that would bring them back (Duttweiler, 1986).

Despite strong resistance from teacher associations in particular to the whole notion of incentive pay, the one inducement that eventually caused them to support the establishment of such programs, as least nominally, was additional teacher salary money that otherwise would not have been available. Pilot districts in Arizona and North Carolina, for example, received more than nonpilots. Taxes were raised in Florida, South Carolina, Tennessee, and Utah specifically to finance educational reform. A part of that cost for the educational community was a willingness to put up with performance-based pay and greater accountability.

So money does talk, and many teachers in all parts of the country report that it was the number one reason for their participation in an incentive pay program. Once they participate, furthermore, the more acceptable it seems. Attitudes of recipients toward these programs, as reported earlier, are typically far more favorable than those of nonparticipants. As they become accustomed to it, furthermore, they do not want it to stop. Teacher ranks become divided on the issue, and the unions lose control and negotiating power. That may be the most fundamental reason for such strong resistance from the teacher associations.

Obviously the extra money for individuals has to be substantial to have an effect. Educators comment (see page 163) that $200 is not worth complicating an already complicated work life; but ten to twelve thousand dollars, as are available in the Utah plan, is a different matter. Even $2,000 to $3,000 obviously serves as a sufficient incentive for many Tennessee teachers to try to reach levels II or III.

Teaching is a highly mobile profession with many persons leaving and others reentering it each year. This high turnover rate is one of the reasons school boards cite for starting incentive pay plans. They want the best teachers to stay as long as possible and not leave for higher pay and better working conditions elsewhere, either to another school system or to private industry and another kind of work. Underlying the development of recent incentive plans was research that indicated college students and teachers with the best academic qualifications were no longer attracted to teaching or interested in making a career of it if they did enter the field (Schlecty and Vance, 1982; Weaver, 1984; Murnane et al., 1989).

By the end of the eighties, however, college students were showing increased interest in teaching. Teacher education enrollments were up substantially all over the country. Perhaps all the reform publicity was not only drawing attention to the problems of the schools but successfully challenging the next generation to do something about them. The fact that since 1984 teacher salaries had risen twice as fast as wages in most other industries might also have contributed to this renewed interest in teaching careers.

Compared with much earlier periods, dissatisfaction with teaching as a career has most certainly increased. National polls conducted by the National Education Association indicated that only 59 percent of those teaching in 1979 would probably become a teacher if they could start over again compared with 78 percent a decade earlier (NEA, 1979). The difficulty and complexity of teaching (Fullan, 1982, p. 110), a feeling that the job is never done (Lortie, 1975), role ambiguity (Bacharach et al., 1986), boredom from teaching the same grade and subject year after year (DiGeronimo, 1985), and increasingly disruptive students are features that exacerbate teacher stress and frustration, and make mere survival from day-to-day a primary motivation for many teachers.

Several other findings of the recent Dade County study reflect the difficulties of teaching and the desire of teachers to make survival easier: In indicating the kinds of students they would prefer to teach, almost half (47 percent verses 36 percent two decades earlier) selected "nice kids, from average homes, who are respectful and hard-working." Twelve percent fewer teachers in 1984 said they wanted to teach "creative and intellectually demanding students who call for special effort" (Kottkamp et al., 1986). They also indicated less satisfaction with their school as a workplace than the 1964 teachers.

An important reduction was reported in the Dade County polls with regard to status and belongingness needs. Fewer teachers in 1984 cited "respect from others" (26 percent verses 37 percent) and "opportunity to wield influence" (32 percent verses 36 percent) as the most satisfying extrinsic rewards. Salary along with respect from others and opportunity to wield influence were the three extrinsic reward options on the questionnaire. The proportion of teachers indicating "no extrinsic rewards" as the "most satisfying" option doubled during the two decades.

Although some satisfaction was indicated from being respected and having influence, Duke, Showers, and Imber (1980) found in another study that high school teachers were hesitant to take advantage of shared-decision-making opportunities in their schools because they felt their involvement would have little real effect. Teacher involvement in site-based management takes time and may not be so attractive to teachers as is often presumed. The potential benefits for participation, such as a sense of ownership and influence, may not actually be realized. Even with extra salary included, which career ladder programs might provide, the overall benefits to an individual might not outweigh the costs.

Teachers' relationships with students and especially their perceptions of the impact they have had on them are much more rewarding than their relationships with other teachers. Among the intrinsic rewards that Lortie (1975) and his later replicators listed, "the chance to associate with other teachers and educators" was only selected as the most satisfying option by one percent of the teachers in each poll. Associating with children or youths (8 percent) and especially knowing one has reached students and they have learned (87 percent) were chosen much more frequently.

The latter, of course, relates to our third need level: sense of accomplishment and self-esteem. In determining how well one is doing as a teacher, the source of assessment is important. Feedback from others is one source, self-assessment another. The Dade County polls show a sharp shift in the sources teachers rely on most in judging their effectiveness. Whereas in 1964, 59 percent of the teachers were most likely to base this judgment on their own observation of what students were learning, that is, self-assessment, only 37 percent did so in 1984. Reactions of other teachers, students, and even parents; assessments by the principal or supervisor; and results of objective examinations and other tests were all more influential than in 1964. Together, these external sources accounted for 63 percent of the 1984 sample.

The implications of this study suggest that teachers have become more other- than inner-directed. How good they feel they are as teachers is shaped more by what others say and do than by how they themselves view the world. This change reflects a loss of autonomy. One would seem to be less in control of one's own destiny as a teacher and less likely to generate one's own notions of how or even what to teach. To the extent that teachers' sense of autonomy is lessened, working conditions made more difficult, and external forces become more influential in shaping the teaching role, uncertainties and self-doubts must be greater as well. Psychologically, then, the combination of changes reduces the opportunity for self-fulfillment as a teacher and satisfaction with a teaching career. Although the most satisfying reward for teachers may still be knowing that one has reached students and they have learned well from one's teaching, as the polls clearly indicate, the opportunities to attain that reward may be less than what they once were.

Evidence is beginning to appear that, in districts which require student outcome data tied to specific teaching objectives, participants are deriving great satisfaction when the results show significant student gain. Program coordinators in two South Carolina districts claim that teachers become quite excited when they obtain actual documentation of how much their students have learned. The focus on student learning and how to measure it presents them with a real challenge. Staff development has been focused on this topic in many places, with apparently increasing success in how to do it. Documenting the fact that student learning has occurred is highly rewarding to those responsible for it.

Attitudes toward teaching and the desire to improve one's performance, then, is a reflection of how well all three kinds of need are satisfied. Undoubtedly, patterns of need satisfaction are highly diverse given variations in school organization and leadership, characteristics of students and communities, home life and avocational interests, teaching assignments and abilities. Which needs shape particular teacher motivation and behavior will vary greatly from one teacher to another, one class and school to others. Teachers who are especially effective with students receive considerably more intrinsically rewarding student feedback than those who have disruptive students and unresponsive classes. On the other hand, those who are struggling with the management of student behavior or other problems of the workplace will be most influenced by basic survival needs. For them, adding pressure in the form of increased expectations and extra scrutiny, as career ladders do, would only increase frustration and make life even more uncomfortable. If, as a third possibility, some of the stress comes not just from teaching but from moonlighting, extra career ladder pay might permit one to give up the outside job and survival pressures would actually be eased.

Married women, according to Lortie (1975), are generally quite satisfied with their teaching positions but not necessarily the most involved. For them, additional expectancies might threaten one of their prime sources of motivation, that is, being able to manage their family life and teaching career simultaneously. Teaching schedules and calendars have permitted the blending of family and career patterns to a greater extent than is possible in other occupations. For those with children in school the mix could not be better. It is likely, therefore, that career ladder expectancies would threaten what otherwise is a tolerable resolution of home and work needs.

For still other teachers, whose coping mechanisms have allowed them to handle classroom and out-of-school pressures smoothly and whose status is established, the job enlargement opportunities provided by the plan, as well as more money, could be highly motivating.

The career ladder, then, is likely to have a highly differential effect on teachers, threatening some and challenging others. In order to investigate what kind of specific needs were threatened or enhanced by the career ladder and new evaluation system in Danville, all teacher interview comments in the summer 1987 data that had been classified as motivational in nature were coded again in terms of the kinds of needs they reflected. Teachers had talked at length about not just the career ladder but school teaching more generally, why they were doing it, what they liked and disliked about it.

Exhibit 5.3 lists all the interview comments that referred to basic survival needs and the number of teachers who mentioned them. For example, of the fourteen who mentioned money, nine indicated it was a major reason for them considering the career ladder, two others disparagingly suggested it was the only reason for participating, and the last three inferred that money was not sufficiently important to make them participate. One of these three, however, did intend to participate for another reason, that is, primarily for a sense of accomplishment. Among the seven teachers interviewed who were already participating, three indicated money was a major, though not sole factor, in their decision.

The extra pressure added to an already tough job by the career ladder and new evaluation system is clearly evident in the next set of comments. Only the last two remarks suggest the new system might provide a needed challenge to better performance. All the rest suggest that, for someone to participate, extra time, energy, and stress can be expected, clear disincentives for many teachers. At least a third of those interviewed referred directly to the difficulties

Exhibit 5.3

Perceived Survival Incentives and Disincentives for Participating or Not Participating on the Career Ladder

Need	Comments	No. of Teachers*	
		Comments	Total
Pay			14(3)
	"Extra money is a big incentive."	5	
	"Probably wouldn't have applied without money."	(1)	
	"Money needed to send kids to college."	2(1)	
	"Career ladder makes it a livable salary in this area."	(1)	
	"Only reason is money."	2	
	"Don't need the money."	2	
	"I was glad for my master's degree supplement."	1	
Job demands and pressure			14(5)
	"Teaching is tough. No time left over from meeting present expectations."	7	
	"Teacher next to me works hard, is burning out."	1	
	"Lots of teachers are apprehensive. Some principals encourage and inform you about career ladder, others don't to ease the pressure."	(1)	
	"Takes a lot of time being evaluated."	(1)	
	"Documentation and PCT related criticism upset older teachers initially."	(1)	
	"Many teachers don't want pressure of six observations."	3(1)	
	"Evaluation tool is better. It makes you interested in applying."	1	
	"It does add pressure. Some need more pressure."	(2)	
Outside obligations			6(1)
	"Some teachers have outside interests."	2	
	"Some teachers who don't want to stay after school to watch the band or come back aren't interested in CL. Lots of Teachers like to teach because it's a convenient job."	(1)	
	"You don't want school to be your whole life."	1	
	"The kids don't drive yet."	1	
	"Many women want summer vacation and after work free when their children are not in school."	2	
Total number of teachers referring to survival needs			18(5)

* Numbers in these columns refer to the number of teachers making a particular comment. Numbers in parentheses identify the number of teachers who were already participating on the career ladder as career teacher, candidate, or evaluator. Total figures refer to the number of teachers making coments about the need category. The total number of teachers interviewed was twenty-three.

inherent in the teaching role and meeting all the expectations demanded of teachers today. This finding is very consistent with what Lortie and many other researchers report about the nature of teaching and the job difficulties to be faced.

The working culture for Danville teachers is obviously a demanding one. Many teachers are so busy trying to do their job as best they can, that they have given little thought to doing anything more. The career ladder is seen as adding extra pressure in the review process itself, with six observations by several observers required along with numerous conferences and documentation. Many teachers are not accustomed to classroom visitation by outsiders, which itself can be threatening. More than a few teachers have already found the extensive specifications of the PCT a nuisance if not a real threat to the relative autonomy of previous years. They would prefer to be left alone, which the previous evaluation system had permitted in most instances.

On top of the added pressure of the review process were the uncertainties of job enlargement in the role of career or master teacher. Admittedly, the comments in Exhibit 5.3 may only hint at those concerns but they appear elsewhere in the ethnographical data as well. For many teachers, life is complicated enough already; unless their own concerns ease about additional pressures the career ladder might bring, they are likely to remain nonparticipants.

The ancillary incentives of flexible schedules, compatible with those of family life and other outside activities, are certainly attractive to some of the Danville teachers. Teaching has historically been a nine-month assignment. While that has limited full-time career opportunities in pay and responsibility for those who want them, it has provided many others with a unique calendar. Tied originally to the agricultural cycle, it is singularly appropriate today for those trying to blend the two careers of white-collar professional activity and child rearing. It is apparent that in Danville, as Lortie found in Dade County, a certain percentage of teachers will not be attracted to the career ladder because participation might complicate their nonteaching world.

It would appear, then, that for at least half of the Danville teachers, the extra money attached to career ladder participation is a strong incentive to participate. It could make the difference in their remaining in teaching, getting the children through college, and having a decent overall life-style. For some teachers, it is currently the only reason for trying to be promoted.

For many teachers, however, teaching is already very demanding. Promotion on the career ladder would mean subjecting oneself to a great deal of scrutiny and extra work, they believe. If one were successful, more responsibilities than one currently has would be assumed. It is not certain exactly what they would be. In all, many teachers have as much, if not more, stress than they want and volunteering for the career ladder is not being considered. Maintaining sanity and coping with present responsibilities is sufficient.

Still other teachers have sufficiently strong family or other outside interests that they do not want to complicate their life further by tackling the career ladder. Life is well balanced, and one can schedule the two worlds of teaching and nonteaching rather smoothly. In several cases, however, as outside needs change, (for example, children going to college), the career ladder offers new, enriching opportunities. The extra pay helps with college tuition, and children going away to school means more time for the work career.

Survival needs, therefore, make the career ladder both attractive to some and unattractive to others. The maintenance of life-style and mental health, both in and out of school, is the most fundamental basic need influencing the career ladder attitudes and decisions of many teachers in Danville. What Lortie refers to as external and ancillary rewards, such as pay and schedule flexibility, are important to many teachers. These are primarily maintenance rewards because they allow one to continue a way of life to which one has become accustomed. I would add survival in the classroom as well to this general maintenance theme, given the increasing complexity of a teacher's world. If one cannot cope reasonably well inside the classroom, one's outside life becomes extra complicated as well. So survival needs are clearly important forces shaping the behavior and attitudes of teachers toward the Danville career ladder.

Exhibit 5.4 presents similar data on relatedness needs. None of the four who commented about relationships and had been involved with the career ladder indicated anything but support from teacher colleagues and principals. They apparently felt well accepted and respected. One or two others indicated as well that showing interest in the plan would not jeopardize colleague relationships, in considerable contrast to the polls taken two years earlier. Only one comment was made suggesting the arousal of jealousy toward those who made it. At least three references were made to the lack of full administrative support or direct criticism from one's principals. Obviously, those who received less than outstanding ratings on the

Exhibit 5.4

Perceived Relatedness Incentives and Disincentives for Participating or Not Participating on the Career Ladder

		No. of Teachers*	
Need	Comments	Comments	Total
Belongingness			9(4)
	"My faculty wanted me to be an evaluator."	(3)	
	"Teachers no longer take it personally if you apply."	2(1)	
	"Colleagues are supportive—didn't want observers to visit my class when I wasn't feeling well."	(1)	
	"Little time to talk—everyone is too busy."	1	
	"I've enough respect for myself. If coworkers make it, I'd not feel inferior."	1	
	"Too much jealousy. Everyone's threatened by those who make it."	1	
Respect			7(3)
	"My principal has always been supportive."	2(1)	
	"Some principals encourage you."	(1)	
	"I'm comfortable with my status—on a lot of committees."	1	
	"I like being recognized even more than the money, especially after being observed by 8 people. Even my own family doesn't think much of my being a teacher."	(1)	
	"Older teachers received criticism for first time."	2(1)	
	"My principal has not been supportive."	1	
	"Dislike seeing teachers toot their own horns, trying to impress others."	1	
Total number of teachers referring to relatedness needs			11(5)

* Numbers in these columns refer to the number of teachers making a particular comment. Numbers in parentheses identify the number of teachers who were already participating on the career ladder as career teacher, candidate, or evaluator. Total figures refer to the number of teachers making comments about the need category. The total number of teachers interviewed was twenty-three.

various PCT items sensed less support for their teaching than earlier when little or no direct feedback was received.

Not unexpectedly, comments relating to the several self-related needs (Exhibit 5.5) came more often from those who had the most to do with the career ladder. Those who were confident of their

Exhibit 5.5

Perceived Self-Related Incentives and Disincentives for Participating or Not Participating on the Career Ladder

| | | No. of Teachers | |
Need	Comments	Comments	Total
Self-fulfillment			5(2)
	"Something to work toward. Sets you apart from colleagues."	1	
	"A challenge to young, enthusiastic teachers. Not for those who want an easy job."	1	
	"The most important thing that has happened to me."	(1)	
	"Personal satisfaction of being approved."	2(1)	
	"I'm a better teacher for being in other classes. Learned a lot."	(1)	
Sense of accomplishment			3
	"Best reward is having students respond well and learn."	1	
	"To influence young minds is important."	1	
	"Some teachers are motivated to teach students. Not the same ones motivated by money."	1	
	"I want better student outcomes."	1	
Self-esteem			4(3)
	"Not uneasy [about being observed] always had lots of confidence. Used to visitors, but I'd be devastated if I didn't make it."	(1)	
	"I'm not the best teacher in the world, but I know I do more than my colleagues and should be paid more."	(1)	
	"Going through classrooms as an evaluator makes you confident in being a model. I'll probably apply."	(1)	
	"Some teachers don't want to be noticed. If named outstanding, they'd be expected never to make a mistake. Everybody makes mistakes."	1	
Sense of autonomy			(3)
	"I didn't do anything different to become a career teacher. Didn't change what I do."	(3)	
	"I like doing things my own way. Don't want CL to thwart that."	(1)	
Total number of teachers referring to self needs			9(5)

* Numbers in these columns refer to the number of teachers making a particular comment. Numbers in parentheses identify the number of teachers who were already participating on the career ladder as career teacher, candidate, or evaluator. Total figures refer to the number of teachers making comments about the need category. The total number of teachers interviewed was twenty-three.

teaching ability and experienced acceptance and respect from their administrators and peers were most likely to try for promotion. While many teachers commented about the extra stress and effort imposed by the career ladder (Exhibit 5.3), three of those reviewed for promotion (Exhibit 5.5) claimed they made no changes in what they ordinarily did in order to make it. It is clear that several teachers, including some not then directly involved, viewed the career ladder as an opportunity to develop themselves and strengthen their teaching skills and their impact on students. For the most part, however, the numbers of teachers who referred directly to these self-related needs was somewhat smaller than those indicating that relatedness and especially survival needs were most pressing. Although it provides only a crude estimate of how the three kinds of need comments are distributed across the 5 percent sample ($N = 23$) of Danville teachers, it is interesting that nine individuals referred to self needs, eleven to relatedness needs, and eighteen to survival needs during the interviews.

Quite a few teachers made references to several kinds of needs, and five, including one career teacher, made no need-related comments whatsoever. It would seem, in summary, that pay among the survival needs, respect and encouragement from peers and administrators, and self-maintenance and enhancement, to use Snygg and Combs's (1959) terms, act as inducements to participate on the career ladder. On the other hand, pressures of the job, perceived extra stress from the review process or job enlargement responsibilities if promoted, outside obligations, and a lack of administrator or peer encouragement serve as deterrents to career ladder participation. During the first year of the program peer discouragement was most certainly a bigger deterrent than it is now.

ORGANIZATIONAL CHANGE

The Danville career ladder was well launched. Its development and implementation provide a clear example of major organizational change. Successful change of such proportions does not come easily, so it is worth noting again some of the key factors that brought this about.

The resistance that followed its introduction was a typical initial response to instructional change attempts and should have been fully anticipated. What so often happens next after change is initiated, however, did not occur with the Danville plan. The major features of the plan were not compromised or watered down as implementation took place. So many change efforts fail by lack of continued attention and leadership during the implementation phase (Fullan, 1982; Sarason, 1971; Schein, 1980; Malen and Hart, 1987; Hart and Murphy, 1989). Education particularly is noted for programmatic fads that come and go with no lasting impact, often because they are never fully implemented. People have come to expect that "this too shall pass" if they just wait awhile. All over the country I have seen such comments in district or state surveys. Most frequently they are made by teachers giving their reasons for not participating in incentive pay plans. They are skeptical that they will last beyond the first two or three years.

Because of sharp differences among various educational constituencies, career ladders seem particularly susceptible to dilution of their original intent due to the political compromises that take place during their development and installation. Malen and Hart (1987) trace the history of career ladder legislation and development in Utah and show how the distinctive features of promotional positions and differential salaries were compromised at both state and local levels. The "reform" was gradually converted into familiar practice.

In Danville, however, the basic notion of identifying outstanding teachers was preserved through its first four years. It is true that, because the plan is voluntary, not all outstanding teachers applied and were therefore selected. Most of those who were chosen during the first few years were recognized by their peers and administrators as at least above average in teaching performance. Many were considered exceptionally good.

As documented earlier, teacher receptivity to the plan increased considerably during its third year (1986–87). By summer 1987 as many teachers liked as disliked the plan, even if they did not intend to participate in it. What were the reasons behind this increased acceptance? Two were suggested earlier, that is, seeing candidates complete the review process, and the board's reaffirmation of its support in August 1986.

For a more extensive analysis I will relate what happened to a change model proposed by Waugh (Waugh and Punch, 1987) and identify Danville implementation procedures that seem congruent with relevant model variables. Exhibit 5.6 portrays this model. My focus will be on five of the six group 2 independent variables because together they are supposed to account for 40 percent of the variance in teacher receptivity.[3] Both groups of independent variables are estimated by Waugh and Punch to account for 60 percent of the

Exhibit 5.6

Model for the Study of Teachers' Receptivity Toward a Planned
Educational Change That Has Been in Operation for a Few Years
(from Waugh and Punch, 1987)

Independent Variables (Group 1)	Independent Variables (Group 2)	Situation Variables	Dependent Variables
Beliefs on general issues of education	Alleviation of fears and uncertainty associated with the change		
	Practicality of the new educational system in the classroom	School	
Overall feelings toward the previous educational system	Perceived expectations and beliefs about some important aspects of the new educational system		
	Perceived support for teacher roles at school in respect of the main referents of the new educational system	Subject	Receptivity toward the new educational system
Attitude toward the previous educational system	Personal cost appraisal of the change	Teacher	
	Beliefs on some important aspects of the new educational system in comparison with the previous one		

variance. Regarding the previous pay system, it is a fairly safe assumption that teachers were generally in favor of higher salaries for all teachers on an across-the-board basis. They also acknowledged that substantial pay raises had been given on that basis for at least three years.

Regarding the specific issue of merit pay, at least half of the Danville teachers indicated their approval of the general principle that pay should also reflect the quality of one's performance. To the extent that this notion is a genuine reflection of how teachers originally felt, eventual support for a specific plan for implementing the idea should exist once people have understood and become accustomed to the procedures. Unless they are offended for other reasons, eventual understanding and acceptance of a well-designed operational plan would seem likely, especially in the absence of better, more universally accepted alternatives.

Design and implementation steps related to the group 2 variables in Exhibit 5.6 can be summarized as follows:

Alleviation of fears and uncertainties

All teachers experienced the new evaluation system directly, beginning in 1984. By summer 1987, they had received at least two summative evaluations via the new system. They knew what to expect and many had improved their ratings on the new instrument from those given the first time it was used in fall 1984.

Uncertainties about how the career ladder review would operate were lessened also by seeing how the first groups of candidates were treated.

Finally, no one was forced to become a candidate; there were no reprisals for not participating on the ladder. Some very good teachers chose not to participate. This fact most certainly eased potential fears of being stigmatized as a poor teacher if one did not participate.

Practicality of the new system

What initially appeared as a highly complex set of procedures, for which many teachers said they did not have time, actually worked. Two groups of candidates had completed the various conferences, observations, and documentation activities demanded by the review process and had been promoted. A few said they even did little more than they ordinarily would have done without the special review. Furthermore, those whose burdens had increased the most, namely the principals and vice principals, were relieved a bit when many of the teachers chose the alternative year option for summative evaluations.

Perceived expectations and beliefs

Waugh and Punch suggest that accurate perceptions and expectations regarding changes facilitate their acceptance, whereas conflicting expectations and misconceptions of problems deter it. Because of the complexity of the plan and the initial vocal opposition, there was conflicting opinion and misunderstanding over many of its features. One example was the difference among teachers over how much of a hassle the review process would bring. The long list of issues discussed in chapter 3 indicates the areas in which opinion differences flourished and confusion reigned. It was only after continued administrative attention and communication during implementation, as well as seeing the plan operate, that some of the confusion subsided and the number of teachers seeing value in the plan increased.

Perceived school support

The importance to individual teachers of having their principals either encourage or discourage their participation on the ladder was shown earlier (see p.000). In a number of schools, principals actively encouraged people to participate and helped them with student outcome planning and documentation. In several instances, principals alleviated negative peer pressure by urging faculty who were not interested in participating not to run down those who felt differently.

The plan forced principals into a more difficult role of not just supporting and assisting teachers, but making important summative judgments about their teaching performance. These judgments determined their eligibility even to apply for promotion. This was a new role for principals and vice principals, one which they took quite seriously.

Differences existed from one school to another in the proportion of teachers who expressed an interest in the career ladder. It should not automatically be assumed, however, that where there were no applicants, the principal did not try to sell the program. Principals did vary, however, in their own feelings about the program; and, as a result, teacher acceptance or rejection of the plan was bound to be influenced to some extent by what they did and said.

Reduction of the strong, early peer pressure not to participate was also very important. Almost all teachers interviewed in July 1987 said they would be supported or even encouraged by their colleagues if they applied. A few indicated they would be kidded about it, but they did not expect real animosity.

Personal cost appraisal

Many school innovations require extra time and effort on the part of teachers with few benefits, only a more complicated life. Therefore, teachers are usually cautious about endorsing new ideas or programs until they can see some real benefits for themselves.

The Danville career ladder is no different. For those who are promoted there are significant increases in pay, status, and personal satisfaction. The potential for job enlargement and empowerment also exists, depending on the extent to which role differentiation and structural change in school organization actually occur in the years ahead. Career and master teachers who serve as evaluators and instructional leaders in their schools would at the same time assume more complete and challenging professional roles than teaching the same subjects year after year to new groups of students. To the extent that job enlargement actually occurs, the career ladder would truly provide a career alternative for those who want it and earn it.

The trade-off for these benefits, of course, would be a more complex role, extra responsibilities, somewhat greater restriction on out-of-school life perhaps, and, probably for many, a longer working calendar throughout the year. For teachers not choosing the career ladder path, the benefits are few if any. Perhaps structural change, if it does occur, would produce a better functioning organization. Increased attention to student outcomes and more direct involvement on the part of career ladder teachers might produce improved student response and better team functioning than the traditional cellular system. Only time will tell whether any of these benefits will accrue in the years ahead.

There has been suspicion that those who do not participate will lose status and perhaps even pay by the establishment of an elite hierarchy of teachers.

Those concerns have been eased somewhat, but not completely eliminated. They should be monitored closely in the years immediately ahead as role differentiation and structural change evolve.

The imposition of the new, more precise and demanding evaluative system for all teachers did, by itself, introduce major change. The presumed benefit, as far as teachers were concerned, was continued and perhaps increased public support. Theoretically, too, instruction might improve and students would respond better than in the past. If that were to happen, the intrinsic rewards of teaching that Lortie writes about and some of the Danville teachers said were most satisfying would increase.

Many Danville teachers, however, questioned the likelihood of instruction improving sufficiently and for these good things to happen. Direct evidence of increased public confidence and support was not apparent. So presumed benefits for many teachers were undoubtedly outweighed by the extra pressure of close scrutiny and explicit expectations brought on by the new summative evaluation system. That pressure was eased in the third year of the program by allowing the year-off option. As a result, the entire innovation became more widely accepted.

The importance of administrator leadership during the early implementation stage is evident in other programs as well. After conducting in-depth case studies of initial implementation of a career ladder (i.e., second year of the program) in five Utah schools, for example, Hart and Murphy (1989) report great diversity in how it was implemented and received. Where teachers viewed the goals and procedures of the career ladder as contributory to the core values of their schools, that is, teaching and learning, greater support prevailed, more positive response to those who were participating, and more awareness of the opportunities it could provide for all persons. The work of career ladder teachers was openly discussed. In faculty meetings and teacher's lounges, teachers talked freely about how their special tasks and responsibilities related to various school needs. While principals, teacher leaders, and teacher specialists were the program's primary advocates, other teachers readily acknowledged the benefits of the program to their schools.

In the three schools where negative attitudes still dominated, it was unclear how the goals of the program related to those of the school and what the restructured work activities for those participating on the ladder had to do with the regular school program. Nonparticipating teachers knew relatively little about what career ladder teachers were doing, and even the latter were unsure about how some of what they were doing fitted in. As a result, they often downplayed their special roles and devalued career ladder work in an attempt to preserve collegial relationships.

Principals' attitudes and behaviors were at least partly responsible for establishing these sharply different reactions. In the first two schools they articulated the potential contributions career ladders could make to teaching and learning. They helped promote the new tasks and roles participating teachers would have as important contributors to school goals. The other three principals saw the reform as an imposition "that used up time without contributing to the core function of the school or as an unmanageable burden to be foisted upon the teachers" (p. 41). The role of principals in helping make sense of school reform efforts and put them into operation cannot be overestimated. Without their understanding and leadership to help teachers see how it relates to other ongoing activity, it is not likely to succeed.

POWER STRUGGLES

Numerous references have already been made to the variety of reactions incentive pay plans inevitably bring forth. Teachers tend to be wary if not outright opposed to most programs because they think that they know the problems involved. Teacher association leadership is even more strongly against the introduction of such programs and prepared to oppose the effort aggressively. Their tactics include raising issues, lengthening debates, and delaying as long as possible easy resolution of the many issues that must be settled (Malen and Hart, 1987).

Certain ground is sacred and must never be disturbed: no quotas, no arbitrary limits on the numbers who can apply and participate, no comparisons, no relative standards, no rankings, no limits to the numbers who can be judged best. Everybody should be able to become a master teacher if she is willing to work hard enough and the standards are clear. How others perform should not affect how one is judged.

> Tell people clearly what they have to do. If they fail when they try, tell them specifically how they failed and help them improve and try again until they succeed. Everything must be fair and objective. If one feels abused or unfairly treated, there must be a way to appeal the treatment or "questionable" decision—and to the highest authority—the school board or an outside arbitration panel if need be. Get basic salaries up so they are competitive with those in outside industry; then we will support merit pay if there is still money available. And, because these programs are to provide incentives for teachers, they should have the most say in how they work, the greatest

representation on various planning committees, the loudest voice in what is decided. Without teachers in favor of a plan, there is little likelihood that it will work.

Yet, teachers did not ask for it. Legislators, councilmen, business leaders, industrialists, and others in the larger community the schools are to serve were the instigators, "What's needed if schools are to improve," they would say, "are ways to reward and encourage the best."

> Our schools have some great teachers—dedicated, hardworking, caring people—but many are not. We need a system to recognize and pay those who excel a lot more than we do, but not everybody deserves more. Some don't deserve what they are already getting. A little competition will shape up those who are sloughing off. If it doesn't, they ought to get out. In the business world the best, most productive workers are paid most and advance fastest. Why shouldn't that happen in education as well? Why is school teaching so different? We all know some teachers are better than others.

And so the rhetoric goes from both sides of the constituency. The rhetoric is only symbolic and tactical, not strategic. Underlying strategies have to do with powerful struggles between primary and secondary actors over who will run the schools. Not only are teachers and taxpayers involved but principals and parents, central office administrators and PTA officers, board of education and city/county council members, local district and state officials, council persons and legislators, business and union leaders, and so on. No institution has a greater yet more diverse group of stakeholders than the public schools. Each has more than one axe to grind as attempts are made to chop away at educational traditions that impede reform. Something as potentially pervasive as incentive pay is bound to threaten change in the dynamic system of human forces and counterforces that shapes and runs public education.

At stake is not only who controls the schools but money, jobs, influence, status, and life-style for many people. Public education expenditures account for the largest segment of state and local budgets. The 2.5 million teachers represent perhaps the largest organized work force in America, and one of the largest voter blocs as well. Low in pay in comparison with many other kinds of workers, especially of the white-collar, college-educated variety, teachers are not quite at the bottom of the list. Librarians, curators, in many instances, nurses, social workers, even bookkeepers are lower when comparisons are made on a twelve-month basis. And teachers' salaries have improved faster than those of many other groups since the current reform movement began. The salaries of public school teachers, furthermore, are significantly higher than for those who are teaching in private schools.

The above discussion serves to highlight the size of the educational establishment and the power it wields, not to suggest teachers are overpaid. It is not only the people involved but the various organizations and associations they represent, or who represent them, which have much at stake also. Undoubtedly, resistance to differential pay from the NEA and its state affiliates derives from its potential to divide the teacher ranks. Teacher association ability to negotiate uniform salary schedules year after year is certainly made more difficult, if not jeopardized altogether, when teachers are at different ranks, with different responsibilities and pay scales. On the other hand, with a single salary schedule the leadership can argue with united backing for a specified across-the-board percentage raise for everyone. As differentiation occurs in teacher status and responsibility, furthermore, it also becomes more difficult to identify other working condition issues for negotiation purposes. Teachers will tend to have different problems and different perspectives depending on their place on the ladder and the particular roles they assume. It is already clear that career ladder participants and nonparticipants perceive these programs and related school issues quite differently. So the strength of the teacher associations is very much at stake if the notion of treating teachers according to how well they perform goes very far.

The power struggles go on at all levels and in all stages of the development of incentive pay programs. As indicated earlier, state legislatures were the battlegrounds for enactment of many of the early plans—Florida, Tennessee, Utah, South Carolina, and Texas among others. In all of these states, strong business and industry coalitions lobbied sufficiently well to pass comprehensive educational reform legislation featuring incentive pay or career ladders, among other items, against opposition from the education establishment. The latter element was temporarily subdued by increases in state taxes to finance the reform. The honeymoon did not last long, however. In Florida, the NEA and AFT state affiliates filed lawsuits within a year to stop implementation of the merit pay program, charging that it violated collective bargaining laws (*Education Week*,

28 June 1989). In Tennessee, negotiations in the legislature itself broadened the base of participation prior to enactment by setting the requirements for the first step on the ladder so that a majority of the states teachers could get on it (Handler and Carlson, 1984, 1985).

In Utah, the story was much the same. The initiative came from Governor Scott Matheson with strong backing from the business community, the Mormon Church, and a number of key legislators. It featured sizable increases in educational expenditures and major changes in the teacher pay structure through the establishment of a statewide career ladder program (Hart and Murphy, 1989).

Although the UEA was put on the defensive, it managed to garner sufficient support of its own to delay final enactment until some of its own agenda could be included and the seeds sown for still greater modification during the implementation stage. The fact that the governor had not given the UEA a place on the career ladder design committee both angered the association and generated extra sympathy among legislators. Behind the scenes the UEA was a highly active lobbyist and eventually sold the idea that without teacher backing career ladders would never succeed. To gain teacher support, furthermore, the performance bonus component had to be minimized and the job enlargement and extended contract features expanded.

None of the various power groups was able by itself to have its preferred brand of legislation passed. The result, therefore, was an eclectic package that contained something for all and therefore received widespread support for the initial enactment.

Another teacher association strategy worked as well, namely, to transfer the responsibility for designing plans to the local districts. There, basic decisions about the many controversial procedural issues could be hammered out one at a time with plenty of opportunity to chip away at less desirable features and negotiate more acceptable ones.

As indicated earlier, further opportunity to alter undesirable program features occurred also during the school-by-school implementation process when the attitudes and leadership abilities of school principals came into play. Increasingly, as the planning and development effort was transferred down the chain of authority from those who started the reform to those who ran it and were most affected by it, educators became more dominant and in control of the planning process. At each step of the way opportunities were found for modifying and softening unwelcome design features with traditional practice.

The final result was a program that increased the pay opportunities substantially for almost all teachers and provided a variety of ways for them to do additional, important school-related tasks. In short, it expanded the teacher's role beyond straight classroom instruction toward that of a more complete professional. The superior teaching component, the main thrust of the original initiative but the source of the greatest controversy, was contained. What remained was a substantial restructuring of teacher salaries and workloads that in many localities was very positively received. Despite the vanishing effects of the original initiative, the Utah career ladder has brought real change to many communities (Amsler et al., 1988; Cornett, 1988).

Similar struggles have taken place around many of the same issues in legislatures and school districts elsewhere. Whereas the Florida, Tennessee, and Utah battles were fought primarily at the state level, many others have played out at the local level as well. In Virginia, most of it has taken place locally without even encouragement by the state.

In Arizona, state NEA affiliates have vacillated between outright opposition to not taking a position about the career ladder pilot programs. Since the money for participating teachers and districts is all state money above what nonparticipants are making and has no detrimental effect on others, it is hard to make a case against the pilot programs. Individuals participating, furthermore, as in Danville, are often strong teachers and respected leaders in local teacher associations. In many instances, the state education leadership has been told by its own members to stop fighting and start supporting the reform. Teacher ranks are clearly divided over the virtue or lack of virtue of career ladder programs. The degree of support or rejection varies with how well they operate locally and the amount of trust and respect that exists among those involved.

SUMMARY

Major educational change is never easy. Sarason (1971), in fact, thinks it is highly unlikely because we seldom examine the underlying regularities of school life, such as never comparing teachers. If schooling cannot be improved, he suggests, needed educational solutions will have to be found in alternative institutions.

In this chapter I have examined together the forces of resistance and the sources of motivation with which career ladder and incentive pay programs interact. Hopefully, I have identified some of the underlying regularities behind teacher motivation and work. My view is not so pessimistic as Sarason's. In spite of entropic trends and vanishing effects here and there, a perception of real change also prevails in numerous states and localities. After six years of strenuous effort to plan and install these programs, they at least have endured so far and gained favor in more than a few places. I will look more closely in the next chapter at what seemingly has been accomplished and where the future lies.

An Interim Assessment

In this chapter I look back at what has happened with this particular reform effort. What was started? How did it turn out ? What impact has it had? What benefits? Costs?

I also review what is currently happening in late 1989. How have programs that have been under development or in operation for a half-decade or more been changed? What do new programs look like? What issues remain and need further resolution?

SCOPE AND NATURE OF THE RESPONSE

A 1988 survey indicated that half of the states had career ladder or incentive programs with state funding or assistance. Nine state programs were also under development or already planned. At least eleven of the states were making major funding commitments to these programs, including during the 1988–89 year: Texas–$104 million;[1] Tennessee– $99 million; California– $63 million; North Carolina–$46 million; Iowa–$42 million; Utah–$41 million; New York–$25 million; South Carolina–$21 million; Arizona, Florida, and Missouri–$10 to $13 million each. In most cases, these amounts represented increased spending over earlier years. In another dozen or so states planning and pilot projects were funded with considerably smaller amounts of money (Cornett, 1988, 1989).

Not all state initiatives have persisted, however. The Florida 1983 Master Teacher Program was replaced within two years by a locally operated career ladder plan. The latter was also repealed in 1988 when the legislature failed to appropriate the required $90 million. Alabama too, after two years of development effort on a state evaluation system, repealed earlier legislation for a performance-based career incentive program. In several states where proposals were made, funding to plan programs or to launch pilot programs was never appropriated, including Arkansas, Georgia, Idaho,

Nebraska, Nevada, and New Mexico; and in Wisconsin funding of initial pilot projects was actually stopped in 1988–89. Overall, then:

> In most states that have put substantial funding into incentive programs, funding increased or held steady in 1988 and 1989; if states had provided no funding for plans, that remains the case.
>
> (Cornett, 1989)

Models and Distinguishing Features

Six program models were identified. For each of five models an exemplary program was described. For the other model, *area incentives*, studies were cited that indicated the nature of specific supplements and the approximate numbers of teachers receiving them.

A superior teacher program is designed to identify and reward the best teachers with promotion and/or extra pay. The quality of instruction presumably will be improved by attracting and retaining those who perform best. The salary system will become competitive with those in other districts, or even other industries, for the most productive personnel.

Of the five models, this one reflects most directly a response to the merit pay mandate contained in several national commission reports (see chapter 1). It is also the model most strongly resisted by educators. The early demise of the Florida Master Teacher program and the relatively low ratings given the performance component of the Utah program are but two of many examples of the failure of merit pay to receive strong, widespread endorsement from the educational community. The great majority of plans under development or consideration in the late eighties emphasized more popular features found in other models. According to one report, Georgia lawmakers failed to appropriate the $11 million needed to start an incentive plan in 1989 that had already been tested in several districts because it would benefit fewer than half the teachers. This action followed strong lobbying by teacher groups for across-the-board raises before giving bonuses to a few (*Augusta Chronicle*, 9 April 1989).

The student learning model also focuses on a major reform theme, that is, rewarding those whose students learn well. In operating these programs attention is drawn to the attainment of important teaching objectives and how student learning can be measured. Whereas performance assessment in the superior teacher model is accomplished by observing and judging how one teaches, determining what students have learned from their teacher is the primary aim in this model. The one stresses process, the other outcome.

Again there is dissent. Whereas the bottom line for the public is how much students learn, educators are particularly sensitive to the many factors that influence learning and the difficulty in telling how much blame or credit should be attributed directly to the teacher. In many incentive pay programs, student learning is one of several items assessed because legislative directives insist it be used. In very few so far, however, are student data the primary source determining incentive pay. The individual bonus plans in South Carolina and the school-based incentive plans in Florida, South Carolina, and Campbell County, Virginia were the major programs underway in 1988 where student learning data were the primary determiners of performance pay.

Staff development programs are considerably less controversial and more widely available. One long-standing practice, paying teachers extra for completing graduate degrees, is one of the two primary reasons in most school districts why some teachers are paid more than others. The other, of course, is years of teaching experience. In many states taking a course or two, or participating in a specified amount of in-service activity every few years, is even a requirement for teaching certificate renewal.

The purpose of such programs is improvement of teaching by broadening the knowledge base or skill repertoire. Their connection with everyday teaching, however, is usually incidental and seldom monitored.

The Orange County, Virginia, program, however, is an exception to the general pattern. The program is conducted during regular classroom teaching. As with other incentive pay models, observation, recording, rating, and clinical conferencing are conducted. What gives this particular program a staff development flavor are that the decision of what to work on is the teacher's, including nothing at all if one so chooses; a limited scope for the performance assessment; and a heavy emphasis on improvement. For incentive pay purposes, no attempt is made to provide summative assessment of one's total teaching performance. To be rewarded one only needs to demonstrate competency or proficiency in one skill area at a time, that is, that one can teach a set of skills; not whether they are used regularly or whether one can or does use other skills as well.[2]

Because of the attention to teacher evaluation caused by the installation of incentive pay and career ladder programs, many districts offer workshops and other in-service experiences built around the particular teaching practices contained in the summative instruments. All North Carolina teachers, for instance, had the opportunity to attend workshops to learn about the five teaching functions and twenty-eight practices contained in the state evaluation instrument when it was first introduced. They were paid $250 each for doing so. In Arizona pilot districts, workshops focused on measurement of student performance and learning were also widely attended and favorably received by career ladder participants.

Those high participation programs that provide incentive pay for almost everybody also trigger relatively little animosity. Egalitarian traditions are not jeopardized. What slight loss of teacher autonomy might be felt from a somewhat intensive, more highly prescriptive evaluation system is softened by everyone but a handful receiving a "merit raise." No attempt is made to distinguish between those who are truly great performers and the mass of teachers who perform up to district expectancies. No one is really stressed, as with the superior teacher or student learning models, by extra scrutiny from multiple observers and the use of several data sources.

The primary purposes are to participate in the movement for public relations reasons, to provide a shot of positive reinforcement for many teachers, and to target trouble areas for those few who truly need to improve or leave teaching. These are not unworthy purposes.

There seems to be an expanding interest in the full career model. Although the Utah career ladder serves to illustrate the model, many other programs also feature extended contract and job enlargement components. They provide teachers who are interested in more work with more paid opportunities to have it. The California mentor teacher program is of this sort. It pays teachers to spend extra time after school or at other times assisting beginning teachers, developing curriculum materials, or conducting school-related research activities. In some districts teachers take turns with these assignments so everyone who is interested will have a similar chance to gain experience and extra pay. Competition between teachers is thus minimized and those who assume these roles come from the experienced teacher ranks. They do not necessarily represent the best teachers in the district. There is no reason to consider them an elite group, compared with other experienced teachers, so petty jealousies are minimal. Meanwhile the school district offers teachers overtime work with extra pay for accomplishing extra duties deemed important. More will be said later about the kinds of responsibilities they are handling and the impact of their work on the overall organization of schools.

I should point out that in some incentive programs, selection priorities for such positions are given to those highest on a performance-based career ladder. In Danville, for example, master teachers will presumably serve as evaluators for other teachers striving for promotion on the career ladder. One of the primary Tennessee teacher association thrusts of recent years was to eliminate the restriction of eleven- and twelve-month extended contract opportunities to level III and level II teachers and to permit any teachers who were interested to be considered for such assignments.[3] Such an amendment was passed by the 1988 legislature, thus reducing some of the special reward features of the upper levels.

Eclecticism and Compromise

Most state and district programs contain elements from more than one of these models. For example, many career ladders feature high participation rates, relatively small pay supplements, limited scrutiny, and relatively easy selection standards at the lowest levels. At the highest levels, however, elements of the superior teacher model often prevail. Considerably fewer persons are selected, pay supplements above the base salary are much greater, performance standards are substantially higher, and evaluation procedures more elaborate.

The Utah career ladder, which serves as our example of the full career model, also has a performance-based merit component, encourages student learning data to be used, and offers pay incentives for teachers in high demand areas. Danville, Virginia, and Amphitheater, along with other Arizona districts, depend on both teaching process assessment and student performance data to make decisions about career ladder promotions. Many career ladder programs, including Danville's, include leadership attributes among the criteria used in determining advancement to the highest levels because these are the teachers who will be expected to become mentors and peer evaluators or to assume other job enlargement and extended contract responsibilities needed by the district. And, as mentioned earlier, most programs relate directly to staff development activities in the district as well. The criteria used for summative assessment serve also as the focus for feedback and training for formative purposes.

The eclectic nature of these programs broadens the basis for participation and the number of people who can be served. Theoretically, it should enhance their overall value by expanding their purposes as well.

In the process of program expansion, however, it is quite possible that its unique features are subverted and the original functions around which it was designed no longer are well served. As has been noted several times, political negotiations take place among various constituencies at every stage in the planning-implementation process—from state legislatures to individual school buildings. Utah provides a classic example, but "vanishing effects" can be seen also in Tennessee with eliminating the requirement that all tenured teachers be placed on the ladder and giving all teachers, not just those on levels II and III, extended contract opportunities in the summer.

Elitism features, in general, have been softened in many programs in response to the expression of resentment and jealousy between those selected and those not selected on performance criteria. The merit pay thrust, so dominant a theme in the national commission reports and early legislation, is already considered passé in many circles (ASCD, 1988).

Complexities of Planning and Installation

Development of incentive pay programs, whatever mode, is more complicated than many people realize. The long history of planning and implementation in Danville reveals the many issues that must be addressed and the many individuals who must be involved. Innumerable decisions are needed. How they can best be made is not always clear. A seemingly endless number of situations must be considered and procedures worked out to cover them consistently and fairly from one setting or time to another. The Texas directives specify among hundreds of other items, for example, that if a school district assigns a teacher to another grade level or subject over her objections, she cannot subsequently be reassigned to a lower career ladder level for three years on the basis of performance appraisals.

Even the basic decision to have or not have a plan is not taken lightly. In Virginia, most school districts in which superintendents said they had never seriously considered incentive pay for teachers admitted under close questioning that one or more of the following activities had occurred: School boards discussed the topic, literature was searched, plans already in operation were reviewed, staff recommendations were received, and special task forces were established to explore the possibilities and make recommendations. Those who more actively considered the idea and ultimately rejected it, and especially those who actually decided to develop a plan, typically took longer and engaged in still more of these and other activities. The national reform reports, outside consultants, and a state pilot study, according to the superintendents in four districts, were influential in deciding to proceed with a plan (Brandt and Gansneder, 1987).

Not only is the planning and development process complicated. It takes time. None of the plans reviewed in this book were thoroughly institutionalized by summer 1989. Tennessee probably came closest, having been implemented at all levels for several years. With changes in the governorship and legislature, however, and subsequently in those persons in charge of the career ladder program, several procedural changes were made in the 1987 and 1988 legislatures and more may be forthcoming. Uncertainty remains over how long something akin to the original career ladder proposal of Governor Alexander will operate in Tennessee.

In Arizona decisions had not yet been made by December 1989 regarding continuation and possible expansion of career ladder programs beyond the five-year pilot activities. In North Carolina difficulties in obtaining agreement about the criteria and measurement processes for the highest level of the North Carolina plan kept it from becoming operational at all levels during the four-year pilot period. In brief, then, such programs demand an extensive amount of planning and leadership over a several year period if they are to have much chance to succeed. Potentially, those who initiated the effort had high hopes for major school improvement once they became operational. But developing and launching them well requires skillful leadership and much time and effort. The cost is great. What about the results? Are they having a positive impact? Is the reform working as it was intended?

IMPACT TO DATE (FALL 1989)

It is still too early to assess the long-term impact of this reform effort. While first-order change is seen here and there in teacher evaluation practices, the monitoring of student learning, and teacher pay policies, second-order change in which new structural arrangements exist for the delivery of instruction and the organization of schools is not yet apparent (Cuban, 1988, p. 235; Watzlawick et al., 1974). The basic structures of school life remain unchanged. Teachers and students, for example, have the same schedules and assignments as before. Principals have the same responsibilities also. The major change in their lives is a much greater amount of time and attention to the monitoring and supervising of classroom instruction; but this is a priority shift, not a new function.

One might argue that the use of teachers to mentor and, in some places, evaluate other teachers is the beginning of second-order change. The increased emphasis on the assessment of quality and the selection of teachers for extra pay and responsibility on the basis of meritorious performance, where it truly exists and has not yet vanished, might also be considered second-order change in perhaps the most egalitarian-oriented of American institutions, the public school. The evidence that much second-order change has actually occurred so far is certainly very limited.

Let me examine what has taken place as a result of the establishment of career ladders and incentive pay programs during the eighties. Various third-party evaluations have been conducted along with district or state reports of activities and sentiments. They, along with the history of various programs as described earlier, provide the basis for this assessment.

On Teacher Evaluation

According to one report (Wuhs and Manatt, 1983), twenty-six states had laws requiring the evaluation of teachers by the time *A Nation at Risk* was published. Two years later, thirty-six had enacted such legislation (NEA, 1985). The stated purposes behind most of these laws were both formative and summative, that is, to improve teachers and to assist with personnel decisions. Few specified criteria to be evaluated or provided guidelines for local districts to follow. In most states the actual design and operation of teacher evaluation were left to the districts (Stiggins and Duke, 1988, pp. 10–11).

What was actually done to evaluate teachers in the early 1980s, especially for summative purposes, was very limited and unsystematic. Principals typically rated their teachers each year on a number of teaching dimensions and general characteristics after only a few, and in some cases no, classroom visits. In the absence of specific criteria and systematic assessment procedures, many teachers were rated at the highest level on the scale on most characteristics and all but a few were never rated below the second highest level on anything. With such positively skewed feedback, it is quite understandable to find that 50 percent of all teachers believe they are among the best 10 percent in the quality of their teaching (MGT, 1988). The ratings most teachers had received indicated there was little, if any, room for improvement.

Not to rate teachers near the top of the scale obligates administrators to show where performance is less than good, which in turn means more observation, record keeping, and feedback communication. As a consequence, many principals were able to avoid such extra hassle as long as the primary purpose of summative observation was to identify a few unsatisfactory performers. When the purpose was extended to merit pay decisions, other tactics were needed.

It was obvious that traditional rating procedures would not discriminate fairly and effectively for merit pay purposes between those who were exceptionally good and everybody else. What happened, therefore, wherever incentive pay was mandated, was immediate attention to the development of adequate evaluation procedures. In several states (Alabama, Delaware, and Oklahoma) legislation and funding promoted improvements in teacher evaluation without starting career ladder programs later (Cornett, 1988).

The most widely recognized immediate effect of the incentive pay and career ladder movement, therefore, was the redesign of summative evaluation systems. Where little if any useful information was generated with previous procedures, newly established systems used for incentive pay are now highly prescriptive, relatively elaborate, and quite costly in the time and resources needed to operate them. They must be designed so they discriminate consistently and well at the upper as well as the lower end of the performance distribution.

Most of the new systems generate various kinds of data and judgments from several people as well. Teaching functions to be included among the criteria assessed are typically selected from research studies of effective teaching, that is, teaching practices which correlate with student learning. Other criteria may be included as well, if there is near-consensus of their importance among those who design the system.

Teacher manuals describe the variables to be studied, indicators to look for, examples to follow, and forms on which to record observational data systematically. Principals are joined by other school personnel, including teachers, to serve as evaluators. Evaluators are given extensive training in the correct use of the rating or low inference coding systems. While the great majority of summative instruments in use today are multistep rating scales, with judgments ranging from very poor to very high performance, evaluators are instructed and trained to write objective, narrative descriptions of teaching behavior and class activity during classroom observations.[4] After each visit evaluators usually retreat to a quiet place to complete the running event record they have made so it is legible and accurate. Evaluators then review these records closely looking for evidence of how the various teaching practices to be rated were actually manifested, and then rate how well they think each practice was conducted. The narrative records, as well as the ratings, are typically used later to share with other evaluators and provide feedback to teachers in post-conferencing.

In North Carolina, evaluators actually code script tapes, assigning numbers of the teaching practices to the various teacher behaviors scripted, prior to filling out a data analysis sheet. For example, the script tape teacher statement, "you have a good memory" was coded 5.1, which refers to the teaching practice:

> Teacher provides feedback on the correctness or incorrectness of in-class work to encourage student growth.

This along with several other 5.1 coded behaviors led the evaluator of this lesson to list 5.1 as one of the strengths observed on the Formative Observation Data Analysis (FODA) sheet that he filled out and used to give the teacher feedback about the lesson, and to provide the principal with a record of it for summative purposes later on.

In addition to a list of teaching practices considered strengths and of those needing improvement, FODAs contain general interpretations of how well each of the five teaching functions (each consisting of several teaching practices) is judged to have been carried out. For this particular lesson, the FODA comments covering the Instructional Feedback function (practices 5.1 to 5.4) were as follows:

> Feedback on in-class work was prompt, specific, and positive. It was incremental and related to each specific task, helping to clarify and elaborate "making lesson understanding and success high."

Late in the school year, to show how this example is used for summative purposes, the principal rereads the FODAs for all of the lessons observed that year and fills out a form in which he makes general comments and rates each of the five instructional functions along with three other functions covering out-of-class responsibilities (such as planning, record keeping, communicating within the school and community). He rated the Instructional Feedback function, in the above case, at the fifth step on the six-step scale ("Well above Standard").

As indicated for the North Carolina teacher appraisal instrument, not all of what teachers do is seen during classroom teaching. Important dimensions of overall teaching performance to be assessed include the quality of their planning, for example, collegiality with other teachers, and professionalism outside as well as inside the classroom. Teacher absenteeism is a major problem in many districts today, so attendance is an important criterion in many teacher evaluation systems.

Highly selective systems typically require several observations (both announced and unannounced) during the year, usually by more than one evaluator. In Lynchburg, Virginia, teachers are often observed by two individuals simultaneously in order to estimate interobserver agreement and enhance the consistency of rating practices. Evaluators are trained extensively in observation, recording, and rating processes both with the use of videotapes and in live classrooms. In Florida and Tennessee, among other places, evaluators had to pass previously scored criterion observation tapes before being allowed to function in these roles.

Assessment of some noninstructional variables does not always depend on so many judges or such systematic procedures as are used in classroom observations. As a result, ratings may be somewhat inflated or deflated depending on general attitudes of the evaluator. Principals' ratings in North Carolina of the three noninstructional functions have typically been significantly higher on average than ratings of the five instructional functions that were derived from a review of several observation reports (FODIs and FODAs) of classroom visits made by two or more evaluators (Division of Personnel Relations, 1988a). In many pilot districts, furthermore, peer observers participate along with principals in the final assessment of these latter functions as well.

As described in chapter 2, seven different instruments are used to collect and score performance data that determine career ladder placement of Tennessee teachers. In this process, a teacher under review for level II or III is observed six times, submits various records, is interviewed three times, takes tests of reading, writing, and professional knowledge; students and principals fill out questionnaires; and three state-trained peer evaluators from outside the district and on leave from their own school systems make a consensus rating from their visits and review of data.[5]

Although other systems are not usually so elaborate, most selective plans do depend on several kinds of data from a variety of sources. Our survey of eleven Virginia school systems found that, other than two districts that based awards completely on student outcome data, all districts used at least two sources, several used three or four, and one (Danville) actually collected data from six sources. Along with observations by both administrators and other teachers, student performance data were collected, students' and parents' opinions were surveyed, and teacher records examined. Student learning and performance data were required in five districts and optional in another. Peer observations were made in five districts as part of the evaluation system. Self-evaluation served as a source of data in three districts; only one of them has a highly selective plan. Although self-evaluation serves a useful function in formative evaluation, its utility in summative evaluation is question-able, especially when it leads to merit pay or promotion. The teacher faces a conflict of interest between providing accurate information and receiving an award.

Prior to the incentive pay movement of the eighties, what passed as summative evaluation did not really differentiate at the upper end of the performance distribution nor, in fact, at the lower end either. It was not very costly in time or effort. It was not taken very seriously by either those who administered it, that is, principals, or those who were evaluated, the teachers. With the advent of incentive pay and career ladder reform, better systems for evaluating teacher performance were needed. The result is an impressive array of new measures and procedures designed for that purpose. A third-party evaluation of the Utah program, after its initial implementation stage, stated succinctly:

> More frequent and effective teacher evaluations is the single greatest effect of the Career Ladder System.
>
> (Amsler et al., 1988)

I shall examine some of the differences these evaluation systems have made in instruction, learning, and other areas in the next sections.

On Instruction

An incentive system for teachers should not be judged on

whether it makes them try harder, rather on how much they improve. Most teachers, I believe, work hard at what is a difficult job. Secondary teachers have five or more classes to teach daily with almost no time for planning, organizing materials, grading, or conferencing with students in between. Preparation, evaluation of student work, and record keeping must be done after school and on the weekends. Moments to reflect seriously about what and how to teach are few and far between.

Despite fewer students to teach, elementary teachers have a wide range of subjects to cover—much wider than earlier in the century—and considerable variation in student abilities and backgrounds with which to contend. There is convincing evidence that home conditions are typically less supportive and children more at risk than ever before. There are certainly many distractions to teaching and learning in most school classrooms today, whatever the grade level or subject.

To bear the teaching burden well and cope successfully with the many tasks and decisions teachers face daily, hourly, class by class, and student by student, they must establish various routines and more than a semblance of order. Materials need to be available when needed, equipment in working order and ready for use, and student work monitored closely. More importantly, students need to stay busy and interested and be successful with most of their work and participation in school life if they are to learn very much. Teachers have a sizable orchestra to conduct, many scores to know and play in the course of a single day; even more in the course of a year. In order not to be overwhelmed by the cacophonous sounds and sights of today's classrooms—and some are—they must take shortcuts in how they teach and streamline their own activities over what they might prefer to do if they had more time and a lighter load.

Although, we believe, most teachers are hardworking, some may be less so. Our Danville ethnographic data include teacher comments about some colleagues working much harder than others. Shortcuts to full involvement include using the same materials they have used before, giving students busywork which is never checked, and leaving school when pupils do without papers to grade, materials to prepare, or lessons to construct. For such persons, summative evaluation might be useful in causing them to shape up or ship out, either of which will improve instruction.

But, I repeat, the vast majority of teachers are viewed both by me and their colleagues as very busy in their jobs and trying hard enough. A good summative system does not improve teaching by causing them to work harder. It does so by giving them a yardstick against which they can compare themselves. It forces them to rethink how they teach and become aware of routines that need to be changed. It concentrates on skills that research shows make a difference in student learning. It provides an outside, impartial, authoritative perspective for examining the quality of instruction. In so doing, of course, it arouses anxiety and adds stress to what is already a stressful job. But years ago psychologists discovered that before new behaviors can replace old behaviors, dissatisfaction with the latter has to occur first. The first stage in learning is increased frustration with what one has been doing. Summative evaluation of teachers serves to reduce complacency with past teaching patterns, adding discomfort in the process, as a prelude to discovering better ways of teaching. Its purpose is to tell how well teaching is conducted so one can attempt to improve. It can be used again and again to see how much improvement has really taken place.

These new evaluation systems have already had a profound influence on both the monitoring of classroom instruction and seeking ways to improve it. Classroom doors have been opened as never before. Principals, assistant principals, and teacher peers are visiting classrooms to observe ongoing teaching much more frequently than they did a few years ago. These are not just casual dropin visits, furthermore. Continuous precise tallying or notetaking of what is occurring provides lengthy descriptive records for later analysis and formative feedback. Those who do the observing are carefully trained in how to observe and record, how to analyze and report, and how to confer with teachers so they are helped, not hurt. Teachers too are literally forced by the assessment process to recognize the teaching practices on which the evaluation is done and consider how congruent their own teaching is with respect to them. In school systems all over the country thousands of teachers have participated in workshops and other staff development activities to examine the generic teaching practices contained in their evaluation systems and the manner in which they can be applied in different grade levels and subjects. In North Carolina alone, stimulated by a $250 stipend, almost all of the state's teachers have participated in a thirty-hour workshop on the various teaching practices of the Teacher Performance Appraisal Instrument.

Evidence that instruction is changing as a result of all this activity is also available. Over a three-year period rating means increased in the North Carolina pilot districts and the standard deviations of evaluations decreased, as predicted. While the differences between years one and two might be attributed in part to observer and evaluator training and experience, skill improvement alone was the more likely reason for the second to third year increases (Holdzkom et al., 1989). In a separate third-party evaluation study, trained readers examined and rated the evaluation records of three hundred teachers and principals over a three-year period. Teacher performance ratings were significantly higher on all five classroom teaching functions in 1988 than in 1986 (Research and Service Institute, 1988).

Similar findings are reported elsewhere. In Orange County, Virginia, for example, where 95 percent of the teachers participate in a pay-for-performance program, 90 percent achieve at least a proficiency rating on at least two of three performance indicators (Manning, 1988). Teaching skills can definitely improve in measurable ways as a result of incentive plans which are developed around a sound evaluation system.

Teachers involved as peer evaluators and teaching mentors engage in a variety of activities that temporarily take them out of their own classrooms. However, what they do contributes to their own as well as others' instructional efficacy. Those who gain the most, we have been told over and over, are the observers themselves. Typically these are among the strongest teachers in a district, yet they are first to admit how much they have learned by watching others teach. And they in turn, quite often, are asked by those whom they mentor to teach their classes and demonstrate various teaching skills. Doors are being opened, and teachers as well as principals are watching each other teach increasingly. This cannot help but improve instruction.

Teacher absenteeism has been cut back in many districts (Danville, Lexington, South Carolina, and so on) after including attendance criteria in the evaluation system. One instance was reported of a father staying home from work to take care of a sick child, so the mother's attendance record would not be ruined. Numerous examples of increased communication with parents and increased attention to other teacher performance criteria can be found in the Danville ethnographic data.

Many educators take offense at the precise, and therefore limited, structure of the particular evaluation systems in place and the threat their use in summative evaluation imposes. They opt instead for a kinder, gentler system that leaves decisions about what needs improvement and how to go about it more with the teacher. This preferred model for improvement is often referred to as clinical supervision. Its goal is formative not summative. Supervisors are to serve as partners in the self-evaluation which teachers engage in as they try to improve one or more aspects of their teaching. Teachers set the objectives for improving their teaching, that is, they determine what to work on, and use the supervisor to rethink how else they might try to teach, to observe and perhaps record attempts to change, and to assess how well their efforts work. The choices of what to work on, how to go about it, and how to judge its effectiveness remain with the teacher. The supervisor is to assist in this self-evaluation and facilitate growth by bringing up other perspectives for the teacher to consider. Under the clinical supervision strategy, improvement occurs best when a teacher recognizes a need to do so and along lines that she thinks might be most productive. The clinical supervisor serves as a mirror against which to reassess one's notions of how best to teach.

The Orange County, Virginia, Pay for Performance program is, in most respects, quite consistent with this theoretical position. So are many other staff development programs. Teachers are paid for participating in in-service or professional development activities of their own choosing. How they participate, however, and what they derive from them are not closely structured or monitored by others. Research evidence of solid improvements in overall teaching as a result of participation in staff development programs is barely existent.

On the other hand, comprehensive summative evaluation of teaching adds needed rigor and objectivity to the assessment process which cannot help but improve teaching. The early evidence suggests this indeed is happening.

On Student Learning[6]

The concomitant and even more important criterion is student learning. Are students really learning more as a result of a career ladder and incentive pay system for teachers? As far as the public is concerned, the answer to that question is the "bottom line" in determining how well the schools are doing and, in this case, the reform is working. Mark Musick of the Southern Regional Education Board believes the South is more committed than ever to improving the quality of its schools; but he adds: "The public will stay committed only if you can prove that students in the South are learning more year after year" (Musick, 1987, p. 8).

Student learning has been written into career ladder and incentive pay legislation and other policy directives as a major criterion for assessing teacher performance in several states and districts. Arizona, South Carolina, and some Utah districts require student achievement data to be used for making decisions about incentive pay or career ladder advancement. Texas requires teachers to assess their own students' learning as part of their summative evaluation procedure, although the data are not scored or used in the final assessment process. School incentive plans, similar to the South Carolina campus model in which the teaching staff receives bonuses if their schools score at or above predicted achievement test targets, are already operating or have been proposed in Florida, Georgia, Kentucky, and Louisiana. Information about student progress has recently been added to the data collected on Tennessee career ladder candidates. The stated purpose of such directives is to reward teachers for superior student learning.

Schools have responded with two kinds of plans. One is the school-based program mentioned above in which schools receive extra instructional resources if their students meet established targets. Teachers also receive individual bonuses on an equal basis, if any other individual criteria, such as attendance, are met. The other type of plan is one in which teachers are judged individually and given bonuses if their students meet or exceed specific learning or performance targets. In many programs of this sort, teachers establish their own goals and select appropriate measurement processes early in the year, and provide data near the end of the year documenting how well they have been met. Ratings are made by peer-dominated panels of the significance and amount of student learning.

Objections have been raised in the educational community about the fairness and validity of these practices and even the general principle of basing the assessment of teaching on student performance. The use of standardized achievement tests as the primary criterion is attacked on many grounds (e.g., Berk, 1988; Glass, 1989). One primary reason is their lack of curricular validity, that is, inconsistency with what teachers are responsible to teach. The local AFT association took the St. Louis School District to court over a policy that put teachers on probation if half of their students did not achieve at the national norm on the California Achievement Test and attain one month's learning progress for each month in the classroom. A comparative analysis of the test, the curriculum guide, and assigned textbooks for the four grades studied showed only a 9.5 percent overlap of all content items (*Education Week*, 3 June 1987).

Where a single test is used year after year, especially with bonus money attached to it, test security becomes particularly crucial. We have heard instances of teacher cheating, i.e. that is, not just teaching to the test but teaching actual items and correct answers (e.g., *Wall Street Journal*, 2 November 1989). Another commonly recognized problem stems from the instability of average pupil gain scores from one class to another and one year to the next. Teachers vary considerably in how much their students learn from one time to another. Different teachers show up as superior teachers from one class to another when student gain scores on standardized tests are the sole criterion (Medley, Coker, and Soar, 1984).

Because of differences in what teachers are responsible to teach and the instability of pupil gain scores, most incentive programs that require the use of standardized tests as a primary criterion are of the school-based variety. For statistical reasons their use is more valid than when one attempts to use them to judge individual teacher performance. To take into account variations in student ability and other population characteristics that are known to influence test results, schools and districts are matched on selected demographic variables so that competition is between schools with similar socio-economic characteristics and student backgrounds.

Most incentive programs that include student data for judging individual teacher performance are of the goal-setting variety. Measures of student performance are taken early and late in a school year to assess how well specific learning objectives have been achieved by particular classes.

Teachers initially need assistance in selecting and refining goals and in designing plans for documenting how well these goals are achieved. Outside or district test experts are often used to provide in-service training in how to specify goals in measurable ways, and even to help with the administration and scoring of performance instruments. In some cases, districts design their own criterion referenced tests or use commercial test-item banks to construct pre- and post-measures for particular grades and subjects.

In Aiken, South Carolina, for example, alternate test forms are constructed annually from a commercial test bank. Teachers express teaching objectives in the form of specific percentage gain scores for their classes. Similar measures are selected and administered by other parties for all teachers of similar subjects and grade levels. According to the program coordinator, teachers are very happy to have this amount of assistance in designing and conducting the measurement processes. They like the objective, impartial adminis-tration and computerized scoring of the process. A panel of teachers helps oversee the design of the tests to ensure appropriate coverage and judges the significance of the target objectives and results.

A major problem with the individual goal-setting approach is the lack of local norms and common standards to help interpret how significant the learning has been. Typically, teacher panels examine the plans and rate how difficult the learning targets are and how substantial the real learning would be if they are attained. Points are assigned in various Arizona, Utah, and South Carolina districts which, when combined with points for other components of the evaluation systems, provide an overall ranking of individual performances for incentive pay purposes.

I have seen few programs so far, however, where student outcome data for individual teachers have been the primary reason teachers have been or not been awarded incentive pay. In many South Carolina districts learning goals have been met by most of the applicants and the numbers of applicants have not exceeded the bonus money available. If greater participation rates occur in the future, the system would become more competitive and the points assigned for documented student learning would become more important.

Flowing Wells School District, Arizona, provides another example of the early cautious use of student outcome data for performance-based pay decisions. Of eighty-seven candidates under review for career ladder promotion in 1987–88, only five did not receive the full ten points possible for their student achievement results. I am told much the same story in Amphitheater, a neighboring district.

In brief, student learning is perhaps the most important criterion in the eyes of legislators, school board members, and community leaders. Educators, for very good reasons, are uneasy about the whole notion of judging teacher performance on how much students learn, but they are carefully experimenting with ways to do it. Much teacher attention is focused on what learning should really be expected and how it can be measured properly. School districts sponsor workshops for teachers in classroom testing and performance measurement. In many cases teachers are excited about seeing tangible evidence that their pupils are learning. Except for school-based pay, where the individual payments to teachers are relatively small, student outcome scores or ratings have served as supportive rather than the primary evaluation data determining awards or promotions.

Looking more comprehensively at the question of whether or

not evidence can be found connecting the operation of incentive pay programs with improved learning, we are fully aware of the difficulties in establishing clear-cut evidence of the impact of any large-scale program on student learning and development. As one third-party evaluator group states (Amsler et al., 1988):

> When policymakers . . . have attempted to attribute increased student achievement to unique program effects, they have generally been discredited. There are simply not enough reliable control variables to allow researchers to isolate the unique effects of a particular program from a host of other factors that influence student academic progress.

It was indeed many years after the launching of such currently established programs as "head start" and "chapter one" before solid and consistent evidence of their effectiveness was available to justify their continued and eventually expanded support. Early evaluation studies reported negative or at best nonconclusive findings. The delay in more positive findings was due to a considerable extent to the slowness with which major change strategies can be operational-ized and perfected. Undoubtedly also, new research designs and strategies were needed as well. In the evaluation of the federally initiated "follow through" program, for example, evaluation had to be focused first on how well various model programs were operating at various sites merely to identify those that were implemented sufficiently well to permit further testing of their effectiveness.

Despite the difficulty of macroevaluation and the uncertainty that accompanies lack of control over the majority of variables, evaluation of the effectiveness of such a major reform is desperately needed. With so many programs underway in different parts of the country, evidence of their long-range effect on the "bottom line" ought to be sought.

In this spirit one of the recommendations made by an outside panel in reviewing the North Carolina Teacher Performance Appraisal Instrument (TPAI) after the third year of the pilot program was to conduct two types of validity studies: one, to compare achievement gain scores of students taught by teachers in the pilot districts rated at standard (level 3 on the rating scale) with those rated at levels 5 and 6; a second, to compare student gains in pilot districts versus those in comparable nonpilot districts. The assump-tion behind both recommendations was that the numbers were sufficiently large and, in the second study if proper matching of districts was accomplished, there was great probability that the hundreds of contributing and counteracting factors determining student achievement would be fairly evenly balanced. If a major difference was found in student gain scores on statewide achievement tests between the two groups of teachers or the two sets of districts, the major independent variables would be strongly supported (Brandt et al., 1988). Importantly, the North Carolina career ladder program does not use student learning as a data source for judging the quality of teaching performance. Evaluation of teaching is done solely through assessing teacher behavior.

It was the second recommendation that was pursued.[7] There was hesitancy, as there should be, to ignore the complex interactions between inputs and outcomes and base the assessment of a single program school district component (i.e., that it has a career ladder) on a single measure of achievement. As many people have observed, much of what is taught and learned is never tested. Fifteen school districts were selected by another outside evaluator to match the fifteen pilot districts on the basis of geographic location, average daily membership, per-pupil expenditure, and percentage of students planning to attend college. On the criterion variable, however, the two groups turned out to have slightly different district averages in 1986 (spring of the first year) with pilot districts three to five percentiles higher.

California Achievement Tests are given near the end of each year throughout the state in grades three, six, and eight. School district average scores were compared over the first three years of the career ladder. For two years in a row students in the pilot districts, taken as a group, evidenced more gain in student achievement than those in the nonpilot districts.[8]

In Arizona, achievement test scores of students (grades 2-6) in the seven original pilot districts were compared with those of students in all non-career ladder districts for a seven year period (1981-1988). Approximately 40,000 students were involved per grade. The California Achievement Test was used through 1985 and the Iowa Test of Basic Skills since then. In one type of analysis adjustments were made for factors which are likely to affect achievement but over which teachers have no control (e.g., age, gender, ethnicity, primary language). Students' actual scores were compared with their expected scores. In all years, average scores of students in the career ladder districts were above expectations while those of students in the non-career ladder districts were below expectations. Furthermore, average achievement on career ladder districts was higher during each of the later years when the career ladder was in effect.

In the second type of analysis, average achievement scores of non-career ladder districts were subtracted from those of career ladder districts. The differences between the two types of districts increased considerably after the introduction of the program in 1985 (from 1½ points in 1981 to more than 3 points for 1986, 1987, and 1988). Overall, student achievement increased on average in career ladder districts; it did not in the others (Braver and Helmstadter, 1989).

Academic achievement gains were reported also for South Carolina schools during the reform years, although no comparisons were attempted between students of teacher participants with those of nonparticipants. Among the findings were improvements in the first five grades on the CTBS in most skill areas and a thirty-five-point improvement on the SAT over a four-year period (Division of Public Accountability, 1988). On the other hand, no appreciable correlation was found between the percentage of teachers in a school receiving individual incentive awards and the school gain index (MGT, 1989).

Other than the Arizona and North Carolina findings, information about the impact of teacher incentive pay on student learning is still quite limited. It comes primarily from the opinions of program participants. Many teachers and principals do believe that instruction and learning have both improved as a function of career ladder and incentive pay programs (Amsler et al., 1988). More substantial data are being collected in the Arizona pilot districts to study the impact of the career ladder program on student achievement production and outcomes. Several research methodologies are being employed: (a) pre-test, post-test, gain score elements, (b) multivariate regression analysis, (c) canonical correlation, and (d) qualitative matrix paradigm (Packard and Dereshiwsky, 1988 a,c).

On School Culture

Many authorities have suggested that reforms will not have lasting effects unless basic changes occur in the structural organization of schools and the roles and responsibilities of principals and teachers (e.g., Tye and Tye, 1984; Martin, Green, and Palaich, 1986). Some organizational characteristics that discourage excellence include (ASCD, 1985):

- lack of peer-support systems

- an expectation and commensurate treatment of teachers as nonprofessionals
- insufficient teacher involvement in meaningful discussions and decisions regarding classroom work
- reduced instructional time from interruptions, paperwork, and bureaucratic requirements
- little control over staff development activities
- little collaboration and lack of processes for self-directed review and revision

For improving the organization, Duttweiler (1987) suggests:

- Career ladder programs should be initiated to vertically restructure the occupation to create a hierarchy of positions in teaching that provide for enlarged responsibilities and for promotion within teaching. . . .
- The talents of outstanding teachers should be used to create a support system for both beginning and career teachers who wish to expand their skills and knowledge.
- Teachers' job descriptions should be rewritten (and the necessary budget provided) to allow time for observing other teachers, for collegial exchange, and for inservice to develop new skills.
- The decision-making structure of the school system should be redesigned. Teachers have knowledge and expertise that should be called upon when considering many of the decisions made at the school and district levels.
- Improvements in the training, selection, and performance of administrators, as well as in the procedures by which they manage the school and judge the performance of others, should become top priority.
- The school climate should encourage teacher autonomy in the classroom, good collegial relations among teachers, and a strong sense of shared values among school staff, students, and parents.

    To what extent have the programs reviewed in this book led to such improvements? My answer must be ambivalent for three reasons: It depends on which model is being considered. It depends on how well a particular program is actually implemented and how good the leadership is at both the district and school levels. It depends on what stage a program is in. Many teachers will feel less autonomous and more heavily burdened with paperwork during the early stages of a program as a result of increased observation and evaluation requirements. Those feelings should ease later on as a function of increased status and experience in handling the requirements.

There is certainly clear evidence that much of what Duttweiler proposes is already happening in many places. Teachers are visiting other teachers' classrooms. Principals have been trained in performance appraisal. Outstanding teachers have been selected to help with summative observation in some instances, mentor beginning teachers and those needing special help, and conduct various kinds of in-service instruction-related activities. The instructional expertise of teachers is being used in Arizona and South Carolina to review and assess the significance of student outcome plans; in North Carolina, in Tennessee, and in Danville, Lynchburg, and Orange County, Virginia to record observational data as part of the performance assessment process; and in many places to help design the programs, select the instruments, set the standards, and serve on various operating committees. Most career ladders are designed so that those who reach the top rungs particularly have expanded instructional responsibilities and higher status. Many have extended contracts in the summer and released time during the year to carry out such activities.

In many places, principals' roles have changed even more than teachers. Amsler and associates et al. (1988) report that the principal's attention to teacher supervision and evaluation in Utah has increased substantially with the result that less time is spent on managing other support services and on parent or community relations. While they found no clear evidence that this shift in roles had negative consequences, the magnitude of the time spent on career ladder activities was far greater than anyone had anticipated (p. 41). The performance bonus requirements demand the most attention, followed by principals' monitoring of the teacher's use of the extended contract time. Teacher accomplishments under job enlargement activities, which are typically under the direction and control of the administration, sometimes actually reduce principals' burdens. Overall, the program provides principals with a powerful tool for exerting leadership in their schools.

Heavy demands on principals' time have been seen wherever performance evaluation for promotion or incentive pay has been established. That is a major reason for creating peer evaluator or mentor teacher positions. These are essential supplemental resources to provide the necessary summative evaluation and related formative assistance required by these programs. Principals are visiting classrooms and observing teaching much more than before; but they cannot, by themselves, do all that is needed. Other people must be used to expand the judgment base both in the number of times a teacher can be observed and the number of people doing the observing.

One result from all this activity is much greater dialogue about instruction between teachers and principals; what good instruction is and is not. It takes place between teachers and evaluators in post-observation conferences. It occurs in training workshops for evaluators and teachers about specific instructional skills and student learning goals and measures. It takes place between principals, assistant principals, and peer evaluators as they review observational records and come to a consensus judgment for summative purposes. Increasingly, in the North Carolina pilot districts, for example, the teacher observer evaluators are helping principals make end-of-the-year summative judgments on the appraisal instrument.

In all this activity, the principal's own expertise as an instructional leader is most important. It is also subject to great challenge. A frequent complaint about summative evaluation is that principals lack sufficient experience and training in classroom teaching to assess teachers fairly and well and to provide appropriate assistance when it is needed. Where they are deficient and training does not improve their instructional expertise, teachers are especially prone to resist participation or support for these programs. In many places, however, training workshops for principals and their increased dialogue with teachers over teaching practices typically improve teacher confidence in the evaluation systems.

Involving expert teachers in the process has increased confidence and strengthened support even more. When asked by third-party evaluators if North Carolina observer evaluators (OEs) should participate along with principals in end-of-the-year summative ratings, most teachers as well as principals and other administrators said yes. Many principals had changed their minds after three years of experience in the pilot program (Research and Service Institute, 1988).

To perfect an evaluation system and to run it well, the assistance of expert teachers is needed (Thomas, 1985). In fact, in one Arizona district, teacher evaluators were found to record and evaluate a videotaped lesson much more completely and accurately than administrators. Their overall agreement with a scoring key was

81 percent, as against only 37 percent for the administrators. Whereas teacher evaluators supplied rich examples from the script itself to justify their ratings, the typical justification response of administrators was merely to repeat instrument descriptors (Kelley and Pope-Rolewski, 1989).

The extended contract and job enlargement components of the Utah program have been highly praised for many other important teacher contributions to school life and effectiveness (Amsler et al., 1988). Speaking of the former, they say (p. 4):

> It is almost unanimously valued by teachers, principals, superintendents, board presidents, and parents. Principals and teachers report that they are better prepared for the opening of school. Teachers are able to spend more student-contact time in direct instruction because planning, grade preparation and conferencing time no longer eat into the school day. Principals are able to convene faculty prior to school to set goals and develop school-wide curriculum plans.

The job enlargement component is typically under the direction of school administrators or committees of teachers and administrators, who determine the kinds of jobs and tasks that are needed to improve the system: What kinds of roles senior teachers ought to assume as they advance through the profession? What special instructional materials need to be developed? Mentoring of new teachers, serving on district instructional committees, and curriculum development are most frequently mentioned.

The increased involvement of teachers in all these activities and the expanded communication and shifting role patterns of principals as well as teachers suggest a changing school culture, one in which better teaching and greater learning are central goals. Along with these changes, however, is more accountability and less autonomy, especially for teachers. Countering greater teacher empowerment, as reflected in higher status and more responsibility for some, is less autonomy and more accountability for others. Thus, there may well be conflicting trends in the drive to make teaching a true profession.

Most teachers have been accustomed to teaching classes in their own style with few mandates about how best to do it. If discipline is under reasonable control and students or parental complaints are not too flagrant, they have usually been left alone to teach as they see fit. This freedom "to run one's own show," in fact, has often been cited as one of the reasons for choosing a teaching career (Lortie, 1975). It is also a major reason why many recommendations for improving teaching practice through the years have been ignored and had little impact on the way schools are run (Goodlad, 1983). Teacher autonomy is one of the profession's most zealously guarded traditions. Loss of it, in fact, lessens the claim that teaching is a profession and presumably discourages those who might otherwise be attracted to it.

Imposing an evaluation system with precise criteria spelled out and assessment by others directly threatens long-standing traditions in which self-evaluation has been the primary determiner of how teaching should be conducted. With it has come a sense of powerlessness, a loss of autonomy. For many good teachers especially, the imposition of summative evaluation is demeaning. To be downgraded if such objective indicators of good practice are not followed as having class rules posted or fully written lesson plans in hand [9] is justifiably insulting. A frequently included criterion, the modeling of accurate spelling and grammar usage, often traps many otherwise "good" teachers with mediocre ratings.

Under summative evaluation, teachers are given new directions about how to teach and outside judgment about how well they do it. Principals, as indicated earlier, are forced to enter classrooms in a substantive way and try to show how teaching can be improved. One of the primary factors underlying early resistance has been teachers' belief that principals are not sufficiently knowledgeable about instruction to provide that leadership or even to evaluate them.

Quite often they are right. Principals traditionally have achieved their positions by taking graduate courses in administration and, after a relatively few years as teachers, being offered roles as assistant principals. They have had to pass no special test as outstanding teachers to be considered for this rank. They are often made administrators at very different grade levels from those in which they have taught. The success of incentive pay programs depends in no small part, therefore, on considerable training for them on instructional evaluation practices and the components of good teaching.

Currently, then, the effort induced by these plans to upgrade the quality of instruction has three immediate effects on personnel relationships: Principals are spending much more time in classrooms dealing with instruction. Role differentiation has occurred among teachers with some, presumably those above average in expertise, having expanded responsibility beyond their own classrooms for improving the quality of instruction. The autonomy of other teachers has been lessened as the result of more explicit expectations about how to teach and closer monitoring of what they do.

Regarding the future of these trends one of two scenarios seems likely. If principals continue to be viewed as the instructional leaders of their schools, they will be selected primarily from the ranks of outstanding teachers. Those currently serving as peer evaluators and mentor teachers, whose leadership skills have been tested in these kinds of programs, will be the primary candidates for principalships. If, on the other hand, expert teachers provide the primary instructional leadership through still further expansion of their mentoring, evaluating, staff development, and instructional research activities, principals' roles will be limited to school management functions. One should be able to judge how these scenarios are playing out in a school or district by monitoring where decisions are made about promotion and merit pay, and whether teacher or principal judgment is the decisive factor.

Although there was considerable early concern with many programs that they would have a negative effect on collegiality and teacher cooperativeness (Division of Public Accountability, 1988), our ethnographic data from Danville and elsewhere suggest these fears are seldom warranted. Traditional organizational patterns preclude much opportunity anyway for teachers to work together in direct instruction roles. Most opportunities to collaborate are after school and in committee meetings, not inside the classroom. Lortie, Goodlad, and many others have focused on the isolation of teachers in the conduct of their primary function. What little evidence I have seen about how teachers relate to each other as a result of these programs suggests they reach out and actually help their colleagues achieve promotion or incentive pay.

However, the fear of direct competition, or at least not wanting to participate in these programs because they are perceived as competitive, is very real. It is a primary reason why many good teachers have not applied.

The fact that egalitarian traditions have been well preserved in most plans may account in part for both the maintenance of the collegial spirit among teachers and increasing participation and greater support after plans have become fully operational and teachers see how they can participate without competing directly with others. Extra pay for extra duty, not better quality performance, is still prevailing practice. The lack of quotas and direct comparison techniques in performance measures provides additional evidence of long-standing egalitarian patterns still in place. Hostility and resentment are strongest wherever selectivity rates are high and performance criteria most demanding. Even politicians who enact these programs become uneasy when they see low participation rates. Among the six models, it is the superior teacher and highly competitive, individually based student learning programs[10] that are most threatening and initially unpopular.

Continued rejection of excellence as a standard beyond what the majority does shows how limited the reform impact has been so far. The clarion calls of Alexander and Graham, among others, in 1983 have been sharply muted through the years since. Changes are occurring in school culture and in the roles the key actors play; but on the deeper level of structural reform that business leaders in particular attempted to impose, the intended effect has diminished in most places almost to the vanishing point.

On Pay and Budgets

It is clear that teachers' overall pay has been increased substantially in many places where incentive pay and career ladder programs were started. An increase in basic pay for all teachers was often cited as a precondition and used as a bargaining chip to gain support from teacher associations in order to start such programs.

Throughout the eighties teacher salaries across the country improved at approximately twice the rate of inflation (Boyer, 1988, p. 7). The reform reports and subsequent debates helped the public realize that teacher salaries were not competitive with those in other fields and had to be improved. Career ladders and incentive pay were considered one means of enhancing the overall expansion of financial support for schools. In Tennessee, South Carolina, and Florida, for example, the introduction of performance-based pay was a major selling point for statewide tax increases. In Virginia, school districts that started plans obtained more money from their communities, according to their superintendents, than what would have been available without them (Brandt and Gansneder, 1987).

In states that funded pilot studies for several years before deciding on longer-term or expanded commitments in this area, participating districts received extra state money to administer programs and provide awards to participating teachers. Incentive pay, therefore, is only a part of the overall response to a widely recognized need for higher teacher pay in general.

It has brought about a much more differentiated salary system with some teachers working longer hours or extra days and carrying heavier responsibilities than others. If they perform particularly well or their students achieve up to designated learning targets, they may achieve a bonus or a promotion to a higher paying rank. Thus, teacher salaries have increased, in some places substantially, as a function of their performance. The establishment of these systems has resulted in substantial reallocation of teacher salaries across districts and states. Although the funding of the supplementary components may be relatively small, as compared with base salaries or operating budgets, differences in overall pay among individuals can be substantial. In Utah, for example, career ladder expenditures amounting to about 7 percent of base pay resulted in some teachers making as much as 20 percent more than others (Amsler et al., 1988). Many of the same differences are seen in Danville and Lynchburg, Virginia, and across the state of Tennessee for those at the highest levels of the career ladder who also choose to work under extended contracts.

The Arizona pilot program provides the most completely restructured pay model. Career ladders were developed in the pilot districts with salary ranges established for each level and specific salaries designated for each of several steps within levels. Movement upward or downward within levels, as well as across levels, is based on annual performance evaluations. The salary schedule is not broken down, as in most places, between basic pay and career ladder supplements. One advantage to such a system is less controversy over whether basic or supplementary pay should be cut if budget reductions are necessary. The two are no longer separated.

A second advantage of the Arizona plan stems from an option teachers have of staying on a traditional experience and degree-based pay schedule. If their performance-based contract offer is not as high as it would be according to the traditional criteria by which teachers in non-pilot districts are paid, they can choose the latter. This feature allows teachers to try for more pay at no risk of salary loss if they do not achieve it. It also serves as a bigger incentive for younger than older teachers because the opportunity for big pay jumps is much greater for those lowest on the traditional scales. Some individuals in their fourth year of teaching are being paid as much as those in their eleventh or twelfth year because of their high performance evaluations. The alternative pay option not only benefits the teachers by giving them a choice; it helps prevent undue pressure from senior teachers to ease the performance standards. They are often the most opposed to merit pay.

Overall expenditures for incentive pay depend on three

variables: the type of award (annual bonus versus promotion to higher levels on a career ladder), the size of bonuses or pay increases for promotion, and participation rates at each award level. Even the type of annual bonus or career ladder movement can make a difference. In South Carolina, for example, individual awards for reaching student learning targets range between $2,000 and $3,000; campus awards distributed in equal amounts to faculty members when their school achieves schoolwide learning objectives range from several hundred to well over one thousand dollars. In Amphitheater, Arizona, movement from one step to another within a career level increases salary between one and two thousand dollars; movement from one level to another enhances salary by two thousand to almost six thousand dollars for the most advanced status.

Although South Carolina districts have considerable flexibility to determine the kind and size of awards and influence the participation rates within designated options and limits, the total amount of money to be spent on incentive pay is set by the state. The larger the participation rates, within these limits, the smaller the increments. Because of the fixed amount from the state, only a minority of teachers are likely to receive awards in any particular year. The chances of receiving them in the bonus model go down as the numbers of teachers trying for them go up. As a percentage of total teacher salary money for the state, incentive pay amounted to only 1.4 percent in 1987–88 when forty-four of the ninety-one districts in the state were participating (Division of Public Accountability, 1988, p. 63).

Although expenditures for incentive pay are relatively small, they represent a new item in school budgets that must compete with other items in the all-important annual review process. With desired expenditures almost always greater than resources available, new items are generally more vulnerable than long established ones. Despite all the reform attempts, the actual expenditures to support them may have been so limited that not much may happen (Inman, 1987). For career ladders and incentive pay, most states have planned and in most cases piloted programs, but few had made heavy financial commitments by summer 1989. Only about ten had spent as much as $10 million a year on them. Almost all of the latter, incidentally, were below the average in per-pupil expenditures, some well below. In 1986–87, with only New York above the average, these states ranked as follows:

27   California
28   Iowa
30   Texas
32   North Carolina
36   Missouri
42   South Carolina
44   Tennessee
46   Arizona
51   Utah

Planned programs in Alabama, Georgia, and Louisiana were not funded in 1988 or 1989. Overall, however, Cornett says (1989):

> Funding for incentive programs has generally fared well, but the programs are new; in most cases there is still debate about them; and the costs of fully operational programs are substantial. All of these factors make funding vulnerable to budget cuts. To determine if programs can achieve intended results they will need to be funded for several more years.

On Teacher Recruitment, Retention, and Career Opportunities

A major concern identified in the reform reports was the declining interest in education careers, especially of academically talented college students. The numbers of entering college students interested in becoming teachers had dropped dramatically over the previous decade. Evidence also existed that the most academically able teachers were the first to leave teaching for other pursuits. As a consequence, a major goal of many incentive pay and career ladder programs is to help attract and retain the best teachers available. They are designed to improve the working conditions and enhance long-term career opportunities for very good teachers so they will remain in the classroom rather than move into administration or out of education altogether. To what extent have these good things come to pass and career ladder and incentive pay programs had the desired effect?

It is probably too early to expect much effect specifically from incentive pay. About the only evidence available comes from surveys of teacher attitudes toward these programs, and these reports indicate skepticism that they have made a difference (e.g., MGT, 1989). There has not been time to see people coming or leaving education in sufficient numbers specifically because of the incentive plans. Most plans are only three to five years old, not long enough to identify changes in applicant pools and retention rates. We have not located current studies of the reasons why people enter or leave teaching in districts which have such programs.

What does seem relevant, however, is the amount of interest in teaching careers five or six years after all the recent reform rhetoric started and a decade or so after women in large numbers began finding high-level competing positions in business and industry. Also relevant is the teacher supply-demand balance now and in the next decade. Both of these factors should affect interest in teaching careers along with whatever incentive value career ladder programs offer.

A recent turn around has indeed occurred in the interest college students have in becoming teachers. Between 1985 and 1986 alone the number of students in four-year colleges preparing to teach jumped 13.5 percent (*Education Week*, 2 March 1988). Where teacher education programs have been upgraded in standards and status, furthermore, application rates have often doubled or even tripled. Grade point averages in courses outside education have gone up as well.

Severe teacher shortages are anticipated for the 1990s with a sizable proportion of the current population approaching retirement age. A generation ago, teachers on average were relatively young and turnover quite rapid. Only 35 percent, according to a survey in the early 1960s, had been teaching for more than four years (Charters, 1970). By 1972, 59 percent had been in the classroom that long (Mark and Anderson, 1978). By 1984 the median teaching experience nationally was reported to be 12.7 years (Harris, 1984).

Predictions of teacher supply and demand have not been particularly accurate. Murnane, Singer, and Willett (1988) found that attrition rates vary by subject specialization and by the age of teachers when they enter the profession. Tracking a cohort of 5,869 white teachers who began their careers in Michigan in 1972 or 1973, they found that between about one-third of the elementary and one-fourth of the secondary teachers who left teaching returned to it after relatively short career interruptions. Of the specialty groups studied, chemistry and physics teachers stayed the shortest time and only 13 percent returned to teaching later on. At that time starting salaries in business and industry for majors in these fields were considerably higher than salaries for majors in biology and other specialties. Ten-month teaching salaries, incidentally, were only slightly below twelve-month starting pay for college graduates in all specialties except chemistry, physics, and mathematics. The temptation to jump ship for better pay by moving to industry was certainly greater for physical scientists, and that is precisely what happened.

One long-standing career problem for teachers is what business management scholars refer to as plateauing. In teaching, it may underlie the early burnout phenomenon so common today. It may also account for some less-than-desirable teaching patterns we have mentioned before of simplifying an overly stressful classroom life by excessive use of worksheets and media which keep students occupied but not necessarily learning.

Plateauing comes from jobs becoming repetitive and routine, and losing whatever appeal and challenge they might initially have for one to grow and develop. One feels secure and stable in handling a job, but at the same time stagnant and no longer stimulated to improve. In business organizations more than in teaching, a form of structural plateauing occurs when one begins to realize that promotion to a higher level position is becoming less and less likely. Content plateauing sets in after one loses the sense of learning in one's present position. Unlike structural plateauing, which is eventually unavoidable for the vast majority of executives, content plateauing is not inevitable. No one ever knows everything. In teaching, for example, various possibilities exist for reducing plateauing.

For those who are overstressed, school-related causes can be identified and steps taken to alleviate them. Reassignment of students, reduction of classroom disturbances, rescheduling of classes, and the provision of mentoring assistance, among other seemingly minor changes in organizational patterns, can all provide substantial psychological benefits if they actually address one or more legitimate sources of complaint for individual teachers. Reduction of even one or two causes of extra stress can indeed alter one's perspective significantly and restore some of the excitement to teaching.

For those who are coping well and not overstressed, content plateauing is just as likely. The sameness from class to class and year to year in assignment, curriculum, and schedule can be just as mesmerizing as for those overstressed by complexity. The secret to improvement lies in bringing a change of focus into what one is doing.

Theoretically, at least, that is what incentive pay and career ladder plans do. They offer opportunities to expand their perspective on what they as teachers do. They sharpen one's awareness that there are other ways to teach, some of which may be better than those with which they are familiar. In many programs, they shift the focus from teaching processes to student learning. The challenge of designing ways to track student performance and documenting the amount of learning that takes place in one's classes is a new one for most teachers (Stiggins and Duke, 1988). Seeing concrete evidence that learning has actually occurred in a year's time, I have often been told by program participants, is reassuring and sometimes even exhilarating. It makes one want to try even harder the next year and reach those who are hardest to teach. The emphasis on student learning is targeted directly at what Lortie, among many others, thinks is the most powerful teacher incentive of all: the knowledge that one's efforts have had an effect.

Milstein (1989) studied ways teachers and administrators who identified themselves as plateaued attempted to cope with this condition by trying to make their role more challenging and rewarding. Their preferred ways ranked as follows:

(1) new methods, new activities, attempts to be more creative, and, for teachers, more intensive focusing on students
(2) personal activities—hobbies, exercise, attitude modification
(3) professional development activities—further education, workshops, reading
(4) changing jobs—different subjects, grades, organizational level
(5) increased involvement in the school organization—committees, extra-curricular activities

While it is too early for definitive data on the question of how much real effect these programs have had on attracting and retaining high-quality teachers, they certainly would appear to offer more career choices and opportunities than traditionally structured schools. Individuals can continue to teach within the confines of a nine-month year with vacations when children are out of school. They can continue to receive pay on the same basis as before, as most incentive plans are voluntary. They can strive for higher pay and recognition on a competitive basis without extending their teaching year. They can work longer hours or more days, without students around, to work up better plans and materials, complete the ever-increasing records and forms that are required today, conduct research or participate in curriculum development, or undertake staff development activities of one sort or another. They can accept extra months of employment in leadership roles of various kinds and approach year-round employment in pay and status as a professional educator. They can strive to become peer evaluators, lead or mentor teachers with considerably more pay and added responsibilities. Many of those I have talked to in these roles have exclaimed about how much they themselves have learned about good teaching from visiting other classrooms and concentrating on assessing what goes on, even though they had been selected because they were already considered very effective. The recognition that there are always ways to improve is an essential condition to the prevention or reduction of content plateauing. As Bardwick (1986, p. 7) states it:

> No one ever knows everything; no one has done everything. There are no limits to change and challenge except those created by personal fear or organizational laziness.

The several options created by these plans are certainly congruent with the various motives underlying teachers' reactions to the Danville career ladder plans and those that can be inferred from evaluation reports of teacher responses and sentiments toward other plans as well. Responses to incentive plans of any sort will always depend on how they impact the ever-changing network of needs and motivations that shape human behavior. The data clearly show that great differences exist in why teachers are teaching and what they want out of their careers. To the extent that these programs open up the options, they should enhance the attractiveness of teaching for increasing numbers of people.

On Attitudes

Much commentary throughout this volume has reported reactions of teachers and others to teacher incentive pay and career ladder programs and their many features. These attitudes vary with the program, the stage it is in when they are assessed, the group whose sentiments are under consideration, and the specific feature under discussion.

They also vary greatly according to the means of assessment. Third-party anonymous surveys, the primary mechanism for many reports, are subject to many weaknesses. Response rates are usually not very high, often under 50 percent. The specific way in which questions are worded may trigger defensiveness or tendencies to give a socially acceptable response, despite the promise of anonymity, rather than true feelings. When individuals are asked if a program has caused them to work harder or teach better, they must first admit at least to themselves that they had not been trying relatively hard or teaching particularly well to respond yes. Psychologically, this is not an easy admission, especially for those who think they are already among the best teachers. More than half of the South Carolina teachers indicated they thought they were among the best ten percent of teachers in their districts (MGT, 1989, p. 38). When teachers are asked if they believe that those doing the best job should receive more pay the majority say yes. Who can be against such a simple principle? Putting this principle into specific practice, however, is another matter; and the initial reaction to many plans of how to do it is often quite negative.

One other tendency, I believe, prevents a faithful reporting of true feelings in many surveys. Polling people's attitudes on just about everything has become common practice in our culture. Media reports include as much about the reactions of people to events as about the events themselves. Polls are used by political candidates to try to influence the elections themselves. In a number of instances, surveys of teacher reaction to incentive pay and career ladder programs have been used to try to force their modification if not elimination. Teachers know that without some semblance of teacher support, school boards and legislatures will be hesitant to mandate their continuance. I have seen survey questionnaires designed to elicit certain results, which are then used to say it is not working and should be discontinued. I have heard of organized efforts to encourage teachers to respond in particular ways in order to gain ammunition to fight its continued promotion. And I have heard concerns raised many times by legislators, board members, and other instigators of this particular reform over low participation rates and a lack of apparent interest on the part of those it is presumed to benefit. Paraphrasing one Danville task force member (Brandt, 1988, p. 121): "If teachers will support it, it will work. If they don't, it won't work."

The use of polls to influence program decisions not only works to some extent; it also distorts the results from reflecting accurately how people feel. In assessing attitudes, therefore, I lean more heavily on ethnographic and interview data than on survey reports. I consider what teachers actually do when they have a choice to make. Participation rates are more important indicators of teacher interest, with all the pros and cons factored in, than what they say they will do.

Having stated a number of caveats, let me highlight what I think are the overarching attitude patterns. I do not intend to report again the many specific reactions that were generated toward various program characteristics or the numerous planning issues that were faced. What I shall attempt are several generalizations, first about teacher reactions and then about those of other stakeholders.

Negative reactions predominate in the early stages of many programs. Teachers are initially upset for several reasons (see pp. 153 - 164). Confusion and concern prevail over how a program will work and what it will mean to each person. Teachers have been accustomed to being treated as a group. No longer will that be so. Some will be promoted and receive extra pay; others will not. It may not even be clear at first who might apply, much less be accepted. There is much uncertainty, and uncertainty promotes discomfort and lowers morale. The vast majority of both teachers and principals in the South Carolina pilot districts responding to a 1989 survey disagreed or strongly disagreed with the statement: "Morale improved at my school as a result of TIP" (MGT, 1989). Yet, teacher morale has been low throughout the country during the eighties, and 40 percent of South Carolina teachers as a whole actually said it improved between 1983 and 1987. This was the highest percentage of such responses reported in any of the states (Boyer, 1988, p. 80).

Negative sentiments soon give way to mixed or more positive attitudes, depending on how well the program is implemented and related to other school goals (Amsler et al., 1988; Hart and Murphy, 1989; MGT, 1989, E–15). Successful participants are typically much more positive than nonparticipants. Feelings about these new programs remain strong in both directions, some individuals highly enthusiastic about what they have accomplished and the opportunities they provide, while others claim they have divided the faculties, imposed more stress, and dampened whatever enjoyment for teaching people previously had. Early complaints about the overburden of record keeping were eased somewhat as districts streamlined procedures and teachers gained experience in dealing with them. Extra evaluation require-ments for program participants, which often are accompanied by extra responsibilities if one is successful, continue to both discourage some good teachers from applying and provide "legitimate" explanations for others not trying. The continued strength of both pro and con sentiments suggests the programs are indeed having major impacts. If little were changed, few would react strongly.

Performance-based components and highly selective programs tend to draw the greatest amount of hostility. In Utah, for example, the performance bonus is the least popular of the four components. Heavy lobbying by the UEA has kept the minimum state requirements for funding it at 10 percent of the overall district allocation (in the original bill, it was to have been increased to 30 percent after the first year). It does have its supporters, however. Although the other three components were rated higher, teacher ratings of the contributions of the performance bonus early in the third year of implementation averaged near the midpoint of the rating scale on most items.

A benefit of the bonus is its emphasis on teacher evaluation (Amsler et al., 1988, p. 5):

> By requiring principals to systematically evaluate teachers, it has served in some schools to reinstate the principal as the instructional leader.

In schools where principals have to choose only a few teachers for bonuses out of a larger pool of teachers considered good by both the principal and their colleagues, fragmented relationships have often resulted and the adequacy and fairness of the evaluation system have been questioned.

Extended contract and job enlargement provisions tend to be evaluated very favorably as long as they are open to all and not restricted to those judged superior. Teachers say, among other things, that they increase their opportunities to plan for instruction, develop curriculum, take care of records, and be paid for work they once did on their own time for no pay (Amsler et al., 1988).

Career ladder components generally include features of the three other components. For successful participants, teaching is judged to be superior and overall performance above average. Responsibilities are expanded outside of one's own classroom teaching. Quite often they must be carried out after school in the afternoon, on weekends, or during the summer months on extended contract.

New roles and responsibilities are not easily defined and incorporated into ongoing organizational structures. Mentoring responsibilities with new teachers, and with experienced teachers who require special assistance, are perhaps the best attempts so far. Teachers who serve as peer observers or evaluators on career ladder review committees are providing very needed expert resources to help run per-

formance-based programs that require extensive, fair teacher evaluation and summative judgments about the quality of teaching. They
expand the judgment base and assistance pool considerably.

Teachers, and teacher unions especially, were divided or even
hostile in some places at first about the extra status and responsibility
conferred by promotion of some individuals to special positions as
mentor teachers or peer evaluators. Formerly clear lines between
management and labor functions were blurred. Some felt it was not
appropriate for teachers to be judging other teachers. That was
management's responsibility. So I find in some systems no
involvement of teachers in the judgment process. In Orange County,
Virginia, for example, teachers observe and record objectively
teaching behaviors that illustrate previously designated indicators of
good teaching practice. Principals then rate these records against
previously designated scoring standards. The teacher observers
themselves make no ratings.

In Danville, Virginia, however, and in an increasing number of
North Carolina pilot districts, peer evaluators sit down with
principals after observations have been made by both parties to come
up with a consensus rating about the quality of performance based
on several observations. According to teachers, the fairness,
objectivity, and acceptability of the teacher evaluation system are
typically enhanced as more and more teachers are involved in the
process (MGT, 1988, p. 43).

Contributions to school and district instructional materials
from teacher job enlargement activities are increasingly heralded.
Under job enlargement components teachers are paid to tackle
important instruction-related assignments at times when they are
not overburdened with regular teaching. New products and
information are obtained for both the school district and individuals as the special expertise of teachers is stimulated to direct
attention on real school problems. New ideas should be generated
for the improvement of schools. For the teachers concerned,
concept plateauing should be detained. The job enlargement
feature of these programs is strongly endorsed by teachers and
administrators alike (Amsler et al., 1988). Although changes in
teacher role so far toward differentiated staffing organizational
patterns are only of a first-order variety, they are both substantial
and viewed quite positively by teachers and administrators.

*Isolating the effects of teacher incentive pay from those of other reform
programs is not easy.* In Utah the career ladder program was the

primary instrument for reform. In South Carolina it was only one component out of several dozen in what may well have been the most comprehensive state reform legislation in the country, the Education Improvement Act of 1984. Included in that act were increasing graduation requirements, limiting interscholastic athletic participation to those who passed their courses, requiring kindergartens in each district, establishing eligibility criteria for gifted and talented programs, and dozens of other provisions. Related directly to TIP were a school incentive reward program, a principal incentive program, competitive grants for schools, a loan program for teachers in areas of critical need, and the establishment of a division of public accountability to monitor all the effort. In between Utah and South Carolina were many states with comprehensive reform packages that included a mandate for teacher incentive pay.

Teacher reactions to the various programs that emerged from these statewide reform efforts were assessed after five years by the Carnegie Foundation for the Advancement of Teaching. Salaries improved 46 percent during that period (1983–87). Three teachers in five across the country indicated salaries were better. One in four indicated job security was greater, and 26 percent (again, one in four) said career ladder options had increased at their school. Twice as many teachers indicated special awards for teachers had increased at their schools as those who said they had decreased (Boyer, 1988).

In the state-by-state comparisons, most of the eight programs that established teacher incentive pay or career ladders as key elements in 1983 or 1984 reform legislation, as evidenced by at least ten million or more in support of such programs in 1988, were in the top half of the teacher grade distribution on the survey questions. South Carolina teachers reported more positive attitudes toward various school changes than teachers in any other state. They gave the highest percentage of A or B grades (52 percent) to their reform movement than did teachers from any other state. South Carolina ranked first of all other states in the percentages of teachers who responded that the following program features or conditions were better than five years earlier. Rankings of other states with TIP/CL programs were as follows:

- clarity of school goals (Texas 3rd, North Carolina 11th, Utah 16th, and Arizona 17th)
- academic expectations for students (Texas 2nd, Arizona 6th, North Carolina 11th, Tennessee 13th, Utah 15th, California 20th)

- leadership of principals (Texas 3rd, Utah 8th, North Carolina 13th, Tennessee 15th, California 16th, Arizona 19th)
- student math skills
- student reading skills
- student writing skills[11]

While teachers may not always be enthusiastic about incentive programs, it would appear that in those places where such programs have been major components of a reform effort, teachers tend to recognize that school conditions have generally improved.

Ambivalent attitudes prevail toward the new summative evaluation systems that accompany incentive programs. Teachers quickly acknowledge they are much better—fairer, more objective, more precise—than they used to be. By the second or third year of use, teachers typically say that principals and the evaluators have improved in their consistency and accuracy. At the same time they continue to question how well these systems distinguish between good and superior teaching. Many authorities contest their use in awarding performance-based pay, complaining that performance measures are not sufficiently developed to provide valid appraisals. Although the multisource, multijudge procedures featured in most plans are a considerable improvement over single evaluations by the principal, they still lack consistency of use from one school to another and one district to another. The reliability of ratings from one situation to another is still too low to satisfy some teachers.

Attitudes toward the evaluation system, of course, vary from one program to another. They depend on how individuals are actually assessed and what use is made of the results. If most individuals are rated sufficiently high to meet performance criteria, teachers feel better on average than they do in systems where only a minority of them have such high ratings.

Many teachers are still very uneasy about being evaluated rigorously. The extensive scrutiny required by candidates for career ladder promotion is a real deterrent to their participation. In programs where limits are set on how many teachers can be promoted, the numbers of those volunteering are quite often no larger than the numbers of openings or awards expected to be made. Many good teachers are not applying.

Underlying these attitudes toward the evaluation and incentive system are one's overall reasons for teaching and the degree of self-confidence one possesses. Such evaluation can indeed be ego-threatening for some individuals. For others, it serves merely to disturb a sense of complacency to the point where one recognizes a need to improve. Evaluation works best and teachers generally favor its use when principals provide strong leadership and communicate with teachers candidly yet supportively.

Almost everyone likes extra pay for extra work opportunities. The extended contract and job enlargement options are very popular. They do not require rigorous evaluation. It is judgments about the quality of teaching or work performance that are new and so often disliked. Numerous surveys report teachers disagreeing with statements that "instruction has improved," "planning is more thorough," or "students are learning more because of the incentive program or evaluation system." To agree means admitting that teaching, planning, or learning was not good before. Many admit in private, however: "These programs are getting principals into classrooms and teachers who used to slough off aren't doing so now."

Performance evaluation is both stressful and disturbing. Negative reactions are certainly understandable. It threatens long-standing, comfortable egalitarian relationships. Because it imposes a measure of accountability that was not there earlier, furthermore, it serves to reduce one's sense of autonomy as well. A new dimension has been added to school life in places where incentive-driven summative evaluation programs prevail. It cannot help but lessen teachers' sense of being trusted as a professional. Differences in teacher survey results from one community to another are only understandable if one takes into account variations in the degree of threat and rigor the evaluation systems impose.

Similar sentiments toward teacher incentive programs are reported for principals and other administrators. In general, however, they tend to be more positive. They tend to credit the programs and accompanying changes in evaluation procedures with improving a whole range of things from teacher attendance and planning to teaching and learning (MGT, 1989). The much heavier instruction-oriented evaluation burden they carry because of these programs has clearly complicated their lives and lessened their activities elsewhere. Increasingly, however, they seem willing to divide the load with teachers and be receptive to assistance and advice about how to improve instruction and learning. Most principals in South Carolina pilot districts were more than willing to let teacher-dominated committees make the judgments of approval-disapproval of student-outcome plans. More than 60 percent of them also indicated that peers and administrators should both be involved in conducting TIP participants' performance observations. Only about one-third of the schools had done so up to that time (1987–88).

The extent to which public confidence in the schools has changed as a function of the incentive movement is not easily determined. The 1988 Gallup poll responses indicated that 25 percent of the public sampled and 39 percent of the parents felt that public schools in their communities had improved over five years earlier versus 19 percent and 16 percent respectively saying they had "gotten worse." In the Carnegie report card, teacher-perceived parental support for teachers and community respect for teachers were virtually unchanged nationally, on balance. In South Carolina and Arizona, twice as many teachers said parental support and community respect were better than those who indicated it was worse. Perceived support and respect were reported as worse rather than better by substantially larger numbers of teachers, on the other hand, in Tennessee, Texas, and Utah. In fact, teacher sentiment in Utah was more negative on both of these questions than in any other state. Only 11 percent said community respect for teachers was better, compared to 47 percent who said it was worse (Boyer, 1988, pp. 83–84).

These responses, of course, relate to the total reform effort, not just incentive pay. Attitudes of community support for these programs are probably best judged by the amount of funding they continue to receive from one year to the next. As Cornett (1989) points out, in states that had already made extensive commitments to incentive programs, funding increased or at least held steady in 1988 and 1989. In states that had provided little or no funding before, little or no new funding was forthcoming; incentive pay may or may not be still under serious consideration.

LATER DEVELOPMENTS AND REMAINING ISSUES

After five years of experimentation with teacher incentive pay in the aftermath of the 1983–84 reform calls, what changes were apparent in such plans? What issues remained? What was the likelihood of their continuance? What form would new programs take?

I look both at what features were enduring and approaching institutionalization in the various programs I have tracked in this volume and new incentive program startups near the end of the decade. I note several emerging patterns.

Outcomes assessment was clearly becoming the guiding strategy. It preserved the accountability demands of the reform legislation while, at the same time, it allowed strong pressures for decentralized control and greater operational flexibility to emerge. Site-based management and work restructuring were other reform themes that were gaining popularity and needed to be tried out as possible answers to the stiflingly bureaucratic, top-down management patterns that had killed so many school improvement efforts. Big-scale experimentation was undertaken with school-based management in Dade County, Florida; Boston, Massachusetts; Rochester, New York; and several other places.

A similar trend could be seen at the state level in Arizona, Iowa, South Carolina, Utah, and more recently in North Carolina, where local districts were given considerable latitude in program design as long as primary guidelines were followed. The 1989 North Carolina legislature failed to expand the state-directed career development program beyond the sixteen pilot districts and provided planning money for local districts to develop their own incentive plans for possible funding in 1990. A majority of the teachers would have to approve a district plan before it would be funded. In Utah, in 1989, career ladder money for six districts was folded into general block grants as a way of giving districts greater flexibility in program decisions. It is anticipated that in several of these districts, teachers will be given across-the-board raises in summer 1990 rather than incentive pay.

Across the country the closing months of 1989 witnessed an increasing acceptance of the need for clear, unambiguous local, state, and even national education goals. The first-ever education summit of state governors and the president began the process of achieving consensus about what the nation's priority outcomes should be and how progress toward them might be judged. Clearly articulated reform goals were to be achieved but schools were to have a freer hand in determining how they were to be accomplished (*Education Week*, 4 October 1989).

School incentive programs were on the increase. Tracking the performance of schools is technically easier and more justifiable, according to many statisticians, than monitoring the performance of individual teachers, especially if the primary assessment data used are derived from measures of student learning. In addition to programs in Florida, Indiana, Michigan, Pennsylvania, and South Carolina that have been operating for several years, legislation establishing such programs was passed in Louisiana and Colorado, and proposals were made in Arkansas, Kentucky, and Texas in 1989 (Cornett, 1989). Some of these state programs permit teachers to receive bonuses; others do not. Faculty in award-winning schools, in the latter cases, determine how the award money should be spent for school improvement purposes (*Education Week*, 27 September 1989). The largest single item of President Bush's first education initiatives was for $250 million to provide school incentive awards averaging $100,000 each.

The mentor teacher role is well established in many schools today. Paying teachers extra for monitoring and assisting interns, beginning teachers, and even experienced teachers in need of special help is now accepted practice. Increasingly accepted also is the use of peer observer evaluators to assist in both summative and formative teacher assessment for incentive pay purposes. Even the master teacher notion is more widely endorsed than earlier, although the term *lead teacher*, as described in the Carnegie Forum, is the preferred title. In 1988 the Rochester, New York, Career in Teaching Program established a lead teacher position and expanded the duties of individuals selected beyond those involved in mentoring. In addition to the increased funding of early mentor teacher programs in California and New York, the mentor teacher role received widespread support through new programs designed specifically for that purpose, or in various components of older programs, in at least a dozen other states, including Indiana ($1.9 million), Oregon ($2.4 million), and Washington ($1.5 million) (Cornett, 1988).

Pay incentives to attract high school or college students into teaching, especially into fields where teachers are in short supply or to work with "at risk" students, are provided in many states today, including New Jersey, New York, and Utah. They are also included in the recent Bush initiatives. In some places, New Jersey for example, special programs were established to attract minorities to teaching. Typically, as described in chapter 2, awards take the form of special scholarships or forgivable loans. They also exist in the form of alternative ways to become licensed to teach. In Montana teachers may serve as principals under supervision while they are still working on certification requirements for their positions. A similar program is available for teachers seeking special education endorsement (Cornett, 1988, p. 23). In Texas, college graduates are hired as interns to teach under the close supervision of a mentor teacher. A year of intern-teaching substitutes for student teaching for certification purposes (Barnes, 1989).

In brief, the end of the eighties witnessed increasing differential pay practices designed to reward teachers or potential teachers for various reasons—for mentoring, serving as peer observer evaluators, performing exceptionally well, having students who score higher than expected on achievement tests, accepting new assignments where teachers are in short supply and especially needed, and entering teacher education programs in fields such as science and special education where teacher shortages exist. Many models were in operation. Others still were under consideration or development (e.g. Schlecty and Ingerson, 1987).

While teachers were assuming new roles and status to a greater extent than before, real structural change had not yet occurred in the cellular organization of schools. Mentor teachers, beginning teachers, and other teachers as well continued to man their own classes in pretty much their own way. With most incentive plans, participation was voluntary and many chose not to apply. Even those who did kept their classes intact and continued to teach the same kinds of students and schedules to which they were accustomed. In Danville, for example, where willingness to be transferred to schools where the special talent of career ladder teachers might be particularly needed was one criterion for promotion, few if any such reassignments actually took place.

More than a few issues were far from resolved. Problems persisted in the assessment of teaching. Distinctions between good and superior teaching were hard to detect in consistent, acceptable ways. Debates continued over how to define effective teaching and especially how to measure it. Complaints continued that the generic teaching skills, which serve as the primary focus of most observation systems, were too confining and proficiency-oriented (McNeil, 1988). Insufficient attention was paid to one's teaching specialty or the type of students one taught. The fairest, most acceptable evaluation systems were costly in the time and resources needed to administer them properly.

Debates raged even more over outcomes assessment. The many measurement problems described earlier of linking student learning to teaching behavior in systematic, valid ways upset many educators when they see it done. Whereas the practice of tracking student change in relation to individually set teacher objectives may be somewhat less objectionable than across-the-board use of standardized tests of basic skills, many of the same measurement problems do in fact exist. It is particularly hard to establish comparable standards when teachers are pursuing different objectives.

Not all educators reject the notion that student data should not be used for individual teacher assessment. After reviewing teacher effectiveness research, Hanusek, for example, states that striking differences exist in teachers' ability to promote student achievement when student background differences are properly accounted for, and advocates the direct use of student performance measures for teacher assessment (Hanusek, 1989). Cautious progress in this direction could be one outcome of the experimentation going on in places like Arizona and South Carolina, where outcome data are important features of the teacher evaluation systems. So far, and probably wisely so, they are not the primary data used in most places for awarding bonuses or promotions.

For years, the media have used standardized test results to compare schools, districts, states, and even countries. Increasingly the public demands such information. Educators too have sometimes promoted such comparisons as indicators of progress, or the lack of it, and as challenges for teachers to try harder to improve test performance. School superintendent John Murphy of Prince Georgia's County, Maryland, received a "Leadership for Learning" award in March 1989, from the American Association of School Administrators for his "outstanding contribution to student achievement" by charting standardized test scores school by school and increasing district averages ten to fifteen percentiles over a four-year period (*Education Week*, 22 March 1989). Not everyone was happy over the accomplishment, however, even in the school district. Complaints were voiced that too much emphasis was placed on test results and not enough on "true measures of achievement" and the important parts of the curriculum.

Introduced by Secretary of Education Terrell H. Bell and continued by his successors, William J. Bennett and Lauro F. Cavozos, a state-by-state "wall chart" of what selected performance indicators show each year sparks similar debate. While Secretary Cavozos expressed alarm over the lack of progress over a three-year period of college admission test scores and high school graduation rates, in spite of increased spending for education (*Education Week*, 10 May 1989), many other educators strongly denounced such comparisons as hurting, not helping, the cause of education. More precise measures were needed and more time for the effects of school reform to become apparent (*Education Week*, 17 May 1989).

As the eighties drew to a close, the push for state-by-state comparison was leading to an expansion and reshaping of the National Assessment of Educational Progress and the search for more useful indicators, not to scuttling the report card practice. The debate continued over ranking states according to overall global scores versus providing specific data that would indicate areas of strength and weakness. The public wanted the former, educators the latter (Linn, 1988). What would be done in assessing progress toward performance goals stemming from the education summit was not yet clear.

Important issues remained over costs and how to fund incentive programs. Even though expenditures were relatively modest compared to total budgets, instructional costs alone, or even basic salaries, they still represented a major new item in ever-expanding and almost always "tight" school budgets. Many programs were not fully implemented in 1989, and long-term cost projections were more sizable than many people had initially thought they would be. What had looked inexpensive and easily funded during the design and pilot-testing years suddenly looked less so as participation rates went up and the size and duration of supplements took on new meaning. In Fairfax County, Virginia, the board of education took another look and decided that the supplements should be 9 percent annual bonuses rather than more "permanent" 10 percent salary increases on the steps of a career ladder. The difference in retirement and other fringe benefits for this 9th largest school district in the country was projected at several million dollars over the next decade. The decision to switch to a bonus arrangement produced angry charges from the FEA leadership of foul play and the breaking of an agreement.[12]

The structure of many incentive programs establishes incentive pay as an extra cost, and at the same time basic pay patterns continue to be based on years of teaching experience and degrees. To the extent that only a few teachers participate and receive extra pay from incentive programs, they remain politically vulnerable. School boards will continue to be pressured to raise basic pay as much as possible. Teachers by and large will continue to present a united front behind this cause. To the extent that increasing percentages of teachers are participating in one way or another, the arguments over funding will tend to disappear or at least counteract each other. If a school board feels strongly that the pay of all individuals should reflect their performance in part, they can use the Hanover County approach: cost of living for everyone, easily-administered merit raise for almost everyone, and highly differentiated pay supplements for various other elements if needed.

The issue that remains when teacher salaries are clearly perceived as divided into basic pay and performance supplements is an inevitable competition between the two for what is perceived as a concrete, limited overall amount of money available. Teachers think incentive pay is taken from the amount of money available for across-the-board raises. Therefore, to receive incentive pay means taking it away from someone else. Unless this issue is faced squarely and openly at the enactment stage it will appear every budget period when the amount of pay is being negotiated.

As the biggest expenditure in state and local government budgets, funds to operate the public schools must always be constricted by the revenues available. Revenues, in turn, are generated primarily by taxes which depend ultimately on the will of the people and their representatives in the legislatures and on governing councils and school boards. The issue that returns each year is this: Can the schools be operated to the satisfaction of the people on the revenues that will be generated by whatever tax structure is in place? If not, how can more funds be raised? What tax changes are needed, and will the public accept them? Or, if revenue surpluses have been experienced, should taxpayers have some relief instead of expanding school budgets?

The most fundamental issue to be faced in the annual budget review is how much money should be spent on public education. Is what we have been doing to support the schools enough? Too much? Too little? Are they doing as good a job as they should be doing with what they have? Will they really do a better job if they have more money? These questions may not actually be stated in public forums very often, but they are implicit in the budget process. They occasionally are tested at election time with voting on millage or other revenue-raising propositions.

In 1983–84 the need for educational reform was strongly articulated by business and political leaders across the country. The public responded in more than a few places with a willingness to accept some increase in overall taxes—a penny more on the dollar in Florida, South Carolina, and Tennessee for example. Out of this came the reform programs and higher salaries. In several states teacher incentive pay was not only included but became a major selling point to gain broad support during the enactment stage. Teachers went along, sometimes reluctantly as we have seen, because big overall salary increases were included. Business and community support came, at least in part, because education was to become more competitive, more productive. The better teachers were to be recognized and rewarded. Higher standards were set and greater learning expected.

After six years of heavy reform, how good was the effort? What were the results? The public perception, stimulated by political rhetoric, heavy media coverage, and in some places actual tax increases, was that major effort had been mounted. It was time to ask serious questions about what had actually happened and how well it had turned out. The increased use of school report cards is no accident. It is a direct result of the heightened expectations emanating from the reform movement.

As the eighties drew to a close, those questions were still being asked. The jury was still out in most places. The evidence was reassuring in South Carolina where a major commitment had been made (in average salaries for teachers, South Carolina ranked thirty-fourth in 1988 verses forty-fourth in 1982; in expenditures as percentage of income per capita, it went from thirty-seventh to seventeenth). SAT averages increased forty-eight points over the six-year period despite an increase also in the percentage of high school graduates taking the test. Academic achievement test scores improved in most areas and at most grade levels as well. On The Carnegie Foundation Report Card (Boyer, 1988), South Carolina teachers were more positive toward the reform effort than teachers from any other state, and both parents and the public were more positive toward the schools than in earlier years and felt schools had improved.

In other states, the public report card was less clear. In Tennessee, for example, despite the tax increase for the reform package, very little change is noted in the state's relative rankings between 1982 and 1987 in average teacher salary (forty-second and thirty-ninth), expenditures per pupil (forty-eighth and forty-fifth), or expenditures as percentage of income per capita (forty-sixth and forty-sixth). In Utah, with the next to lowest per-pupil expenditures in the country, the highest pupil-teacher ratios, and one of the lowest average teacher salaries, a major shift took place in expenditures for teachers as a percentage of total current expenditures (forty-second to fourteenth). What money was available, apparently, went into increased support of teachers (*Education Week*, 10 May 1989).

The struggle between teacher associations for more pay overall and the business and community leaders for performance-based pay goes on, but at a reduced level. While I do not know how many innings are left on this issue, the score is clearly lopsided in favor of the teacher groups at this point. Teachers' pay and school budgets more generally escalated during the first five years of the reform. Few of the later programs contained performance bonuses or attempted to restrict the upper rungs of career ladders to those judged superior as teachers, at least where fewer than half of those who were eligible and applied for promotion actually made it. True, that most of those programs contained some quality assessment, so below-average performers were unlikely to be advanced. The problems of distinguishing between good and superior performers and of the elitism that was bestowed on those who made it apparently discouraged those developing later programs from using the superior teacher model. Florida was dismantled early and Tennessee, the other statewide superior teacher plan, has lost some of its singular emphasis on meritorious performance. Extra pay for extra work is the accepted standard by the educational community; and a close look at most plans that were operating in 1988–89 reveals that was what was featured. Even in South Carolina, the majority of teachers and principals considered what was going on as paying the dollars for extra work. The extra work, of course, was designing student learning plans and documenting how they turned out (MGT, 1989, E–39).

A Look Ahead

PROSPECTS

It is still uncertain how long the incentive pay movement will last and what structural changes it will leave. The trends toward differential staffing, as displayed in new roles and responsibilities for teachers, are unmistakable. It is too soon to tell, however, whether they will eventually lead to substantial reorganization of school assignments and new decision-making patterns. In this final chapter I will summarize my end-of-decade assessment of the likelihood of a continuation of this reform and make recommendations for those interested in accomplishing it.

The public demand for increased accountability and greater productivity in education has certainly not diminished. The unprecedented meeting of President Bush and the governors to attempt agreement on national education performance goals illustrates the depth of concern over the state of public education.

On a 1989 survey of several hundred corporation executives, 62 percent reported that educational shortcomings were hurting their companies' hiring practices, productivity and/or competitiveness (*Education Week*, 26 April 1989). Barely a day goes by without fresh statements by the nation's business and political leaders about how critical education is for the future of this country. For example, a Committee for Economic Development report concluded that 30 percent of the nation's school children are educationally disadvantaged, which could lead to a "severe employment crisis" and "seriously damage the country's competitive position" (*Wall Street Journal*, 8 September 1987. At an Emerging Issues Forum in North Carolina, "Education for a Comparative Economy," Xerox chairman David Kearns, Apple Computer chief John Sculley, and AFT president Albert Shanker all stressed the need for greater productivity, not just higher salaries (*The Fayetteville Times*, 21 February 1989).

They all appealed for managerial reforms which will permit and reward teacher performance, as measured by student achievement.

A column in *Forbes* magazine (19 September 1988) titled "What's Ahead for Business" reminded its readers that overall education spending surpassed defense spending in the 1970s and stayed ahead even through the Reagan years. It then reraised Education Secretary Bennett's question: Is the U.S. getting value for all this spending? Its concluding sentence was just one more warning: "Most parents-cum-taxpayers . . . are fed up with kids who can't find South Korea on a map."

Noting that education consumes 59 percent of Iowa's overall budget and that about half of its college seniors plan to leave the state, Iowa's agriculture secretary suggested that some educational expenditures might be better used for agricultural marketing and food processing (*Wall Street Journal*, 30 August 1988).

The concern is that education is already a costly venture. The ante has been upped in recent years. At 14 percent annually, per-pupil expenditure increases from 1983–88 actually doubled the rate of the previous five years. Mentioned several times at the Charlottesville summit, per-pupil expenditures in Japan are only half as great. Schools had better become more productive and student learning increase substantially. The nation's standing in a competitive world demands it. If education does not improve, tax dollars might be better spent on other priorities.

Business and community leaders were the principle promoters of the incentive pay movement. They saw a need to recognize and encourage quality. They enacted legislation and policies that would increase competition within the school culture as one means of stimulating greater productivity. The current pressure for more parent and student choice in education reflects the same underlying philosophy.

Rejecting the basic theme, the educational community gradually whittled down the competitive element in most incentive programs. Whether policymakers will continue to support such expensive programs with competition so reduced or turn their attention instead to alternative hopes for reform is still to be decided. Earlier reform advocates must be disappointed about what has vanished of what they had suggested and persuaded others to finance.

Competition will continue as a major theme only as long as

policymakers insist that it be so and provide extra money for it to happen. Even then it may be limited to comparing matched schools and districts rather than individuals. The early history of merit pay discredited the notion that, unlike their counterparts in the world of business and industry, school principals should rate or promote teachers for pay purposes. Their ability to do so fairly was questionable. Whatever authority they might have once had had gradually eroded. The more recent multijudge, multisource systems that were developed during the reform movement have added fairness and authority to a system of differential pay, but with only a modest and, in some cases, symbolic gesture toward increased competitiveness.

Policymakers, of course, could be persuaded that the other effects that have taken place are sufficiently beneficial so that extra competition is not really necessary. If the several indices being tracked—achievement test scores, NAEP results, graduation and literacy rates—show sufficient improvement, public confidence in educators should improve and less outside concern expressed about how schools actually operate. Quality schools is the primary reform theme, not competition per se.

Business involvement is as great as ever before, and might even strengthen in the years ahead. Approximately 40 percent of public elementary and secondary schools had established partnership agreements in 1987–88 with business or community organizations for the betterment of schooling. This was more than double the number in 1983–84 (NCES, 1989). Illustrative of the arrangements is the Boston Compact. It was established in 1982 with businesses and universities pledging jobs and college admissions for Boston public school graduates in exchange for improvements in the schools. More recently, however, business leaders expressed disappointment with the pace of reform and the performance of the graduates on the job or in college (*Education Week*, 19 April 1989).

Across the country there are six hundred councils of school authorities, business and labor leaders that meet regularly to organize and oversee job training and placement for unemployed workers, as part of the National Alliance program under the overall direction and funding of the U.S. Department of Labor. Much of the training is on basic literacy skills and general work performance standards.

Increasingly, also, parent-dominated boards are being established at individual schools to oversee school improvement efforts. In Chicago, for example, under the direction of a fifty-four-member summit group of top business, education, and civic leaders appointed by the mayor, individual school boards at each site are given unusual powers, including the hiring and firing of principals, reviewing budgets, and suggesting curriculum changes, in order to meet such 1993 targets as 50 percent of the students scoring above national achievement norms, reduction of dropout rates by 5 percent a year, and one-percent attendance increases annually (*Education Week*, 30 March 1988).

With continued dissatisfaction of many business and community leaders and rising expectations about what the schools should do, I predict continued close monitoring and increased imposition of client-oriented standards. If the majority of teachers resist the incentive pay programs in their communities and choose not to participate, other mechanisms for school improvement will be tried. If, on the other hand, the majority of teachers are held to higher standards and at the same time receive increased benefits from these programs, I believe that they will ultimately produce lasting changes in the way schools are run, better teaching, and improved learning.

The teacher incentive programs of the eighties provided alternative models of how teachers might be paid and rewarded for what they do in the service of this nation. Differential pay exists today in those communities that took the trouble to implement such programs. Teachers have greater career options than before. More precise quality standards have been articulated, more attention is focused on instruction and good teaching methods, and there is at least a hint of greater learning. I believe that, if this movement expands in the years ahead and these early programs continue to the point of full institutionalization and second-order structural change, the quality of schooling in this country will have taken a categorical leap upwards.

I believe, further, that the public will not continue to increase its overall support of the public schools beyond the somewhat stepped-up level of the late eighties. Taxpayer resistance remains high. Employment cutbacks have been occurring in more and more businesses, and wage rises in industry have been slowing as teacher salaries have improved. According to an American Management Association survey of more than one thousand corporations, two out of five reduced the number of their employees in 1988 (*Wall Street Journal*, 15 August 1989). Several states (e.g., Georgia, North Carolina) stopped their plans to launch an incentive program statewide in 1989 because of funding problems; and many other states were moving slowly, if at all, toward any new educational reform. I suspect that, if this particular reform is really judged a failure, after the great rhetoric of the mid-1980s and the several-year experimentation that has been described in this volume, it will be ever more difficult to mount a successful new school reform of any sort in the nineties. Disillusionment with what can be done to improve our public schools will be greater than ever.

RECOMMENDATIONS

If there is so much at stake with this movement, what can be done to improve the efforts so far? What has been learned that can serve as advice for others who might wish to start such programs? What might be done to strengthen those already underway?

Throughout this volume, where I have described issues that were confronted and procedures that were developed and followed, the descriptions themselves of what happened provide direct guidance of what to consider and what works or does not work. I will not attempt to repeat all these suggestions, but concentrate instead on some of the more general and important policy recommendations that stand out.

Thorough, long-range planning is needed with a full understanding of the major issues at stake and the critical program features to be enacted. Policymakers need to recognize the several long-standing norms that performance-based, selective systems disturb. They should know that close attention will be needed for several years. Starting a program will be costly in administrator time and teacher morale in the early stages. It may be more expensive after it is fully operational than was anticipated unless appropriate standards and measurement procedures are adopted early. It is especially important to realize that real structural change does not come easily, and that is what quality assessment and performance-based pay are supposed to accomplish.

Educators, for the most part, will resist performance-based pay strongly. They will accept extra pay for extra work, but they will typically reject extra pay for better work. Their primary reasons are that it cannot be assessed fairly, and it generates too much dissension.

That it does cause trouble, I do not doubt; but that it cannot or should not be done, I disagree. The experimentation described in this book has clearly shown that it can be done with some very promising results. Even though the performance-based theme has been compromised here and there, it still provides the yeast for the movement and in some places remains the driving force. I doubt if real change is likely without it being at least part of the reform response. Quality assessment is the primary new dimension whether it shows up in process or outcome measures. That is what this particular reform was all about. It is up to the policymakers, after weighing potential costs against benefits, to decide if it is worth doing. If the decision is to proceed, they must intend to see it through to full execution.

The recognition and improvement of quality should be the guiding theme. Glaring failures in our public education system are what instigated the calls for major change. The voices of protest have not subsided and are actually louder than a decade ago.

The primary notion to be promulgated over and over is that improvements are needed in all aspects of our educational system. There is room for improvement in almost everything we do. We expect the best teaching and greatest learning possible. We know that differences exist in how well teachers teach and how much students learn. We understand that some will improve more than others. We expect everyone to try to do his best.

Qualitative differences exist in teaching and learning. They have been ignored too long, because of problems in assessing them perfectly and the likelihood of creating disappointment and hurt feelings. We must begin to acknowledge and reward those who are performing best and improving most. To alleviate the disappointments and hurt feelings, we may need to expand the reward system to ensure the recognition of smaller accomplishments and improved performance, not just a small number of best performers. It is important not to let those who complain that it cannot be done fairly or without distress prevent it from being done at all.

With quality performance as the overriding yardstick, it is particularly important that the people selected to design and operate the program are among the best available—strong and respected teachers with constructive, open attitudes; knowledgeable, sensitive administrators; and far-sighted board members and community representatives. Their selection should not be left to chance or even to some kind of automatic voting process. Selection of individuals from a large pool of applicants ought to allow for sufficient consideration of appropriate personal characteristics. It is also important that those who are the first to receive whatever promotion or awards are at stake be generally recognized as good, if not outstanding, individuals. How this can be engineered has to be left to those doing the planning, but it ought to be an important item on their agenda.

The administration and board must not delegate the planning and monitoring of the program. If they cannot assign it high priority as a means of accomplishing several important long-term objectives, they should not launch such a program. It is too threatening, too easily diluted. Too much potential damage is likely if it is not done well. It represents big change, at least for programs of the superior teacher, student learning, or even full career models. Its design and implementation should not be left to any but the best leadership available.

Policymakers need to be clear about their long-term plans for the roles of both principals and teachers and the organizational changes they ultimately expect. Do they want principals to remain and improve as instructional leaders, or do they see them more as business managers, with teachers responsible for organizing and operating the instructional program on some kind of differentiated staffing arrangement? If the former position is taken, principals must strive to improve their instructional expertise. They must earn the respect of teachers and be skilled in providing instructional leadership and assistance. Extensive training and careful selection of principals may be necessary to bring the level of instructional capability up to what is needed.

For teachers to assume greater leadership, they must be willing to take on new responsibilities, including assisting and evaluating colleagues. They must accept the obligation of passing judgment about the quality of teaching and learning. Those who have served as peer evaluators or panelists to rate and approve or reject teachers' student outcome plans have been making such judgments. One of the reasons they have been willing to do so is the sharing of the judgment responsibility with others and the degree of anonymity it provides. They are not the sole individuals who decide how a colleague is rated.

Good arguments have been made for and against teacher empowerment, participatory management, and new roles for teachers and principals in connection with school reforms today (e.g., Geisert, 1988; Sheive, 1988; Urbanski, 1988). They need to be reviewed and understood as a part of long-range planning.

Career ladders have the potential to produce major changes in the way schools are organized and run. Policymakers should understand that potential early in the planning process, and make sure that the requirements for the various steps on the ladder, as well as its overall shape, will allow the changes they seek to be realized. The shape of a ladder refers to the proportions of the teacher population on each step and whether it is conical, like Tennessee's program, with fewer individuals on each upward level; an inverted cone; or a parallel pole ladder with equal numbers on each of the steps. The organizational changes can vary enormously, so early discussion and resolution of what is desired is wise planning.

Policymakers must remember that, first and foremost, the public schools are to serve their clients—their students, parents, and citizens. Teachers and administrators are not the primary clients. Incentive pay incites political differences and augments power struggles among public education's stakeholders that need to be recognized and accommodated if possible. Policymakers are prone to believe that change can be brought about in a rational way. Our studies of this particular movement remind us of how irrational and political it can become. Others remind us also of how political schools are when such changes are attempted (Bacharach and Mitchell, 1987; Johnson and Nelson, 1987). Timar and Kirp (1988) believe the excellence movement will fail unless policymakers shift the focus from "regulation and compliance monitoring to mobilization of institutional capacity" (p. 75). They cite the South Carolina reform effort as their prime example of how this can be done.

The end runs attempted around the organized teacher unions during the enactment stage in Florida, Tennessee, and Utah were never completely successful. Teacher association leaders bided their time and lobbied behind the scenes and in the districts during implementation. When mistakes were made, they were the first to say so. In time, the union agenda were gradually reconciled, more in some places than in others.

A shift from outright resistance by the national union leadership to conditional support for differential pay seems to have occurred over the half-decade due particularly to the positions taken by AFT president Al Shanker. Local teacher association leaders have been in the forefront of design efforts in Rochester, Dade County, and Toledo, among other places. In each instance, governing councils have included strong representation from the union, overall salary hikes have been substantial, and the decision-making authority granted to the councils has been extensive. Obviously, the union agenda are being accomplished. Hopefully, the public's agenda will be treated just as well. Ensuring that happening might be best accomplished by monitoring the outcomes of education closely. If policymakers are sufficiently sensitive to the needs of various stakeholders to let them work out their differences while at the same time sharing responsibility for that accomplishment, major improvements might indeed occur.

Most programs should include features from more than one model. The models were introduced to provide a taxonomy of different types of programs. Programs serve different purposes. Hopefully the taxonomy clarifies the distinctions among them and highlights the critical features of each model. Even the programs that were described to illustrate a specific model contain elements of other models. While the Tennessee career ladder serves as a prime example of the superior teacher model at the upper two levels, for instance, level one exemplifies the high participation model and is quite similar to Hanover County, Virginia's, program.

The combination of elements from different models provides an eclectic and politically more easily sustained program than most single models, especially for highly selective programs. More individuals can participate. As participation rates go up, the animosity goes down; selection processes typically are simpler and less costly as well.

Multimodel programs also provide greater choice in how teachers can participate. In Utah's career ladder, which contains elements from at least five models, essentially all teachers in the state participate in one way or another. As teachers become accustomed to salary and role differentiation, increased acceptance of further change in one or more of the primary components seems likely, for instance performance-based pay, without a devastating toll on morale.

In general, incentive pay programs should allow for voluntary participation rather than require all teachers to take part. In the most fundamental sense, an incentive system should be designed so individuals try to improve in the hopes of recognition, reward, and a sense of accomplishment. Mandatory participation, on the other hand, emphasizes doing something because it is part of one's job; the primary motivation is to avoid being uncooperative or unsatisfactory in job performance. The proverbial "carrot" rather than "stick" approach is more positive and more enticing. The less heavy-handed the program appears, furthermore, the more likely it is to be favorably received. The fact that most teacher incentive programs are imposed by the outside world, rather than sought by educators, already stiffens the resistance. So, not forcing teachers to participate is important. Designing programs instead that appeal to appropriate segments of the population and offer a variety of incentives should be the guiding principle. Mitchell and Peters (1988) provide a useful description of incentives available.

Another important reason for making participation voluntary is that it establishes self-evaluation as the first screening device. Self-assessment alone is not always accurate. If half of the teachers really believe they are among the best 10 percent of the teacher population (see p. 60), not only will a great many be disappointed with any highly selective assessment system that is established but some reassessment of one's professional self is also likely. It is this reassessment that leads to trying harder or retreating from the challenge.

One of the strengths of the Danville system is that teachers, including some very good ones, can have some very legitimate reasons for not participating. One need not be embarrassed over not being on the ladder, because the additional burdens of the extensive review and additional expectations if one is promoted provide good reasons not to participate. Face-saving is easy. And it should be. As nonparticipants see others participating and reaping rewards, they will continue to weigh the potential benefits against the costs and the likelihood of their own chances against whatever hurdles the system presents. They are in the best position to judge whether and when to participate.

Teacher performance assessment should be based on multiple criteria, multiple judges, and multiple data sources. Teaching embraces a complex set of functions and tasks. To assess it properly, criteria have to be established to cover the wide range of activities in which they are engaged. If the overall quality of performance is to be estimated, a variety of situations need to be observed and representative samples of relevant data collected in objective, systematic fashion. To reduce the influence of personal biases about the nature of good teaching and maximize the attention to the specified criteria and performance variables to be judged, several procedures should be followed:

- Variables and related performance indicators should be

clearly described and illustrated in a widely distributed, written form.

- Evaluators should be trained in the collection and judging of data and demonstrate competency in their own knowledge and use of the evaluation system. This will typically be done by comparing their ratings of particular data with consensus ratings of others. Data collection and data judging are separate processes and evaluators need to be trained in both.

- Final performance ratings should be based on the independent judgments of two or more trained evaluators. The judgment process is strengthened and made more objective when evaluator teams reach agreement about final ratings and the reasons underlying them.

- Data should be derived from a variety of resources to reflect the range and complexity of teaching activities and the variety of relevant information available. Single sources of information not only oversimplify teaching, but they can often be manipulated to provide an erroneous performance picture. Judgments based on a variety of data from a number of sources are likely to reflect more accurately the quality of overall teaching.

- Experimentation with the collection and use of student performance data should be continued. Although much caution is advised about the possible misuse of such data in the evaluation of teachers, student learning is the "bottom line" reason for the existence of schools. We ought to find ways to use information about how well students are learning as at least one means of determining how well schools and teachers are doing. I am fully aware that many educators say it cannot be done fairly and therefore should not be done at all. I think otherwise. Those districts that are using outcome data are proceeding cautiously and using them primarily as supplementary or confirming information in the final judgment process. One clear benefit to such a district is a healthy attention to the question of how much its students are really learning. Hopefully, the educational research establishment will eventually offer a helping hand.

The complexities of teaching defy easy assessment. For this reason as much as any other, summative evaluation of teachers was virtually nonexistent until the emergence of the incentive pay movement in the eighties. The most visible residue of this movement so far is the installation of comprehensive, moderately objective, systems of teacher performance assessment in many states and school districts. Disturbing as personnel evaluation can be, they have refocused the educational spotlight on the quality of teaching and learning in precise, definable ways. I think that response is congruent with what the reform called for. I see the installation of summative evaluation as a tool for sharpening and improving formative evaluation as well.

For those who would argue that the incentive movement was not necessary if the main product is summative evaluation, I say that the evaluation models would not have happened without it. Until there was true need to evaluate teaching for differential pay purposes, there was no reason to spend so much time and energy on developing and operating such elaborate systems. In fact, I predict that if the need for rigorous, objective teacher appraisal is eliminated by the disappearance of performance-based pay and promotion practices, continued use of summative instruments will decline as well.

I do not wish to overstate the accomplishment. Further development of teacher evaluation criteria and procedures is truly needed. The upper levels of many career ladders have more teachers than policymakers originally expected or school budgets can readily support. Measurable ways to distinguish clearly, fairly, and consistently between good and outstanding teaching are still hard to find. Although the progress to date is impressive, measurement problems in the assessment of teaching are considerable, not the least of which is the cost of administering a system once it is developed. Much more work needs to be done.

Continuous research and evaluation are needed to perfect program procedures and monitor the change process. Monitoring the pilot efforts and early installations of incentive programs through annual reports of participation patterns and surveys of teacher sentiments helps modify and improve procedures as they unfold. Such research provides policymakers with ongoing accounts of what is happening in order to tell what problems have been encountered and whether or not objectives are being met. In North Carolina, for example, annual reports of district distributions of teacher ratings on the eight functions of the TPAI have been used to determine how consistently the instrument is being applied across the pilot districts and where additional training may be needed.

In almost all the state programs, third-party evaluations have also been conducted by outside organizations to study program implementation patterns, survey the attitudes of teachers, administrators, and others, and make recommendations for procedural changes and needed research. In Arizona, Florida, North Carolina, South Carolina, and Utah, third-party reports have been cited throughout this volume for the information they provide about program development and success.

Judgments by policymakers about long-term funding and continuation of incentive programs presumably will depend heavily on the findings and recommendations of such outside evaluations. In Arizona, for example, where a major project was undertaken at one of the universities in response to program legislation to study and report on the pilot effort, a model was developed to determine the readiness of districts to participate successfully in the movement. It is proposed that, if the movement is to be funded beyond the five-year pilot stage, expansion to other school districts would depend on empirical data collected that might indicate which ones were most ready to operate a program successfully (Packard and Dereshiwsky, 1989b).

The use of outside consultants, third-party evaluators, and research and measurement specialists is essential. District and state departments typically do not have sufficient resources to conduct the research or provide the technical assistance that is needed during the early stages of these programs.

Sources for long-term funding of incentive programs must be identified early and procedures developed for keeping program participation rates congruent with whatever multiyear cost projections are established. More than one program has faltered because the number of participants meeting standards established for promotion and/or incentive pay exceeded what had been budgeted. A common demand of the teacher associations is that no arbitrary quotas be set (see p. 183) in judging how many can qualify for extra pay or placement on a ladder. Standards should be absolute and not comparative.

Yet, school resources are finite, and annual expenditures for specific purposes are precisely budgeted and carefully audited. There must be limits set annually on how many can receive incentive pay, and procedures must be established to limit the numbers receiving it to whatever is budgeted. If more teachers apply than can be paid extra, some ranking system is needed to determine who will and who will not be recipients in a given year. If the program is supposed to reward high-quality performance, the quality of performance should also be the basis of the ranking.

In South Carolina, teacher-dominated review panels do the essential ranking by assigning points to indicate the significance of student learning objectives and the evidence of their attainment. In many districts, in the early years of these programs, the number of qualified applicants did not exceed the number who could be paid; but in those with more applicants than what were budgeted for, the rankings served an essential function.

In Lynchburg, Virginia, a point system is used for combining judgments of data from several sources so that promotions stay within revenue limits. In addition, the actual salary raise occurs one year later than the year in which one is formally reviewed.

An early resolution of the quota issue is important in favor of the necessity of finite budget limitations. It would clear the air for a full understanding yearly of the approximate numbers of teachers who might expect to be rewarded or advanced to particular levels. It would clarify the general purpose of the plan and allow individuals to see how and where they might fit in. Ambiguity over this issue in the planning stage will only lead to trouble and disappointment later on.

Early ideas about how many might be interested and accommodated at various times and places in the reward system will help determine the size and kind of pay increments to be used. Such decisions should help determine the standards and measurement procedures that will be needed as well.

The source of extra funds for merit pay is an especially sensitive issue. Teachers do not want to feel that any performance bonus they receive comes from less raise for other teachers. One of the best means of downplaying this potential disincentive is to have a separate source of funding for the awards. Extra state funds were made available to pilot districts in Arizona and North Carolina so teachers who participated could only gain, not lose, over what they would have been paid by traditional methods. In Virginia, six superintendents with incentive programs indicated that local governing bodies provided special funds for this purpose beyond what regular salary schedules contained (Brandt and Gansneder, 1987).

The thrust of revenue cutbacks each year, however, always raises the question of which of these two salary pools takes precedent. If basic salary raises are decreased and performance supplements are not, a high volume of complaints can be expected. If relatively small performance supplements are reduced still further, their value as an incentive is decreased as well.

I recommend establishing the principle during the enactment stage that some significant portion of overall salary expenditures will always be used to reflect performance. Whatever salary raises will be negotiated each year will be increases in average salaries. Individual teachers will vary somewhat above or below this amount depending on how much of their pay is performance-based. Politically, this makes the original policy directive more difficult to sell; but once the principle is set, it should ease the annual struggles considerably. The long-term principle is more firmly established, and the message clear that an incentive program of some sort is here to stay.

Temporary sources for extra pay tend to disappear a few years after all the debates that start such programs. If the principle of folding both kinds of pay into one salary pool is established early, I believe the program will be on solid ground for long-term survival. Of the various plans I have reviewed, the Arizona model, accomplishes this salary restructuring best.

The long-term policy to be established is that while all teachers can be expected to receive some increase based on cost of living, extra duties, and perhaps years of experience and extra degrees, some percentage of their salaries will also reflect the quality of performance. To the extent that that policy can be set firmly in place, yearly squabbles over which source of funds to cut should be lessened and realistic long-term projections of salary expenditures can be accomplished.

An appropriate blend of state and local leadership and support enhances the likelihood that incentive programs will be successful. Although successful programs can be established without state help (e.g., Lynchburg, Virginia), the task is probably easier if state resources can be used and nearby school districts are involved in similar efforts. Common problems can be shared and mutual assistance given. The extra state funds for pilot districts in Arizona and the Carolinas, for example, served first as an incentive for districts to participate in an experiment without having to deplete their own funds, provided the stipends for award recipients, and financed extra personnel (e.g., program coordinators and peer evaluators), training workshops, and other administrative costs associated with the programs. In addition, state funds were helpful in developing training materials, providing technical assistance and support services, and in conducting the necessary research and evaluation studies cited above.

In the places where state incentive programs were established, the state's role is always limited to some extent by the fact that local districts actually operate the schools. Great differences were noted among Utah districts, for example, in the distribution of career ladder funds among the four program components and the teacher activities for which extra pay was given. Differences in program implementation were noted even between one school and another within the same district.

The role of the state should be to enact the legislation to define the kind of programs desired, and to provide the extra funds and resources needed and the conditions for their equitable distribution and use. It also has a monitoring and reporting responsibility regarding the proper implementation of legislated policies and appropriate use of state money.

The amount of state direction and control varies extensively among the states I reviewed. In Tennessee, for example, the state retained control of the design of the program and the development and even use of the performance measures for selecting level II and III teachers. A special cadre of teachers was employed by the state and trained to visit districts as outside evaluators to collect the data needed to assess career ladder candidates. In Texas and North Carolina, state-developed instruments served as the primary tools for gathering classroom observation data and other performance information, even though district personnel did the collecting and interpreting.[1] In Arizona, South Carolina, and Utah, at least during the initial years, districts developed their own measurement tools, and the states reviewed them along with other program elements in connection with continued funding decisions.

Extensive attention, early on, to consensus building among policymakers, business leaders, and educators, first about the need for reform and later about the specific agenda and program strategies, was responsible for the apparent success of the South Carolina reform movement. Because of early involvement of teachers and administrators in the policy-making process, along with business leaders and politicians, people were knowledgeable about the intent of the reform and generally in agreement with the strategies enacted by the legislation. Debates over major issues, particularly money, occurred before implementation. Districts were given considerable latitude to work out their own program and assessment plans. They were to be held accountable primarily through outcomes assessment. As Timar and Kirp (1988, p. 87) note:

> South Carolina's approach to school reform is instructive for state policymakers for two reasons. It demonstrates the need for balance between state accountability and local autonomy.

State and local relationships will always vary in accordance with differing state governance traditions and financial patterns. Responsibility for the development and installation of reform programs like teacher incentive pay can also be expected to vary as well. Given the complexity of the issues involved and the extensive time and resources it takes to design and successfully install such programs, policymakers need to consider carefully what the state and district responsibilities should be and how they should be monitored in the years ahead. Legislative and policy directives alone will not ensure successful reform. Long-term attention will be needed by all parties involved if the potential of this particular effort is to be realized.

A FINAL COMMENT

The incentive pay movement of the eighties resulted from the cries for reform of the nation's schools heard in *A Nation At Risk* and other national reports about the condition of education in this country. Those suggesting this particular thrust were from outside the educational community, primarily from business and industry where incentive pay is common practice.

Since this was an imposed, top-down policy, it was and continues to be strongly resisted in many places. Many educators question how long it will continue. There are indications that its time has almost passed. The president of the National Education Association makes no mention of career ladder or incentive pay programs in reviewing the 1980s, describing it as an era of debate rather than real reform (Futrell, 1989). Career ladder presentations and discussions are no longer center stage at education conventions. School-based management, teacher empowerment, and work restructuring are more fashionable themes as the decade comes to a close. Recent startups of incentive programs feature extra pay for extra duty, job enlargement, and extended contract opportunities, not performance-based bonuses and promotions. Few examples of the superior teacher model can be found. For those that do exist, pressures continue to erode the merit features.

Yet, where programs were installed well, they have lasted longer already than some skeptics thought they would. The short-term impacts, as described in chapter 6, have been substantial; long-term effects promise even more. Participants and administrators are quite enthusiastic in many places where the initial storms have been weathered and the sunny side of improved performance, increased recognition, and extra status and responsibility have come on the horizon. Participants now realize, quite vividly, what they will lose if these programs are dropped. And there are more and more participants as programs become fully implemented.

I still do not take bets on how long this particular reform effort will last. It could disappear quickly. Changes in key places—in governors, legislators, board members, superintendents—can shift priorities dramatically. And the forces against structural change in schools are always powerful. Even where programs seem to be functioning well, they lurk just below the surface ready to return the educational scene to what it was before, should leadership falter or unanticipated problems erupt. It is still too early for those who instigated this particular reform to relax their vigilance if they want it to continue. The swell of other believers is not yet sufficient to ensure its endurance.[2]

Notes

CHAPTER 1. RESPONSE TO A MANDATE

1. For a more detailed account and analysis of the charges, see Brandt, 1981.

2. A Gallup Poll finding in May 1983 indicated that Americans would be willing to pay more taxes if they would help raise the quality of public education.

3. My ensuing discussion of compensation practices in business, industry, and the military was first included in a third-party review of the Florida master teacher program in 1985. Permission is granted for its use here, with slight revisions, by MGT of America.

4. Proponents of the Arizona programs described later in this book would probably dispute this statement. (see pp. 132-146).

5. For reasons why not to assess teachers by how much their students learn, see Berk, 1988; Soar, Coker, and Medley (1983); and Glass, G., 1989. For arguments that such assessment is possible, see Hanusek, 1989 and Packard and Dereshiwsky, 1988c.

6. The Gallup Poll in 1984 indicated the reverse: teachers opposed "the idea of merit pay" by a two to one margin. A Louis Harris Poll indicated that 71 percent of the teachers said merit pay "could work if merit could be judged objectively." (Cornett, 1984).

7. The latter was set at 200 days plus additional time each day.

CHAPTER 2. A PROGRAM TAXONOMY

1. Program designers and administrators refer to it as a career ladder rather than a merit pay program. The quality of one's performance, however, not the assumption of extra duties, determines whether or not one receives extra pay.

2. Through out this volume such unidentified quotations about specific program features can be assumed to have been taken from one or more program documents.

3. Many states today offer scholarships or loans to help individuals

attend college to prepare to teach science or some other selected specialty. Such loans are often forgivable for teaching in the state following graduation. Even though their actual salaries may not differ from those of other teachers, they receive an extra reward for teaching which amounts to thousands of dollars of erased debt for each year of teaching.

4. The plan also provides for the selection and employment of a limited number (four in 1987–88) of lead teachers to participate in curriculum development and assist other teachers, including beginning teachers, on an extended contract basis with an additional 5 percent salary supplement. Lead teacher specialists have been selected so far in Art, English, Mathematics, Science, and Special Education. Because so few teachers are involved as lead teachers so far, the overall plan illustrates the high participation model well.

5. A fifth component, incentive funding for teacher shortage areas, was used by only a few districts and is not included in this description.

6. Many districts deliberately did not fund the third level of the career ladder at the time. They were waiting to see if the program would be continued.

CHAPTER 3. PLANNING: ISSUES AND PROCEDURES

1. No extra pay is received for being on CLI. CLIV is expected to be implemented in 1991–92.

2. Tenured teachers are now evaluated in summative fashion only every other year unless they request such evaluation annually. Their requests for annual evaluation give school authorities an early indication for budgeting purposes of how many potential candidates to expect the following year.

3. Excludes the fourteen teacher evaluators who were already participating and temporarily ineligible to apply. Their special assignment will be assumed by career and master teachers once a sufficient number have been selected and trained.

4. Beginning in 1989, teachers can ask their principals to replace one of the three outside evaluators. If they accept the invitation, they participate in the same way as the others: observing classroom teaching, having their observations scored, and helping determine the team consensus.

CHAPTER 4. CHANGING SENTIMENTS AND PROCEDURES

1. Single spaced indented statements in this section are direct quotations from participants or respondents.

2. The numbers cited in this section refer to the twenty-nine issues described in chapter 3 and listed in Exhibit 3.1.

3. In the absence of any official projections of future salaries, I conservatively estimated a 5 percent basic salary annual increase in deriving this percentage as well as no change in the size of the teaching force.

4. See also the earlier description of this program in chapter 2 (pp. 40–44).

5. To be continued through 1991.

6. Many districts elsewhere require all new teachers to participate.

7. Defined as limiting the amount of dollars a teacher could earn for a given year during a phase-in period.

CHAPTER 5. TEACHER MOTIVATION AND ORGANIZATIONAL CHANGE

1. Legislation also limits use of the extended contract component to 50 percent of a district's career ladder allocation.

2. Elementary and middle school teachers met separately and notes were not taken covering their discussion. In general, however, later reports of task force visits to the various schools suggested similar concerns were expressed throughout the school system during fall 1984.

3. Neither group 1 variables nor the sixth group 2 variable were considered because of insufficient teacher attitude data prior to 1984.

CHAPTER 6. AN INTERIM ASSESSMENT

1. For 1989–90, Texas increased state funding of the career ladder program from $70 per student to $90. At the same time certain discretionary money which some districts had also used for career ladder funding was eliminated.

2. Each teacher also receives summative evaluation by the principal every two or three years to ensure that minimum competency standards are maintained and to identify those in need of special assistance (as in the high participation model).

3. CLII and CLIII teachers continue to have priority over other teachers.

4. The term "scripting" is used by Madeline Hunter and others to refer to this process of making a noninterpretive record of what is happening in a classroom while it is taking place. Various abbreviations and symbols are used, along with words, to keep on-the-spot recording up to time.

5. See chapter 3 footnote 4 p. 260.

6. Selected portions of this section were prepared for publication by the SREB Career Ladder Clearinghouse. Permission has been granted by the Southern Regional Education Board for using the material in this publication.

7. A later study was underway consistent with the first recommendation at the time this book went to press.

8. More pilot than matched districts had higher scores in 1988 than in 1986. In the third grade pilot districts, twelve were higher and three lower versus eight higher and seven lower for the matched districts. In the sixth grade, eleven pilots had higher scores and four lower versus six higher and seven lower for the matched districts. In the eighth grade, pilots had ten higher and three lower versus eight higher and four lower for the matched districts. Eighth-grade students in 1988 were essentially the same students as those tested in 1986 when they were in the sixth grade. Scores all increased for the five districts with the lowest sixth-grade scores in both the pilot and matched groups, but more matched districts in the middle and upper range had declines and somewhat larger declines on average than those in the pilot districts. In 1989 the differences were even more striking: In pilot districts, the percentages with improved scores were 81, 75, and 81 for the third, sixth, and eighth grades respectively versus 40, 53, and 53 for the nonpilots (Division of Personnel Relations, 1988b).

9. Although some evaluation systems might list such specific items as indicators of a more generic teaching practice, I do not recommend their use as absolute criteria in this fashion.

10. Many student learning programs, I found, are not highly competitive. Most participants are successful in reaching targets and receiving a bonus.

11. In general, teachers from the eight states tended to believe conditions had improved over the five years on most of the fifty-four items to a greater extent than other teachers, and their rankings will not be continued here. See the original reform report card (Boyer, 1988).

12. The school board's response was that they had never officially voted on an agreement since budgets must of necessity be approved annually.

CHAPTER 7. A LOOK AHEAD

1. As stated earlier (p. 233), the 1989 North Carolina legislature sharply changed the locus of control of the future direction of incentive pay by offering districts money to develop their own programs and stipulating that the majority support of teachers would be needed for further funding.

2. As final page proof corrections were being made in April 1990, I learned of a recent decision to begin phasing out the Danville program as teachers' terms on the career ladder expired. Behind the demise of this carefully launched program was the discontinuance of solid support and constructive attention to it from the chief administrator during the final implementation stage. There had been four changes in the superintendency and an almost complete turnover of board members since Superintendent Truitt's departure in August 1987.

Bibliography

Amsler, M., Mitchell, D., Nelson, L., and Timar, T. (1988). An evaluation of the Utah career ladder system: Summary and analysis of policy implications. San Francisco, CA: Far West Laboratory for Educational Research and Development.

ASCD Task Force on Merit Pay and Career Ladders. (1985). *Incentives for excellence in America's schools*. Alexandria, VA: Association for Supervision and Curriculum Development.

Bacharach, S. B., Bauer, S. C., and Conley, S. (1986). Organizational analysis of stress: The case of elementary secondary schools. *Work and Occupations*, 13 (1), 7–32.

Bacharach, S. B., and Mitchell, S. M. (1987). The generation of practical theory: Schools as political organizations. In J. W. Lorsch, (Ed.), *Handbook of Organizational Behavior*. Englewood Cliffs, NJ: Prentice-Hall.

Balkan, D. B., and Groenemans, S. (1985). Effect of incentive compensation on recruitment: The case of the military. *Personnel Administrator*, January, 29–34.

Banks, H. (1985). What's new in pay? *Personnel Management*, February, 20–23.

Bardwick, J. (1986). *The plateauing trap*. New York: American Management Association.

Barnes, S. (1989). Alternative teacher certification in Texas. Paper presented at the annual conference of the American Educational Research Association, San Francisco, CA.

Beal, J., Olstad, R., and Harder, K. (1986). A study of incentive programs for mathematics and science teachers in the fifty states and District of Columbia 1983–85. *School Science and Mathematics*, 86, December, 666–671.

Berg, N. A. (1959). What is different about conglomerate management? *Harvard Business Review*, November-December.

Berk, R. A. (1988). Fifty reasons why student achievement gain does not mean teacher effectiveness. *Journal of Personnel Evaluation in Education*, 1, 345–363.

Bobbitt, S. A. (1989). Teacher Incentive programs in the public schools. National Center for Education Statistics survey report, April. Washington, D.C.: U.S. Department of Education OERI–CS89–063.

Boyer, E. L. (1988). *Report on school reform*. Princeton, NJ: Carnegie Foundation for the Advancement of Teaching.

Brandt, R. M. (1981). *Public education under scrutiny*. Washington, D.C.: University Press of America.

————. (1986). An ongoing ethnography of career ladder planning. Paper presented at the annual meeting of the American Educational Research Association, San Francisco, CA.

————. (1987a). An ethnography of career ladder planning and implementation. Paper presented at the annual meeting of the American Educational Research Association, Washington, D.C.

————. (1987b). Improving the quality of student outcome data used in career ladder promotion decisions. Paper presented at the annual meeting of the American Educational Research Association, Washington, D.C.

————. (1988). A study of career ladder planning and implementation. Final report submitted to the Office of Educational Research and Improvement, U.S. Department of Education, April. Charlottesville, VA: Curry School of Education, University of Virginia.

Brandt, R. M., Duke, D. L., French, R. L., and Iwanicki, E. F. (1988). A review with recommendations of the North Carolina Teacher Performance Appraisal Instrument. Report submitted to the Education Subcommittee of the Joint Legislative Commission on Government Operations, North Carolina General Assembly, 21 May.

Brandt, R. M., and Gansneder, B. M. (1987). Teacher incentive pay programs in Virginia. Charlottesville, VA: Curry School of Education, University of Virginia.

————. (in press). School district planning for teacher incentive pay. In L. Frase, ed., *Teacher compensation and motivation: A book of readings*. Lancaster, PA: Technomics Publishing.

Brandt, R. M., and Kingston, E. A. (1986). Survey of teacher reactions to Danville career ladder program. Report submitted to the Danville School Board, summer 1986.

Braver, M. W. and Helmstadter, G. C. (1989). Executive Summary: Impact of career ladder on student achievement. Document presented to the

Joint Legislative Committee on Career Ladders, State Capitol, Phoenix, AR, 30 November.

Bruno, J. E. (1986). Teacher compensation and incentive programs for large urban school districts. *Elementary School Journal*, 86(4), 426–447.

Bruno, J. E., and Negrete, E. (1983). Analysis of teacher wage incentive programs for promoting staff stability in a large urban school district. *Urban Review*, 15(3), 139–49.

Burden, P. R., ed. (1987). *Establishing career ladders in teaching: A guide for policymakers*. Springfield, IL: Charles C. Thomas.

Charters, W., Jr. (1970). Some factors affecting teacher survival in school districts. *American Educational Research Journal*, 7, 1–27.

Cole, B. S., and Smith, A. W., Jr. (1979). Trends in bank compensation. *Bankers Magazine*, September-October, 60–65.

Cornett, L. (1984). News from the states. *Career Ladder Clearinghouse*. Atlanta, GA: Southern Regional Education Board, December.

———. (1987). More pay for teachers and administrators who do more: incentive pay programs, 1987. *Career Ladder Clearinghouse*. Atlanta, GA: Southern Regional Education Board, December.

———. (1988). Is "paying for performance" changing schools? *Career Ladder Clearinghouse*. Atlanta, GA: Southern Regional Education Board, December.

———. (1989). Funding performance pay plans. *Career Ladder Clearinghouse*. Atlanta, GA: Southern Regional Education Board, April.

———. (1990). Paying for performance—Important questions and answers. The 1989 Career Ladder Clearinghouse report. Atlanta, GA: Southern Regional Education Board, January.

Crews, V. J. (1984). Teacher attitudes toward merit pay. Ph.D. dissertation, University of Virginia, Charlottesville, VA.

Cuban, L. (1988). *The managerial imperative and the practice of leadership in schools*. Albany, NY: State University of New York Press.

Darling-Hammond, L. (1988). The futures of teaching. *Educational Leadership*, 46(3), 4–10.

Dickson, L. A., DeGracie, J. S., and Guy, V. (1989). Student achievement and career ladder status, 1989. Mesa, AR Public Schools, Department of Research and Evaluation.

DiGeronimo, J. (1985). Boredom: The hidden factor affecting teaching exoders. *The Clearing House*, 59, 178.

Division of LEA Personnel Services, Department of Public Instruction. (1989). Student achievement in career development program pilot units, 1985–89. Report submitted to the North Carolina State Board of Education, Raleigh, September.

Division of Personnel Relations, Department of Public Instruction. (1988a). Analysis of teacher performance ratings in career development program pilot units 1987–88. Report submitted to the North Carolina State Board of Education, Raleigh, December.

_____. (1988b). Student achievement in career development program pilot units 1985–88. Report submitted to the North Carolina State Board of Education, Raleigh, November.

Division of Public Accountability. (1988). What is the penny buying for South Carolina? Columbia, SC: South Carolina Board of Education, December.

Doyle, D. P., and Hartle, T. W. (1985) . Excellence in education: the states take charge. Washington, D.C.: American Enterprise Institute.

Duke, D. L. (1984). Teaching—the imperiled profession. Albany, NY: State University of New York Press.

Duke, D. L., Showers, B. K., and Imber, M. (1980). Teachers and shared decision making: the costs and benefits of involvement. Educational Administration Quarterly, 16(1), 93–106.

Duttweiler, P. C. (1986). Educational excellence and motivating teachers. The Clearinghouse, April, 371–374.

_____. (1987). Organizational changes to attract and retain qualified teachers. Organizational Changes, 61, 150–153.

Edwards, M. R., and Sproull, J. R. (1985). Making performance measures perform: The use of team evaluation. Personnel, March, 22–32.

English, F. W. (1984). We need the ghostbusters! A response to Jerome Freiberg. Educational Leadership, 42(4), 22–25.

ERS Report. (1979). Merit Pay for teachers. Arlington, VA: Educational Research Service.

_____. (1983). Merit pay plans for teachers: Status and descriptions. Arlington, VA: Educational Research Service.

Freiberg, H. J. (1984). Master teacher programs: Lessons from the past. Educational Leadership, 42(4), 16–21.

French, R. L., Malo, G. E., and Rakow, E. A. (1988). What we have learned from Tennessee's career ladder experience. Educational Leadership, 46(3), 70–73.

Fullan, M. (1982). *The meaning of educational change*. New York: Teachers College Press.

Futrell, M. H. (1989). Looking back on educational reform. *Phi Delta Kappan*, 71(1), September, 8–14.

Gallup, A. M. (1985). The 17th annual Gallup Poll of the public's attitudes toward the public schools. *Phi Delta Kappan*, 67(1), 35–47.

Gansneder, B. M., and Brandt, R. M. (1988). Factors influencing the implementation of merit pay plans. Paper presented at the annual conference of the American Educational Research Association, New Orleans, LA.

Garbett, M. J. (1987). *Career ladders in Utah*: 1986–1987. A content analysis of district career ladder plans. Report of the Utah State Board of Education, March.

Geisert, G. (1988). Participatory management: Panacea or hoax? *Educational Leadership*, 46(3), 56–59.

Glass, G. (1989) Using student test scores to evaluate teachers. In J. Millman, and L. Darling-Hammond, eds., *The new handbook of teacher evaluation: Assessing elementary and secondary teachers*. Newberry Park, CA: Sage.

Goodlad, J. (1983). *A place called school: Prospects for the future*. New York: McGraw-Hill.

Goodlad, J. I., and Klein, M. F., and Associates. (1970). *Behind the classroom door*. Worthington, OH: Charles A. Jones.

Governor's Special Advisory Committee. (1984). Master teacher plan and career ladder. Report submitted and revised by the Virginia Board of Education, Richmond, 9 January.

Haberman, M. (1987). *Recruiting and selecting teachers for urban schools*. New York: ERIC Clearinghouse on Urban Education, Columbia University.

Hall, G. E., and Hord, S. M. (1987). *Change in schools*. Albany, NY: State University of New York Press.

Handler, J. R., and Carlson, D. L. (1984). Shaping Tennessee's Career Ladder Program—1983. Part 1: Improving teacher quality through incentives project. Knoxville, TN: University of Tennessee. Report submitted to the U.S. Department of Education, spring.

———. (1985). Shaping Tennessee's Career Ladder Program—1985. Part 2: Improving teacher quality through incentives project. Knoxville, TN: University of Tennessee. Report submitted to the U.S. Department of Education, summer.

Hanusek, E. A. (1989). The Impact of differential expenditures in school performance. *Educational Researcher*, 18(4), 45–51.

Harris, L., and Associates. (1984). Metropolitan life: A survey of the American teacher. New York: Metropolitan Life Insurance Company.

Hart, A. W. (1987). A career ladder's effects on teacher career and work attitudes. *American Educational Research Journal*, 24(4), 479–503.

Hart, A. W., and Murphy, M. J. (1989). Work redesign where it happens: Five comparative cases of schools. Paper presented at the annual conference of the American Educational Research Association, San Francisco, CA.

Hatry, H. P., and Greiner, J. M. (1985). *Issues and case studies in teacher incentive plans*. Washington, D.C.: Urban Institute.

Herzberg, F., Mausner, B., and Snyderman, B. (1959). *The Motivation to Work*. New York: John Wiley.

Holdzkom, D., Stacey, D., and Kuligowski, B. (1989). A longitudinal study of teacher performance evaluation. Presentation at the annual meeting of the American Educational Research Association, San Francisco, CA.

Inman, D. (1987). *The fiscal impact of educational reform*. New York: Center for Educational Finance, New York University.

Jacobson, S. L. (1989). Merit pay incentives in teaching. In L. Weis et al., eds., *Crisis in teaching: Perspectives on current reforms*. Albany, NY: State University of New York Press.

Johnson, H. C., Jr. (1985). *Merit, money, and teachers' careers: Studies on merit pay and career ladders for teachers*. Lanham, MD: University Press of America.

Johnson, S. M., and Nelson, N. C. W. (1987). Teaching reform in an active voice. *Phi Delta Kappan*, 69, 591–598.

Kelley, M. F., and Pope-Rolewski, M. (1989). Administrator and peer evaluations: An examination of accuracy of judgments and organizational impact. Paper presented at the annual meeting of the American Educational Research Association, San Francisco, CA.

Klein, K., ed. (1983–84). *Merit pay and evaluation*. Bloomington, IN: Phi Delta Kappan Center on Evaluation, Development and Research.

Korman, A., Glickman, A., and Frey, R. (1981). More is not better: Two failures of incentive theory. *Journal of Applied Psychology*, 66, 255–259.

Kottkamp, R. B., Provenzo, E. F., Jr., and Cohn, M. M. (1986). Stability and change in a profession: Two decades of teacher attitudes, 1964–1984. *Phi Delta Kappan*, 67, 559–567.

Linn, R. L. (1988). State-by-state comparisons of achievement: Suggestions for enhancing validity. *Educational Researcher*, 17(3).

Lortie, D. C. (1975). *School teacher: A sociological study*. Chicago, IL: University of Chicago Press.

Malen, B., and Hart, A. W. (1987). Career ladder reform: A multi-level analysis of initial efforts. *Educational Evaluation and Policy Analysis*, 9(1) 9–23.

Manning, R. C. (1988). *The teacher evaluation handbook*. Englewood Cliffs, NJ: Prentice-Hall.

Mark, J., and Anderson, B. (1978). Teacher survival rates—a current look. *American Educational Research Journal*, 15, 379–384.

Martin, J., Green, J., and Palaich, R. (1986). *Making teachers partners in reform*. Denver, CO: Education Commission of the States.

Maslow, A. H. (1954). *Motivation and personality*. New York: Harper.

McLarty, J. (1987). Career ladder instrumentation: The Tennessee experience. Paper presented at the annual meeting of the American Educational Research Association, Washington, D.C.

McNeil, L. M. (1988). Contradictions of control, part 3: Contradictions of reform. *Phi Delta Kappan*, 69, 478–485.

Medley, D., Coker, H., and Soar, R. (1984). *Measurement-based evaluation of teacher performance: An empirical approach*. New York: Longman.

MGT of America. (1985). A project to provide a review of the implementation of the Florida master teacher program. Report submitted to the Florida Department of Education. Tallahassee, FL: 30 December.

———. (1987). Evaluation of teacher self-appraisal practices. Report submitted to the Texas Education Agency. Austin, TX: MGT consultants, September.

———. (1988). An evaluation of the teacher incentive program 1987–88 pilot-test implementation. Report submitted to the South Carolina Department of Education. Tallahassee, FL: 10 June.

———. (1989). An evaluation of the teacher incentive program 1987–88 pilot-testing following the payment of incentive awards. Report submitted to the South Carolina Department of Education. Tallahassee, FL: 27 March.

Millman, J., and Darling-Hammond, L., eds. (1989). *The new handbook of teacher evaluation: Assessing elementary and secondary teachers*. Newberry Park, CA: Sage.

Milstein, M. M. (1989). Plateauing as an occupational phenomenon among teachers and administrators. Paper presented at the annual meeting of the American Educational Research Association, San Francisco, CA.

Mitchell, D. E., and Peters, M. J. (1988). A stronger profession through appropriate teacher incentives. *Educational Leadership*, 46(3), 74–78.

Murnane, R. J., and Cohen, D. K. (1986). Merit pay and the evaluation problem: Why most merit pay plans fail and a few survive. *Harvard Educational Review*, 56(1), 1–17.

Murnane, R. J., Singer, S. D., and Willett, J. B. (1988). The career paths of teachers: Implications for teacher supply and methodological lessons for research. *Educational Researcher*, 17(6), 22–30.

_____. (1989). The influences of salaries and "opportunity costs" on teachers' career choices: Evidence from North Carolina. *Harvard Educational Review*, 59(3), 325–346.

Musick, M. (1987). A Time for testing. *Southern Magazine*, December.

National Center for Education Statistics. (1989). Education partnerships in public elementary and secondary schools. Washington, D.C.: Office of Educational Research and Development (CS89–060).

NCES. (1990). School and staffing survey. Washington, D.C.: National Center for Education Statistics, U.S. Department of Education.

National Commission on Excellence in Education. (1983). *A nation at risk: The Imperative for educational reform*. Washington, D.C.: U.S. Government Printing Office.

NEA. (1979). *Teacher opinion poll*. Washington, D.C.: National Education Association.

_____. (1985). *School personnel education manual*. Washington, D.C.: National Education Association.

Nelson, D. E. (1986). A statewide survey of teacher opinions concerning Utah's career ladder program. Report submitted to the Utah State Office of Education, January.

Packard, R. D. (1987). Descriptive and analytical results for the 1986–87 career ladder data cycles. Research document presented to the Joint Legislative Committee on Career Ladder Programs, Arizona State Capitol, 10 November.

Packard, R. D., and Dereshiwsky, M. I. (1988a). Research findings on effective program designs and methodologies. Evaluation research: Study of the effects of a career ladder intervention program with focus on the production and outcomes in student achievement. Research document presented at the Arizona Educational Research organization's annual conference, Phoenix, 10 November.

―――. (1988b). Educational change and reform: A focused design to improve teacher development and student achievement for enhanced school effectiveness. Document presented to the Joint Legislative Committee on Career Ladders, Arizona State Capitol, 11 November.

―――. (1988c). Research findings on effective program designs and methodologies: Quantitative levels of program acceptability by career ladder placement. Document presented to the Joint Legislative Committee on Career Ladders, Arizona State Capitol, 29 November.

―――. (1989a). Summative report and recommendations for program modifications of the Arizona career ladder research and evaluation project. Report presented to the Joint Legislative Committee on career ladder programs, Arizona State Capitol, 14 September.

―――. (1989b). Evaluating school effectiveness: A matrix comparison of research findings and policy implications assessing readiness to implement educational reform and improvement. Paper presented at the AASCD/PDK fall conference, Phoenix, Arizona, 17–18 November.

Packard, R. D., and Nickols, W. (1987). Qualitative analysis and results for the 1987 data cycle by career ladder program strengths and improvement areas. Research document presented to the Joint Legislative Committee on Career Ladder Programs, Arizona State Capitol, 10 November.

Printz, R. A., and Waldman, D. A. (1985). The merit of merit pay. *Personnel Administrator*, January, 84–90.

Research and Service Institute. (1988). Evaluation of North Carolina's school career development pilot program: A report of an outside evaluation. Prepared for the Joint Legislative Commission on Government Operations. Raleigh, N.C.: 31 December.

Rist, M. C. (1983). Our nationwide poll: Most teachers endorse the merit pay concept. *American School Board Journal*, 170(9), 23–27.

Robinson, G. E. (1983). Paying teachers for performance and productivity: Learning from experience. *Concerns in Education*. Arlington, VA: Educational Research Service.

Rosenholtz, S. J., and Smylie, M. A. (1984). Teacher compensation and career ladders. *Elementary School Journal*, 85, 151–166.

Sarason, S. B. (1971). *The culture of the school and the problem of change*. Boston, MA: Allyn and Bacon.

Schein, E. H. (1980). *Organizational psychology*. 3d ed. Englewood Cliffs, NJ: Prentice-Hall.

Schlecty, P. C., and Ingerson, D. W. (1987). A proposed incentive system for Jefferson County teachers. *Phi Delta Kappan*, 68, 585–590.

Schlecty, P. C., and Vance, V. S. (1981). Do academically able teachers leave education? The North Carolina case. *Phi Delta Kappan*, 63, 106–112.

_____(1982). The distribution of academic ability in the teaching force: Policy implications. *Phi Delta Kappan*, 64(1), 22–27.

Schuster, J. (1984). *Management compensating in high technology companies*. Lexington, MA: Lexington Books.

Sheive, L. T. (1988). New roles for administrators in Rochester. *Educational Leadership*, 46(3), 53–55.

Sibson, R. E. (1974). *Compensation*. New York: AMACON.

Snygg, D., and Combs, A. W. (1959). *Individual behavior: A perceptual approach*. New York: Harper.

Soar, R. S., Coker, H., and Medley, D. M. (1983). Teacher evaluation: A critique of currently used methods. *Phi Delta Kappan*, 65(4), 239–46.

Stiggins, R. J. (1988). Revitalizing classroom assessment: The highest instructional priority. *Phi Delta Kappan*, 69(5), 363–368.

Stiggins, R. J., and Duke, D. L. (1988). *The case for commitment to teacher growth: Research on teacher evaluation*. Albany, NY: State University of New York Press.

Task Force on Education for Economic Growth. (1983). *Action for excellence*. Denver, CO: Education Commission of the States.

Thomas, M. D. (1985). Educational personnel evaluation. *Educational Leadership*, 42(4), 32–33.

Thomsen, D. J. (1978). Compensation and benefits. *Personnel Journal*, October, 538–540.

Timar, T. B., and Kirp, D. L. (1988). State efforts to reform schools: Teaching between a regulatory swamp and an English garden. *Educational Evaluation and Policy Analysis*, 10(2), 75–88.

Tye, K. A., and Tye, B. B. (1984). Teacher isolation and school reform. *Phi Delta Kappan*, 65(5), 319–22.

Urbanski, A. (1988). The Rochester contract: A status report. *Educational Leadership*, 46(3), 48–52.

U.S. Department of Education. (1984). *The nation responds: Recent efforts to improve education.* Washington, D.C.: U.S. Government Printing Office.

Watzlawick, P., Weakland, J., and Fisch, R. (1974). *Change: Principles of problem formation and problem resolution.* New York: Norton.

Waugh, R. F., and Punch, K. F. (1987). Teacher receptivity to systemwide change in the implementation stage. *Review of Educational Research,* 57(3), 237–254.

Weaver, W. T. (1984). Solving the problem of teacher quality. *Phi Delta Kappan,* 66, 108–115.

Wuhs, S. K., and Manatt, R. P. (1983). The pace of mandated teacher evaluation picks up. *American School Board Journal,* 170(4), 28.

Index